Principles of Music

PHILIP LAMBERT

Baruch College
and the
Graduate Center,
City University of New York

New York   Oxford
OXFORD UNIVERSITY PRESS

Oxford University Press is a department of the University of Oxford.
It furthers the University's objective of excellence in research,
scholarship, and education by publishing worldwide.

Oxford New York

Auckland   Cape Town   Dar es Salaam   Hong Kong   Karachi
Kuala Lumpur   Madrid   Melbourne   Mexico City   Nairobi
New Delhi   Shanghai   Taipei   Toronto

With offices in

Argentina   Austria   Brazil   Chile   Czech Republic   France   Greece
Guatemala   Hungary   Italy   Japan   Poland   Portugal   Singapore
South Korea   Switzerland   Thailand   Turkey   Ukraine   Vietnam

For titles covered by Section 112 of the US Higher Education
Opportunity Act, please visit www.oup.com/us/he for the latest
information about pricing and alternate formats.

Published by Oxford University Press
198 Madison Avenue, New York, New York 10016
http://www.oup.com

Library of Congress Cataloging-in-Publication Data
Lambert, Philip, 1958-
  Principles of music / Philip Lambert.
      pages cm
  Includes bibliographical references and index.
  ISBN 978-0-19-997556-3
1. Music—Instruction and study.   2. Music theory—Elementary works.   I. Title.
  MT7.L1645 2013
  781—dc23
                                    2013009910

Audio samples recorded by Mix Mobile. mixmobileinc.com

Printing number: 9 8 7 6 5 4 3

Printed in the United States of America
on acid-free paper

CONTENTS

PREFACE

THIS BOOK EXPLORES core principles of most of the music you hear on the radio or at the theater or concert hall. It helps you understand the sound and notation of this music. It teaches you some of the techniques and materials used by composers and songwriters. It prepares you for more advanced study of harmony and music theory. It gets you started on pathways of investigation and discovery.

It's intended for advanced high school or college students or adult learners taking courses with titles such as "Fundamentals of Music" or "Elements of Music" or "Basics of Music" or "Music Theory 101." It starts at the very beginning, assuming no previous experience with musical notation or music theory. It begins with an introduction to the piano keyboard, followed by notation of rhythm and pitch, major and minor scales, key signatures, intervals, triads, and seventh chords. It leaves off where courses in basic harmony usually begin.

The book is organized as a series of lessons focusing on specific steps in the learning process. Here are some distinguishing features of the lessons:

- Early lessons are oriented around the piano keyboard. Then, after the basics of staff notation have been introduced, the remaining lessons are oriented around examples from musical repertoire. Some music, such as the patriotic song "America" and the opening of a well-known piano sonata by Mozart, appears in several different lessons, in deepening levels of inquiry.

- Each lesson includes a list of study questions and written exercises designed to reinforce concepts from that lesson and build on previous lessons and exercises.

- HELP boxes appearing throughout the written exercises provide information from the current lesson that is essential to understand and complete the exercises that follow.

- In addition to lessons in pitch notation and tonal materials, the book includes six lessons in various aspects of rhythm and meter, which are accompanied by performance exercises for practicing rhythm reading. These lessons are interspersed throughout and can be studied out of sequence.

- Throughout each lesson, important terms and concepts are highlighted in bold and defined in the *Glossary* (starting on p. 376).

- Some of these terms, plus other common musical symbols and markings, are also summarized as annotations on a musical score in *A Brief Guide to Common Musical Symbols and Markings* (p. 384), and in an alphabetized list of definitions in *Mini-Dictionary of Score Indications* (p. 385).

- Each lesson concludes with a CREATE! section, which presents suggestions for exploring central concepts in imaginative ways, including improvisation and model composition.

- The final lesson, "Music in Motion," is a gateway into more advanced concepts and materials, intended for students who are interested in extending their studies beyond musical fundamentals and flexing their creative muscles.

- Included on the website for this book (www.oup.com/us/lambert) is a list of *Suggestions for Listening* for each lesson, offering tie-ins between central concepts and other music, often encompassing a variety of styles and genres. Almost all of the music in the listening lists is easily accessible on the Internet. Students can use these lists as starting points for processes of exploration that could take them even deeper into the world of music. Instructors can use them as a source for additional musical examples or supplementary assignments or projects.

Because of its keyboard orientation, the book is well-suited to complement a course in basic piano. The material of the lessons can always be profitably reinforced and drilled at the keyboard. Many of the CREATE! activities specifically involve the piano.

Further, the website for the book (www.oup.com/us/lambert) includes a set of original compositions, "Fifteen Character Pieces," that can supplement and reinforce the lessons. Some of these are specifically designed for a class-piano setting and can accommodate pianists of differing abilities. They connect to individual lessons via the listening lists and CREATE! activities.

A call-out symbol ( ) in the margin next to a musical excerpt directs you to one of the recordings that accompany this book, available at http://www.oup.com/us/lambert. The best way to absorb the material of the lessons is to listen to these recordings each time they appear. You will also benefit by playing excerpts and demonstrations at a keyboard, in addition to listening to the recordings.

As an option for students who desire extra, more independent drilling on music fundamentals, Oxford offers a special online software program, Music Theory Skill Builder, that allows users to complete practice exercises on key concepts at their own pace. The software includes brief self-exams on important topics in the text, providing immediate feedback and the ability to focus drills on areas that need more work. Throughout this book, a reminder appears wherever online drills have particular relevance to a topic being studied. The software is offered at a discounted price when it is packaged with this text or can be purchased separately. See www.oup.com/us/lambert for more information.

ACKNOWLEDGMENTS

I am grateful to the following reviewers for their insights that helped shape and refine this book:

Adriana Tapanes-Inojosa, Harold Washington College
Debra Benoist, San Jacinto College South
Christine Gengaro, Los Angeles City College
Donna Ham, South Plains College
Rebecca Jemian, Ithaca College
Reed Hoyt, University at Albany
Bryan Heath Vercher, Lamar State College, Port Arthur
Julie Moffitt, Harrisburg Area Community College
Shafer Mahoney, Hunter College and the Juilliard School
Mark Zanter, Marshall University
Robert A. M. Ross, Community College of Philadelphia
Nick Vasallo, California State University, East Bay
Steven Young, Bridgewater State University
Peter Purin, Oklahoma Baptist University

I also thank my colleagues Steven G. Laitz (Eastman School of Music), Diane L. Taublieb (Lucy Moses School), and Zachary Bernstein (City University of New York). For help with the recordings, I thank the performers Margaret Kampmeier and Nils Neubert; sound engineers Joe Krachie and P. J. Meyers of Mix Mobile; and John Malatesta of the Baruch Performing Arts Center. At Oxford, I am indebted to executive editor Richard Carlin for his support and expert oversight, project editor Marianne Paul, editorial assistants Katy Albis and Sheena Kowalski, and the rest of the editorial and production team. I also acknowledge my testers, Charlotte and Alice.

LESSON 1
THE PIANO KEYBOARD

1.1   THE C KEY

Look at the arrangement of white keys and black keys on a piano keyboard:

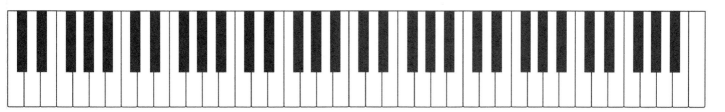

The white keys all touch other white keys on both sides. Sometimes they touch for their entire lengths. Other times, a black key comes between them, and the white keys only touch at one end.

The black keys are arranged in groups of two or three. These groups alternate as you move across the keyboard. Find a group of two black keys in the central area of the keyboard and look at the white key just to the left. That's called **Middle C**:

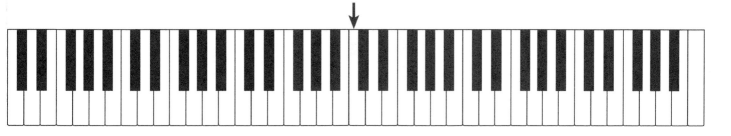

It's called "middle" because it's in the approximate center of the piano. It's called "C" because we label each key with a letter, and our traditional notational system assigns the letter C to that key.

To refer to that key as C is one way of classifying it as a musical **pitch**. Pitch is the highness or lowness of sound. Middle C is a pitch in the middle range of the piano. As you move to the right on the keyboard, the pitches get higher; as you move to the left, they get lower.

Every time you find a group of two black keys on the keyboard, the white key to the left is called C. There is more than one key on the piano called "C," although only one of them is "middle" C:

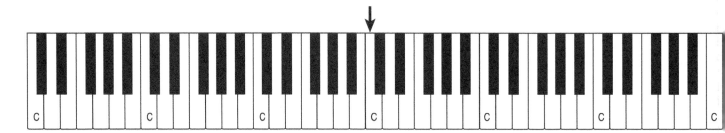

We reuse the letter C for all these pitches because they all have a very similar sound. The distance between two pitches with the same letter label is an **octave**. If you measure the frequencies (sound waves per second) of two pitches an octave apart, you find a simple 2:1 ratio: the frequency of the higher note (the one on the right) is exactly double the frequency of the lower one.

Our keyboard diagram has seven Cs, including the one at the far right, which would be to the left of a group of two black keys if the keyboard continued in that direction. The actual standard piano keyboard has another octave beyond this one to the right (eight Cs in total), and two white keys and one black key to the left, for a total of eighty-eight keys (fifty-two white and thirty-six black).

1.2   NAMES OF THE WHITE KEYS

Let's focus just on one octave, from one C to another. As you move upward (from left to right), continue forward in the alphabet, starting over after G:

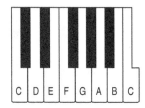

Presenting all the pitches in this manner, spanning an octave and using all the letters in the **musical alphabet** in order, is called a **scale**. That comes from the Italian word "scala," meaning "ladder." Since this scale starts (and ends) on C, we call it a C scale.

These same letter labels apply to the keys in any octave on the piano. Just as any white key immediately to the left of a group of two black keys is C, now we can see that any white key immediately to the *right* of a group of two black keys is E. Any white key just to the left of a group of *three* black keys is F. Any white key situated between a group of two black keys is D. Any time you have two white keys that aren't separated by a black key, those two notes are E/F or B/C. And so forth.

So we can start on any white key on the keyboard and play all the white keys within an octave and we'll have a scale. We can start not only on C (CDEFGABC) but also D (DEFGABCD) or G (GABCDEFG) or on any other white key. Because there are seven different letters in the musical alphabet, there are seven different starting points for these octave spans, seven different sequences. These are the **white-key scales:**

C scale	C D E F G A B C
D scale	D E F G A B C D
E scale	E F G A B C D E
F scale	F G A B C D E F
G scale	G A B C D E F G
A scale	A B C D E F G A
B scale	B C D E F G A B

To play one of these scales on the piano, use these finger numberings:

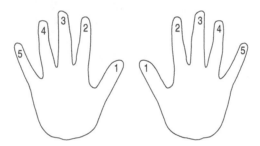

The finger sequence for a white-key scale in the right hand is 1-2-3-1-2-3-4-5. When you shift from finger 3 to finger 1 between scale tones 3 and 4, pivot your hand using your middle finger as an axis while bringing your thumb underneath your palm. The finger sequence for a white-key scale in the left hand is 5-4-3-2-1-3-2-1. When you shift from finger 1 to finger 3 between scale tones 5 and 6, pivot your hand using your thumb as an axis while reaching over with your middle finger.

1.3   THE CHROMATIC SCALE

Let's also think about spanning an octave using both white and black keys. We'll have not only seven different white keys but also all five black keys for a total of *twelve* white and black keys within a one-octave span. That's called a **chromatic scale**. If we start on C, for example, we would play this sequence of white keys (*w*) and black keys (*b*) to complete the octave: *wbwbwwbwbwbww*.

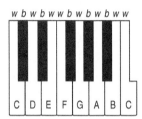

To complete the octave starting on any other note involves a different sequence of white and black keys. Here it is starting on G, for example:

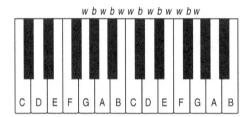

 For suggestions for further listening, go to www.oup.com/us/lambert

► **STUDY QUESTIONS FOR LESSON 1**

1. Define these terms:
   chromatic scale
   middle C
   musical alphabet
   octave
   pitch
   scale
   white-key scales

2. How do you find middle C on the piano?

3. How are the black keys organized on the piano?

4. Which white keys don't have black keys between them?

5. How many different white-key scales are there?

6. Indicate the number of different notes in these scales (not including the repetition of the first note at the end):
   white-key scale
   chromatic scale

▶ EXERCISES FOR LESSON 1

As we learned in Lesson 1, the white keys of the piano are named with the letters of the musical alphabet: A–B–C–D–E–F–G. We remember their names by noticing their location with respect to the black keys. C is situated just to the left of a group of two black keys. F can be found to the left of a group of three black keys. A is nestled between the second and third black keys in a group of three. And so forth.

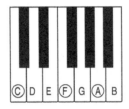

A. Write the letter names for the numbered keys in the blanks with the corresponding numbers:

| 26 | 4 | 14 | | 2 | 20 | | 18 | 25 | | 10 | 21 | | 1 | | 13 | | 6 | | 19 | | 11 | | 15 | 7 | 5 | | 17 | | 22 | 9 | | 12 | 24 | 23 | 3 | | 8 | 16 |

___ 1	___ 2	___ 3	___ 4

___ 5	___ 6	___ 7	___ 8	___ 9	___ 10	___ 11

___ 12	___ 13	___ 14	___ 15	___ 16	___ 17	___ 18

___ 19	___ 20	___ 21	___ 22	___ 23	___ 24	___ 25	___ 26

___ 8	___ 15	___ 10	___ 26	___ 9	___ 18

___ 20	___ 7	___ 3	___ 22	___ 14	___ 5

___ 4	___ 24	___ 11	___ 2	___ 9	___ 21

A white-key scale (Lesson 1.2) uses all the letters of the musical alphabet, filling the distance between two keys with the same name, called the "octave." The D white-key scale (or just "D scale"), for example, fills the distance between two Ds:

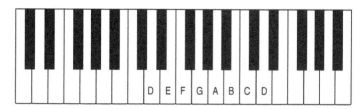

B. Demonstrate your knowledge of the white keys and white-key scales by filling in the blanks and following the instructions.

1. The name of the starred key is _____. Draw a star on the key one octave lower.

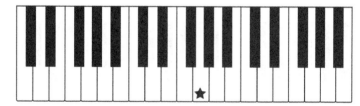

2. The name of the starred key is _____. Draw a star on the key one octave higher.

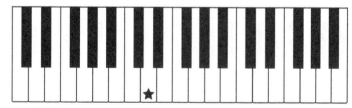

3. The name of the starred key is _____. Draw stars on all other keys with the same letter name in the diagram.

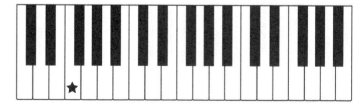

4. Draw a star on each B in the diagram.

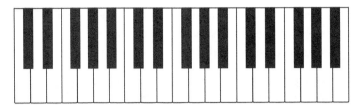

5. Draw a star on each E in the diagram.

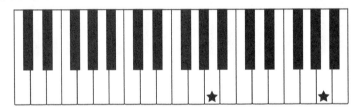

6. What is the word that describes the relationship between the two starred keys? _____

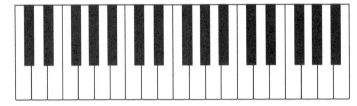

7. On the keys of the keyboard diagram, write the letters of one G white-key scale.

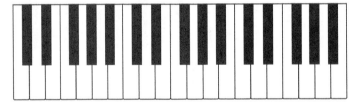

8. On the keys of the keyboard diagram, write the letters of one B white-key scale.

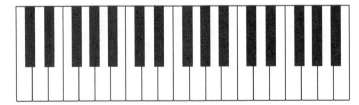

9. On the keys of the keyboard diagram, write the letters of two E white-key scales.

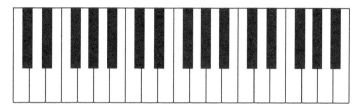

10. On the keys of the keyboard diagram, write the letters of two A white-key scales.

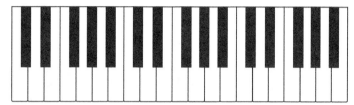

A chromatic scale (Lesson 1.3) uses all the keys, white and black, within an octave. For example, the chromatic scale between one D and another uses this sequence of white (*w*) and black (*b*) keys: *wbwwbwbwbwwbw*.

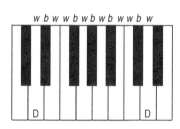

C. **Demonstrate your knowledge of the chromatic scale by filling in the blanks and following the instructions.**

1. The name of the starred key below is _____. Draw a big ring around all the keys of a chromatic scale **starting on** the starred key and ending one octave higher.

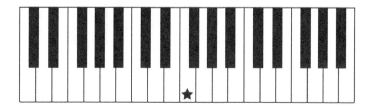

2. The name of the starred key below is _____. Draw a big ring around all the keys of a one-octave chromatic scale **ending on** the starred key.

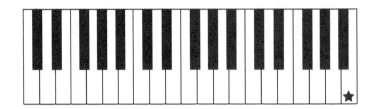

3. Draw a star on the starting key of a chromatic scale with this sequence of white (*w*) and black (*b*) keys: *wwbwbwbwwbwbw*.

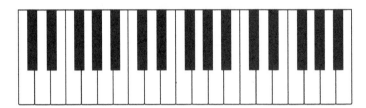

The name of your starred key is _____.

4. Draw a star on the starting key of a chromatic scale with this sequence of white (*w*) and black (*b*) keys: *wbwwbwbwwbwbw*.

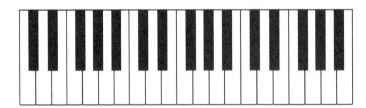

The name of your starred key is _____.

5. Draw a star on the starting key of a chromatic scale with this sequence of white (*w*) and black (*b*) keys: *wbwbwbwwbwbww*.

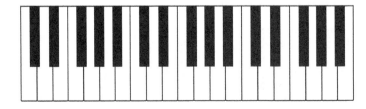

The name of your starred key is _____.

6. Draw a star on the starting key of a chromatic scale with this sequence of white (*w*) and black (*b*) keys: *wwbwbwwbwbwbw*.

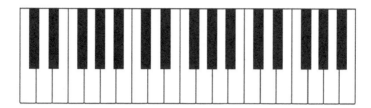

The name of your starred key is _____.

7. Point an arrow to the starting key of a chromatic scale with this sequence of black (*b*) and white (*w*) keys: *bwwbwbwbwwbwb*.

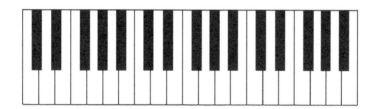

8. Point an arrow to the starting key of a chromatic scale with this sequence of black (*b*) and white (*w*) keys: *bwbwwbwbwwbwb*.

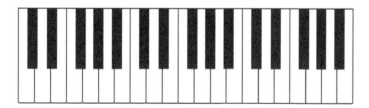

❧ create!

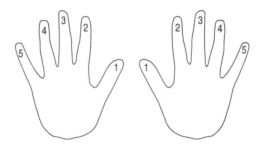

Place your left pinkie (finger 5) on middle C. Place the remaining fingers in your left hand on the next four notes of the C scale (finger 4 on D, 3 on E, 2 on F, 1 on G).

At the same time, place your right thumb (finger 1) on the black key just to the right of middle C, and place the remaining fingers of your right hand on the remaining four black keys to the right. Your right hand, on the five black keys, should be hovering over your left hand on the first five white keys of the C scale.

With your hands in these positions—and without moving those fingers from those keys—improvise sequences of scale tones in your hands. Here are some possibilities:

- Play all the notes in one hand one at a time, up and down, then do the same in the other hand.

- Play all the notes in both hands one at a time, up and down, at the same time.

- Play the left hand notes going up (starting on middle C) while the right hand notes move down (both hands starting with finger 5). When you finish, do the same thing in reverse (both hands starting with finger 1) to get back where you started.

- Make up melodies consisting of some notes from one hand and some from another.

- Experiment with the different sounds you can get by playing one note from each hand at the same time.

- Play a segment of a chromatic scale, up and down.

ACCIDENTALS

2.1 NAMES OF THE BLACK KEYS

In Lesson 1 we learned that a chromatic scale contains all the notes, white and black keys, within an octave. Here's another definition: a chromatic scale consists entirely of **half steps** within an octave span. All those distances between adjacent keys—white to black, black to white, or white to white—are called half steps.

An **accidental** is a symbol that specifies a certain action on a white key. The three most important types of accidentals are:

> **sharp** (♯): move up one half step, to the next key higher (to the right) in the chromatic scale
> **flat** (♭): move down one half step, to the next key lower (to the left) in the chromatic scale
> **natural** (♮): neither sharp nor flat

If you are on **G**, for example, and you want to make it sharp, move up one half step, to the next black key to the right. To make it flat, move down one half step, to the next black key to the left:

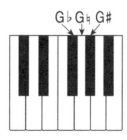

Similarly, A♮ is surrounded by A♭ and A♯:

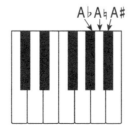

Notice that the black key in the middle of a group of three has two different names, G♯ and A♭, depending how it is approached. By the same logic, G♭ could also be F♯, A♯ could also be B♭, and so forth. Two different spellings for the same key are called **enharmonics**. G♯ and A♭ are enharmonically equivalent. So are G♭/F♯, and A♯/B♭. An enharmonic equivalence is meaningful only to the eye; to the ear, enharmonics are indistinguishable.

A sharp or flat doesn't always refer to a black key. The definition simply requires moving by half step to the next adjacent key in the chromatic scale. That means that if you apply a sharp or flat to a white key that is *not* surrounded by black keys, you may land on another white key. We know, for example, that if we apply a *sharp* to an F, we get a black key, F♯, which is enharmonic with G♭. But if we apply a *flat* to an F, we get to another white key, also known as E♮:

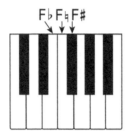

F♭ and E♮ are enharmonically equivalent. So are E♯ and F♮, C♭ and B♮, B♯ and C♮. We usually refer to white keys as natural notes, not as sharps or flats, but in later lessons we'll learn instances when it makes sense to refer to them using sharps or flats.

Context also determines exactly which names we use for black keys. Sometimes when you're moving upward it makes sense to use sharps, and when moving downward, use flats. In the chromatic scale, for example, you can use sharps while ascending and flats while descending:

C C♯ D D♯ E F F♯ G G♯ A A♯ B C B B♭ A A♭ G G♭ F E E♭ D D♭ C

But we will also study contexts where it makes more sense to do just the opposite, to use flats while ascending and sharps while descending:

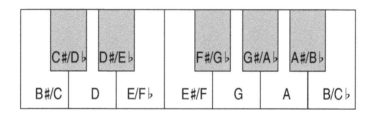

A **pentatonic scale** is the five-tone scale consisting of only black keys, in order. We have two choices for notating this scale also: C♯–D♯–F♯–G♯–A♯ or D♭–E♭–G♭–A♭–B♭. In this case, however, the choice of one or the other may not be immediately obvious and may simply reflect the personal preferences of the notator.

2.2 SUMMARY OF NAMES FOR WHITE AND BLACK KEYS

Here's a summary of the various note names involving flats and sharps within an octave:

C♯/D♭	D♯/E♭		F♯/G♭	G♯/A♭	A♯/B♭
B♯/C	D	E/F♭	E♯/F	G	A	B/C♭

As usual, these names are equally valid in any octave, no matter where you are on the piano keyboard.

 For suggestions for further listening, go to www.oup.com/us/lambert

▶ STUDY QUESTIONS FOR LESSON 2

1. Define these terms:
   accidental
   enharmonically equivalent
   flat
   half step
   natural
   pentatonic scale
   sharp

2. What are the two possible names for each black key within an octave?

3. Which white keys can also be named with sharps or flats?

4. Give the names of three different piano keys, all containing the letter "D."

5. Give the names of three different piano keys, all containing the letter "B."

6. What are the two ways to notate a chromatic scale?

7. What are the two ways to notate a pentatonic scale?

▶ EXERCISES FOR LESSON 2

In Lesson 2 we learned about using accidentals (♯ ♭ ♮) to name black keys and, sometimes, to rename white keys. One result is that the same key can have different names ("enharmonics"). For example, the black key between G and A can be named G♯ or A♭:

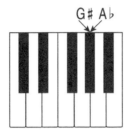

The E key can also be called F♭:

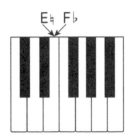

A. Give two possible spellings for each of the numbered keys.

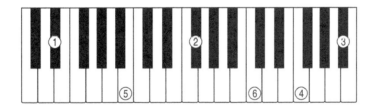

1. _____ or _____

2. _____ or _____

3. _____ or _____

4. _____ or _____

5. _____ or _____

6. _____ or _____

B. Demonstrate your knowledge of the piano keyboard by filling in the blanks and following the instructions.

1. The two possible names for the starred key are _____ and _____.
   Draw a star on the key one octave lower.

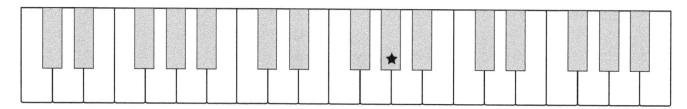

2. The two possible names for the starred key are _____ and _____.
   Draw stars on all other keys the diagram with the same two possible names.

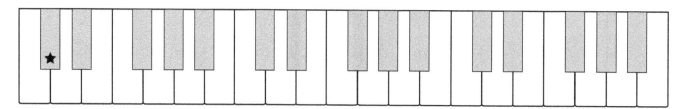

3. Draw a star on each B♯ in the diagram. The enharmonic equivalent of B♯ is _____.

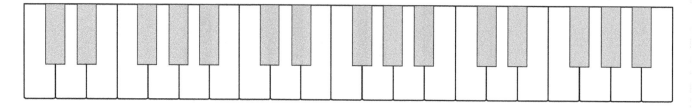

4. Draw a star on each F♭ in the diagram. The enharmonic equivalent of F♭ is _____.

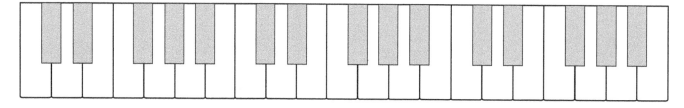

Name: _____

5. Write note names on the keys of a chromatic scale starting on D and ending on D one octave higher. Use natural names for white keys, sharp names for black keys (don't use any flats at all).

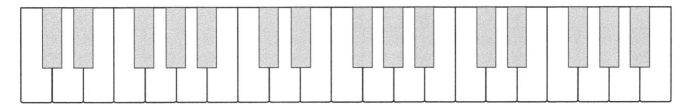

6. Write note names on the keys of a chromatic scale starting on G♭ and ending on G♭ one octave higher. Use flat names for black keys, natural names for white keys (don't use any sharps at all).

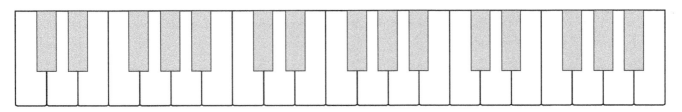

7. Find the starting note of a chromatic scale that has this sequence of white (*w*) and black (*b*) keys: *wbwbwwbwbwwbw*. Write the note names of this chromatic scale within one octave on the diagram. Use natural names for white keys, sharp names for black keys (don't use any flats at all).

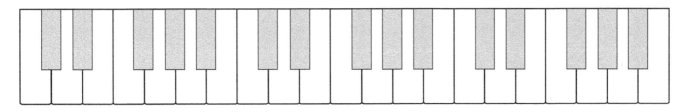

8. Find the starting note of a chromatic scale that has this sequence of black (*b*) and white (*w*) keys: *bwbwwbwbwbwwb*. Write the note names of this chromatic scale within one octave on the diagram. Use sharp names for black keys, natural names for white keys (don't use any flats at all).

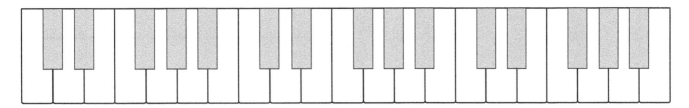

9. Find the starting note of a chromatic scale that has this sequence of black (*b*) and white (*w*) keys: *bwwbwbwwbwbwb*. Write the note names of this chromatic scale within one octave on the diagram. Use flat names for black keys, natural names for white keys (don't use any sharps at all).

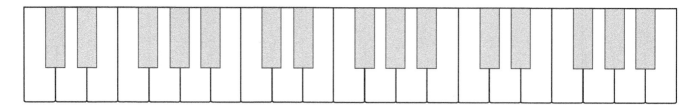

10. Find the starting note of a chromatic scale that has this sequence of white (*w*) and black (*b*) keys: *wbwbwwbwbwbww*. Write the note names of this chromatic scale within one octave on the diagram. Use natural names for white keys, flat names for black keys (don't use any sharps at all).

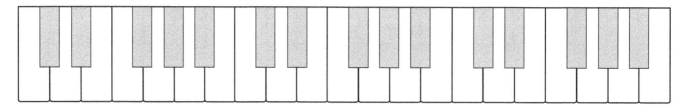

create!

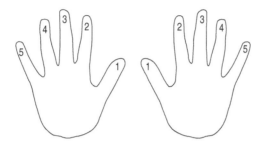

In any range of the piano keyboard, rest your left hand fingers on the notes C (finger 5), C♯ (4), D (3), D♯ (2), and E (1). Rest your right hand fingers on the notes F (finger 1), F♯ (2), G (3), G♯ (4), and A (5). Then try this:

1. Play an entire chromatic scale by following this sequence:

   - Play your left hand fingers 5–4–3–2–1.

   - Play right hand fingers 1–2–3–4–5. While your right hand is playing, reach over it with your left hand.

   - Play the rest of the scale with your left hand: A♯ (finger 3), B (2), and C (1).

   - Play all that in reverse to return via the descending chromatic scale to the note you started on.

2. Experiment with different sounds you can make such as:

   - All fingers playing together at the same time.

   - All fingers in each hand playing at the same time.

   - Both hands playing together, one finger at a time, moving left to right or right to left (LH 5 + RH 1; LH 4 + RH 2; etc.).

   - Both hands playing together, one finger at a time, moving toward or away from each other (same number sequence in both hands).

3. Improvise using finger patterns such as:

   - Alternating notes selected from different hands.

   - A finger pattern in one hand imitating a finger pattern in the other.

   - A finger pattern in one hand contrasting a finger pattern in the other.

   - Finger patterns in dialogue with each other, perhaps in disagreement, or in a conversation that evolves from agreement to argument to resolution.

LESSON **3**

HALF AND WHOLE STEPS

3.1   STEPS IN MUSIC

In Lesson 1 we learned that a chromatic scale contains all the notes, white and black keys, within an octave, and in Lesson 2 we described the distances between those notes as half steps. Let's explore these concepts further.

Most of the time within the chromatic scale, half steps are formed between a white key and a black key, like C and C♯, or G♯ and A:

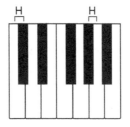

H = half step

In only two instances within an octave do we find half steps between two white keys, E to F and B to C:

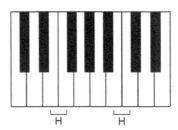

A distance of two half steps combined is called a **whole step**. Any two white keys with a black key between comprise a whole step:

W = whole step

Black keys within groups are also separated by whole steps:

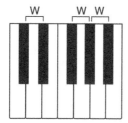

And when E and F or B and C are involved, whole steps are formed between a white key and a black key:

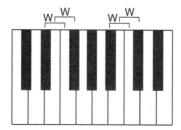

3.2 SPELLING CONVENTIONS FOR HALF AND WHOLE STEPS

We'll follow certain spelling conventions when notating steps. Always spell whole steps using letters that are adjacent in the musical alphabet. Between white-key whole steps, C–D (not B♯–D), A–B (not A–C♭), and so forth:

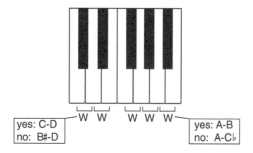

Between black-key whole steps, C♯–D♯ or D♭–E♭ (not C♯–E♭), A♭–B♭ or G♯–A♯ (not G♯–B♭), and so forth:

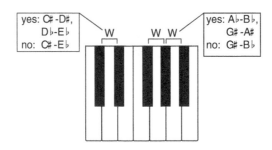

Between a white and a black key, E♭–F or D♯–E♯ (not D♯–F or E♭–E♯), B–C♯ or C♭–D♭ (not B–D♭ or C♭–C♯), and so forth:

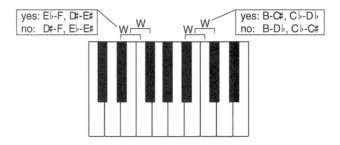

Half steps may be spelled using the same letter or adjacent letters. (Later we'll study reasons for using one spelling or the other.) Half steps spelled with the same letter (C–C♯, E♭–E, F♭–F, A♭–A, and so forth) are known as **chromatic half steps**. Half steps spelled with adjacent letters (C–D♭, D♯–E, E–F, G♯–A, and so forth) are called **diatonic half steps**. Never spell a half step using letters that aren't adjacent (B♯–D♭, D♯–F♭).

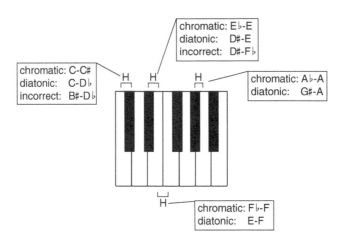

3.3   THE WHOLE-TONE SCALE

A scale consisting entirely of whole steps is called a **whole-tone scale**. Because a whole step is a combination of two half steps, it's easy to think of a whole-tone scale as an extraction of every other note of a chromatic scale. Out of twelve, you select six, every other note:

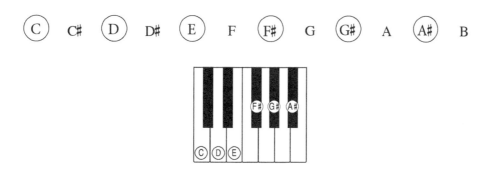

The six notes you jumped over also make a complete series of whole steps—a whole-tone scale with completely different notes:

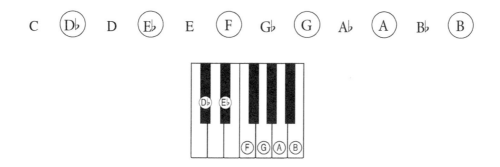

Notice the spelling change to flats for black keys in the second example, to ensure that all the steps are spelled with adjacent letters.

Unlike the white-key scales we studied in Lesson 1, which use all seven letters of the musical alphabet, the whole-tone scale uses only six.

For suggestions for further listening, go to www.oup.com/us/lambert

► STUDY QUESTIONS FOR LESSON 3

1. Define these terms:
    chromatic half step
    diatonic half step
    whole step
    whole-tone scale

2. Within one octave on the piano keyboard, which pairs of white keys are separated by whole steps?

3. Within one octave on the piano keyboard, which pairs of white keys are separated by half steps?

4. Within one octave on the piano keyboard, which pairs of black keys are separated by whole steps?

5. Give the number of different notes in these scales:
    whole-tone
    white-key
    pentatonic
    chromatic

6. What spelling convention is common to both the whole step and the diatonic half step?

▶ ## EXERCISES FOR LESSON 3

According to the spelling conventions explained in Lesson 3, a half step is "chromatic" if its two notes are both spelled with the same letter, but "diatonic" if its notes are spelled using adjacent letters. Whole steps are always spelled using adjacent letters. Suppose, for example, we start on D:

starting note	chromatic H ↑	diatonic H ↑	W ↑	chromatic H ↓	diatonic H ↓	W ↓
D	D♯	E♭	E	D♭	C♯	C

The same rules apply if we start on a note that has an adjacent white key:

starting note	chromatic H ↑	diatonic H ↑	W ↑	chromatic H ↓	diatonic H ↓	W ↓
B	B♯	C	C♯	B♭	A♯	A

A. Fill in the blanks with note names showing distances in half steps (H) and whole steps (W) up or down from the numbered keys.

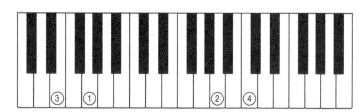

numbered key	chromatic H ↑	diatonic H ↑	W ↑	chromatic H ↓	diatonic H ↓	W ↓

1. _____ _____ _____ _____ _____ _____ _____

2. _____ _____ _____ _____ _____ _____ _____

3. _____ _____ _____ _____ _____ _____ _____

4. _____ _____ _____ _____ _____ _____ _____

B. Fill in the blanks with note names forming the specified steps from the starting note.

1. F: chromatic H ↑ = _____

2. F: diatonic H ↑ = _____

3. G#: chromatic H ↓ = _____

4. A♭: diatonic H ↓ = _____

5. F: diatonic H ↓ = _____

6. E♭: chromatic H ↑ = _____

7. G#: W ↓ = _____

8. A♭: W ↓ = _____

9. F: W ↑ = _____

10. G#: W ↑ = _____

11. A♭: W ↑ = _____

12. D#: chromatic H ↓ = _____

13. E♭: W ↑ = _____

14. E♭: W ↓ = _____

15. C#: diatonic H ↑ = _____

16. C#: W ↑ = _____

17. C#: chromatic H ↓ = _____

18. C#: W ↓ = _____

19. D♭: W ↓ = _____

20. D♭: W ↑ = _____

21. F#: chromatic H ↓ = _____

22. G♭: chromatic H ↑ = _____

23. G♭: W ↑ = _____

24. B#: diatonic H ↑ = _____

25. B#: chromatic H ↓ = _____

26. F♭: chromatic H ↑ = _____

27. F♭: W ↑ = _____

28. B♭: W ↑ = _____

29. B♭: W ↓ = _____

30. A#: diatonic H ↑ = _____

✒ create!

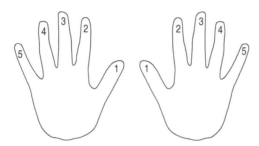

1. Rest the third finger of your right hand on any white key. Let's call this the "anchor." Place your other right-hand fingers as follows:

> 1: whole step below the anchor
>
> 2: half step below the anchor
>
> 3: anchor
>
> 4: half step above the anchor
>
> 5: whole step above the anchor

Play:

- This finger sequence: 3–4–3–5–3–4–3–2–3–1–3–2–3.

- The same finger sequence using different white keys as anchors.

- The same finger sequence using various black keys as anchors.

- Similar sequences in your left hand.

- Improvised finger sequences in hands separately or together.

2. Arrange fingers 2, 3, and 4 of your left (L) and right (R) hands on the notes of the whole-tone scale as follows:

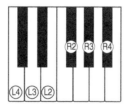

Try different combinations of these notes to explore the sound of the whole-tone scale. First, just play it as a scale. Then play all the notes at the same time. Try playing just the first three together, then the last three. Look for other interesting combinations.

Then shift your fingers to the other whole-tone scale:

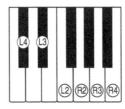

Explore this one as you did the other one. Try moving back and forth between the two. Make patterns in one and then play the same patterns in the other. Improvise a melody in your right hand and an accompaniment in your left hand, using the two scales in alternation or in combination.

LESSON 4
RHYTHM AND METER

4.1   NOTATION OF RHYTHM

Music is sound, and sounds have duration. The specific durations used in a musical presentation, and their organization, are known as musical **rhythm**. Our study of musical notation starts with a set of symbols for notating musical durations. After we've surveyed the possibilities, we'll explore some musical contexts in which they might be used.

This is a **quarter note**:

The head of a quarter note is a black oval. The stem extends upward from the right or downward from the left:

A **half note** is notated exactly like a quarter note but with an open note head:

A half note is twice the length of a quarter note. In a series of quarter notes and half notes played together, two quarter notes take up the same amount of time as one half note:

half notes:

quarter notes:

31

To notate a duration twice the length of a half note—in other words, the equivalent of four quarter notes—use the **whole note**. It's an open note head without a stem. In a series of quarter notes, whole notes occur every other half note, or every fourth quarter note:

To notate durations that are half the length of the quarter note, use the **eighth note**, which is a quarter note plus a flag:

Two eighth notes have the same duration as one quarter note. In a series of quarter notes, two eighth notes occur in the same space as one quarter note:

We often replace flags with **beams**:

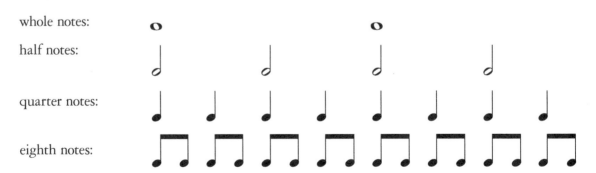

Here the beams group the eighth notes in pairs to show their relationship to quarter notes. Later in this lesson, we'll explore the use of beams in greater detail.

To notate durations that are half the length of the eighth note—in other words, one fourth the length of the quarter note—use the **sixteenth note**, which is a quarter note plus two flags or beams:

Two sixteenth notes have the same duration as one eighth note. Four sixteenth notes have the same duration as one quarter note:

Again, the beams for the eighths and sixteenths show groupings of these notes within the space of one quarter note.

For note values even shorter than a sixteenth, add more flags/beams to make thirty-second notes (three flags/beams) or sixty-fourth notes (four flags/beams). The longest note value in modern notation is the **breve**, which is twice as long as a whole note and looks like this:

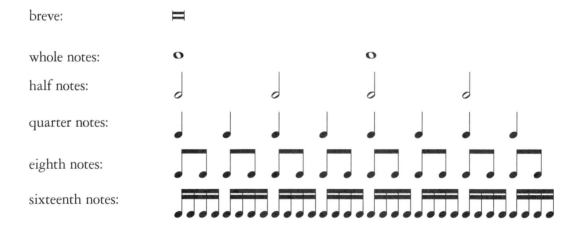

4.2   PATTERNS AND GROUPINGS

Most music has a pulse, just like you do. It's called the **beat**. The beat is regular and predictable; it divides time into equal parts. When music makes you want to dance, or march, or rap, or just tap your foot, you're responding to the beat.

For now, instead of visualizing beats as musical notes, let's imagine beats as syllables in the names of fruits and vegetables. Suppose you're fantasizing about a summer picnic and find yourself chanting the name of a favorite treat, one syllable per beat:

WA - TER - MEL- ON   WA - TER - MEL- ON   WA - TER - MEL- ON

You're not only keeping a steady beat. You're also organizing those beats into groups of four. Each full expression of the word makes a group:

| WA - TER - MEL- ON | WA - TER - MEL- ON | WA - TER - MEL- ON |

We place a little emphasis on the first syllable of this word. This helps establish where each grouping begins. The grouping of beats into regular patterns is known as **meter**. Musical notation involves not just specifying durations (Lesson 4.1) but also grouping them into units of meter.

Let's explore some possibilities. If you're chanting "wa-ter-mel-on" or "ru-ta-ba-ga" or "ap-ple" or "cher-ry," with one syllable per beat, you're grouping even numbers of beats. You could chant while you walk and always step with the same foot on the same syllable:

left	*right*	*left*	*right*	*left*	*right*	*left*	*right*	*left*	*right*	*left*	*right*
WA -	TER -	MEL-	ON	WA -	TER -	MEL-	ON	WA -	TER -	MEL-	ON
RU -	TA -	BA -	GA	RU -	TA -	BA -	GA	RU -	TA -	BA -	GA
AP -	PLE	AP -	PLE	AP -	PLE	AP -	PLE	AP -	PLE	AP -	PLE
CHER-RY		CHER-RY		CHER-RY		CHER-RY		CHER-RY		CHER-RY	

Groupings of four beats ("wa-ter-mel-on" or "ru-ta-ba-ga") are known as **quadruple meter**. Groupings of two beats ("ap-ple" or "cher-ry") are called **duple meter**.

The second type of grouping is known as **triple meter** because it organizes beats into groups of threes:

STRAW - BER - RY	STRAW - BER - RY	STRAW - BER - RY
BLUE - BER - RY	BLUE - BER - RY	BLUE - BER - RY
PINE - AP - PLE	PINE - AP - PLE	PINE - AP - PLE
AP - RI - COT	AP - RI - COT	AP - RI - COT

Waltzes and minuets are in triple meter. They have three-part step patterns, emphasizing every third beat, by contrast with the two-part, left-right, back-and-forth patterns of duple and quadruple.

4.3   NOTATION OF METER

Let's translate these principles into musical notation. Each grouping is called a **measure** or **bar**. The vertical lines separating them are called **bar lines**. A **meter signature** consists of two numbers shown at the beginning of the music. These numbers can mean different things (as we'll see in Lesson 10), but in this case, the top number indicates the number of beats per measure, and the bottom number indicates which type of note represents the beat. Here's one possibility:

$$\begin{array}{|cccc|cccc|cccc|} \frac{4}{4} & & & & & & & & & & & \\ \text{WA - TER - MEL - ON} & & & & \text{WA - TER - MEL - ON} & & & & \text{WA - TER - MEL - ON} & & & \end{array}$$

The "4" on the top indicates four-beat groupings. The "4" on the bottom indicates that each beat is notated as a quarter note.

$$\frac{4}{4} \quad \longleftarrow \text{ number of beats ber measure}$$
$$\quad \longleftarrow \text{ note value used to represent one beat}$$

A duple meter might look like this:

$$\begin{array}{|cc|cc|cc|cc|cc|cc|} \frac{2}{4} & & & & & & & & & & & \\ \text{AP - PLE} & & \text{AP - PLE} & & \text{AP - PLE} & & \text{AP - PLE} & & \text{AP - PLE} & & \text{AP - PLE} & \end{array}$$

. . . indicating a two-beat grouping with beats notated as quarter notes. And a triple meter might look like this:

$$\begin{array}{|ccc|ccc|ccc|} \frac{3}{4} & & & & & & & & \\ \text{STRAW - BER - RY} & & & \text{STRAW - BER - RY} & & & \text{STRAW - BER - RY} & & \end{array}$$

. . . indicating a three-beat grouping with beats notated as quarter notes.

The notes in one measure must always add up to the required number of beats for that measure. It might be any combination of the note values we surveyed at the beginning of this lesson, but they must always come together to form a complete measure in the notated meter.

A big "C" as a meter signature means the same as $\frac{4}{4}$. That's called **common time**:

The beat isn't always notated as a quarter note. In a meter signature with a "2" as the lower number, the beat is notated as a half note:

$\frac{2}{2}$ can also be notated as a big "C" with a line through it, called **cut time**:

And in a meter signature with "8" as the lower number, the beat is notated as an eighth note:

When you change the notation of the beat, you don't necessarily change the way it sounds, only the way it looks.

Composers and arrangers—notators of music—may have many different reasons for choosing one beat notation over another. Sometimes they associate a certain meter signature with a certain style of music. Marches and upbeat show tunes are often notated in cut time, for example (as opposed to $\frac{2}{4}$ or $\frac{4}{4}$). Waltzes are typically notated in $\frac{3}{4}$ (as opposed to $\frac{3}{8}$ or $\frac{3}{2}$). In many instances, the decision to notate in duple versus quadruple meter can seem fairly arbitrary, given that two measures of duple can easily be heard as one measure of quadruple (and $\frac{4}{4}$ can easily become $\frac{2}{2}$ by speeding up the beat). Regardless of customs or other factors, notators try to choose a meter that will communicate their ideas most effectively to the person who will convert their symbols into sounds—the performer.

4.4   BEATS AND BEAMS

Beams can help organize the rhythm in helpful ways. Look at this rhythm, for example:

It's easy to lose your place in a long series of flagged eighth notes, but if you replace the flags with beams, the difficulty disappears. The most helpful way to beam this measure would be to group the notes into pairs that correspond with the four beats in the measure:

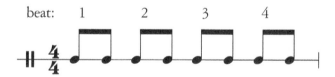

Sometimes you'll also see beams that divide the measure in half . . .

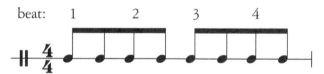

. . . but don't let a beam cross over from one half of the measure to the other:

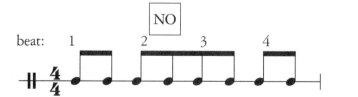
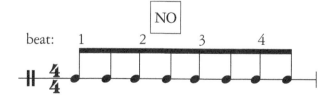

To add beams in place of flags in any rhythm, first identify the notes that fall on the beats:

Then add beams to group together notes within the same beat:

Here are some incorrect beamings of those same rhythms:

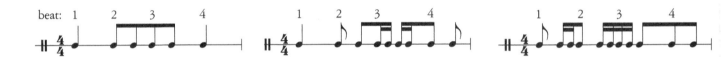

4.5   LEARNING AND PERFORMING RHYTHMS

The process of translating notational symbols into music-making can vary from student to student, teacher to teacher, place to place. For many, it's a very personal undertaking, a result of inexplicable internal neuron-firing. For others, it's a process that can be systematized and strategized.

Let's strategize. Suppose you want to perform this rhythm:

First, establish a regular beat. You can tap your foot, but you might find it easier to use a metronome. Choose a moderate tempo. Notice where each note falls in relation to the beats in the measure:

Play (or sing) the notes, always keeping track of your position in the measure relative to the beat. In the first measure, simply play a note on each beat. In the second, play half notes, the first one starting on beat 1 and continuing through beat 2, the second starting on beat 3 and extending through beat 4. In the third measure, play along with the beats on beats 1 and 4, but on beats 2 and 3 you play notes with half-beat durations: play these eighth notes so that they evenly divide the space between beats 2 and 3 and between beats 3 and 4. And in the last measure, start a note on beat 1 and hold it for the entire measure, stopping the sound on what would be the first beat of the next measure.

For eighth and sixteenth notes, it might help to use a counting system that associates distinctive syllables with particular durations. For notes with half-beat durations, add "&" [and] or "te" halfway between the beats:

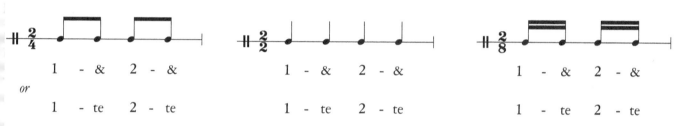

For notes with quarter-beat durations, subdivide the space between beats into four equal parts by adding "e-&-a" or "ti-te-ta":

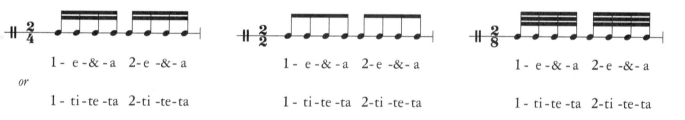

Here's how the syllables would be used for one of the rhythm exercises at the end of this lesson:

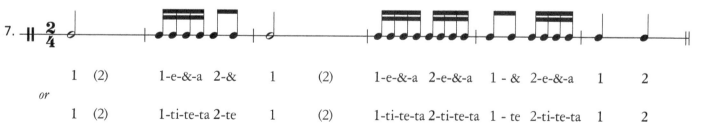

4.6   TEMPO

Beats come in many speeds. In music expressing elation or excitement, they may zip by pretty quickly. In dirges or lullabies they can follow a snail's pace. Plenty of music, from military marches to rock anthems, falls somewhere in between. The musical term for the speed of the beat is the Italian word for "time"—**tempo**.

The specification of tempo appears above the first measure of a musical score. An Italian word or phrase is common, although other languages, such as English, French, or German, are also used, often reflecting the nationality of the publisher (and/or composer). Also above the first measure it's common to find a numerical measurement of beats per minute on a metronome ("M.M." = "metronome marking").

Here are some common tempo specifications:

	M.M. *(approx.)*	*Italian*	*French*	*German*
Extremely Slow	40	Grave	Très lent	Sehr langsam
Very Slow	56	Largo or Adagio	Lent	Langsam
Slow	66	Lento	Un peu lent	Etwas langsam
Moderately Slow	84	Andante	Très modéré	Mässig langsam
Moderate	92	Moderato	Modéré	Mässig bewegt
Moderately Fast	100	Allegretto	Un peu animé	Etwas bewegt
Fast	120	Allegro	Animé	Bewegt or Schnell
Very Fast	148	Vivace	Vif or Vite	Lebhaft or Eilig
Extremely Fast	160	Presto	Très vif	Ganz schnell or Sehr lebhaft

 For suggestions for further listening and online exercises and drills, go to www.oup.com/us/lambert

STUDY QUESTIONS FOR LESSON 4

1. Define these terms:

bar	meter
bar line	meter signature
beam	quadruple meter
beat	quarter note
common time	rhythm
cut time	sixteenth note
duple meter	tempo
eighth note	triple meter
half note	whole note
measure	

2. Describe the difference in the appearance of these notes:

    quarter note and half note

    half note and whole note

    eighth note and quarter note

    eighth note and sixteenth note

3. Describe the mathematical proportion between these notes:

    quarter note and half note

    quarter note and eighth note

    sixteenth note and quarter note

    eighth note and whole note

    breve and whole note

    thirty-second note and whole note

4. What numbers would you expect to find as the lower values in meter signatures? What numbers would you never find as the lower values of meter signatures? Why?

5. How do beams make music reading easier?

6. Where do you find the tempo indication in a musical score?

7. Give some standard musical terms you could use to indicate these tempos in a piece of music:

    the ticking of a clock

    your normal walking pace

    your heartbeat

RHYTHM READING

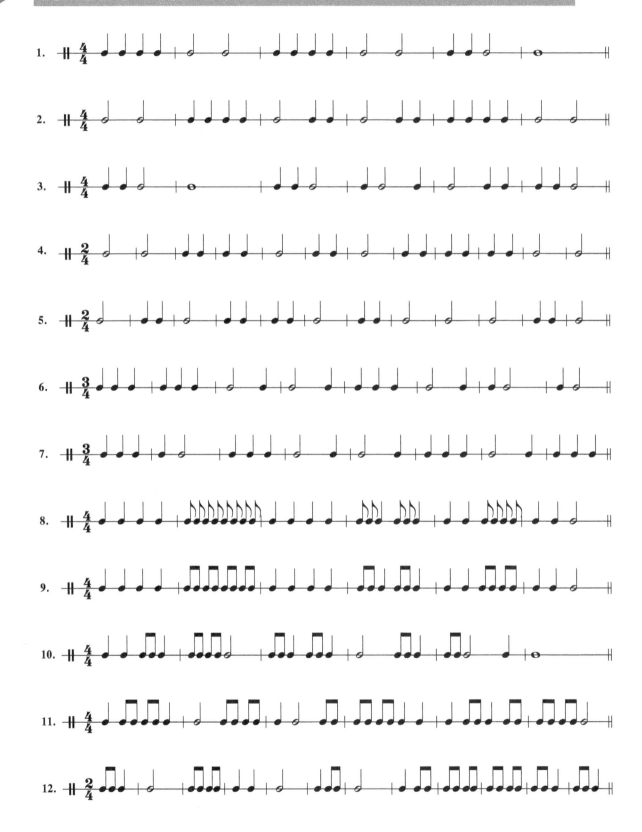

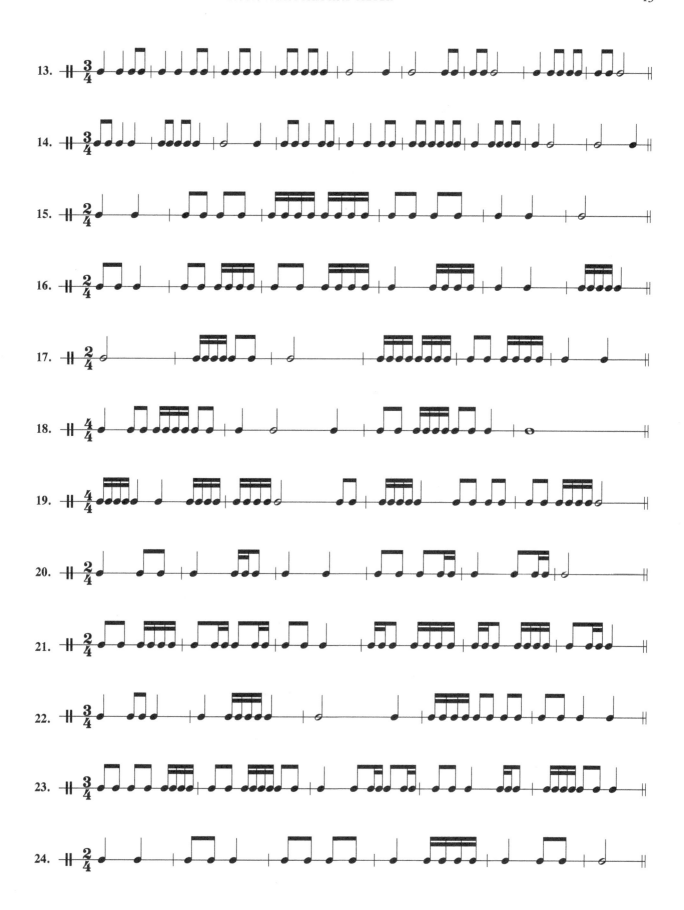

► EXERCISES FOR LESSON 4

Note values are defined in relation to each other. A quarter note is twice the duration of an eighth note but half the duration of a half note. (As a math equation, $1/4 = 2 * 1/8$ but $1/4 = 1/2 * 1/2$.) The commonly used rhythmic values, in order from shortest to longest, are:

♬	♪	♩	𝅗𝅥	𝅝
sixteenth	eighth	quarter	half	whole

In this array, each note is half the duration of the note on its right, double the duration of the note on its left.

A. Write one note in each blank to complete the equations.

1. ♩ + ♩ = _____

2. 𝅗𝅥 + 𝅗𝅥 = _____

3. ♪ + ♪ = _____

4. 𝅗𝅥 + 𝅗𝅥 + 𝅗𝅥 + _____ = 𝅝

5. ♬ + ♬ + ♬ + ♬ = _____

6. ♪ + ♪ + ♩ + 𝅗𝅥 = _____

7. ♩ + ♪ + _____ = 𝅗𝅥

8. ♬ + ♬ + ♩ + ♪ = _____

9. ♬ + ♪ + ♬ + ♩ + 𝅗𝅥 = _____

10. ♪ + ♬ + ♬ + ♪ + _____ = 𝅗𝅥

The notes in a complete measure of music must be equivalent to the number of beats defined by the meter signature (Lesson 4.3). To find the location of missing bar lines for the series of notes below, for example, make groups that are equivalent to two quarter notes:

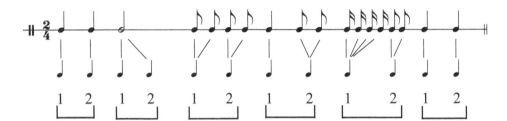

Insert bar lines to make each grouping a separate measure:

Use beams to group together flagged notes within the same beat:

B. Rewrite the rhythm in the space provided, inserting bar lines in the proper places. Replace all flags with beams to show the organization of the music into individual beats.

1.

2.

3.

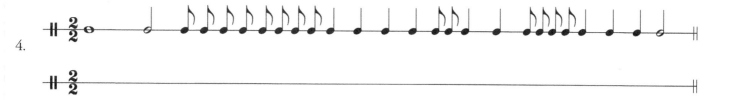

4.

5.

6.

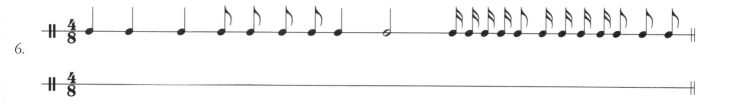

7.

A passage of music can be renotated in a different meter by redefining the beat as a different note value. The top number of the meter signature doesn't change (because the number of beats per measure doesn't change), but the bottom number does. Let's say we want to renotate this measure:

If we redefine the beat as the half note, the meter signature becomes $\frac{4}{2}$ and all the note values are doubled:

If we redefine the beat as the eighth note, the meter signature becomes $\frac{4}{8}$ and all the note values are halved:

In any of the three notations, the measure sounds exactly the same, assuming we haven't changed the tempo. In other words, each note in the original meter must have its counterpart in the corresponding measure of the new meter—a one-to-one correspondence.

C. Renotate the given rhythm on the next line in the specified meter. The new version should sound exactly the same as the original.

1.

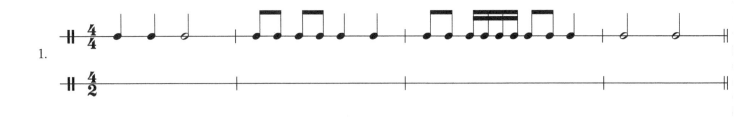

2.

3.

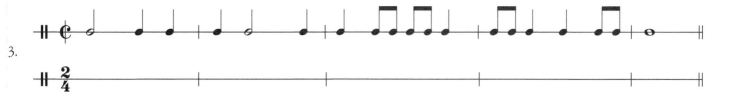

4.

5.

ᴄ✍ᴏ create!

1. Rest your left hand on the first five notes of the C scale starting one octave below middle C. Rest your right hand on the first five notes of the C scale starting on middle C. With your left hand, play this pattern over and over in quarter notes: C–E–G–E . . . (fingers 5–3–1–3 . . .). At the same time with your right hand, improvise a melody using a variety of rhythmic values.

2. Invent different accompaniment patterns using those same three notes in your left hand, and improvise a melody in your right hand. Switch among duple, triple, and quadruple meters.

3. Try some of the same patterns starting on different white or black keys.

4. Try reversing the roles of your hands: Improvise a melody in your left hand while your right hand provides the accompaniment.

LESSON **5**
STAFFS AND CLEFS

5.1   TREBLE CLEF

To express the pitches and scales we learned in Lessons 1 through 3 in musical notation, we will first need a **staff**:

We will assign a letter name to each of the five parallel lines in the staff, and to the spaces between them. Exactly how we do that is determined by the **clef sign**. This one is **treble clef**:

The treble clef is also called **G clef** because it curls around the note G. It indicates that if we place a note head on the second line of the staff, that note will be the G lying a few steps above middle C on the piano:

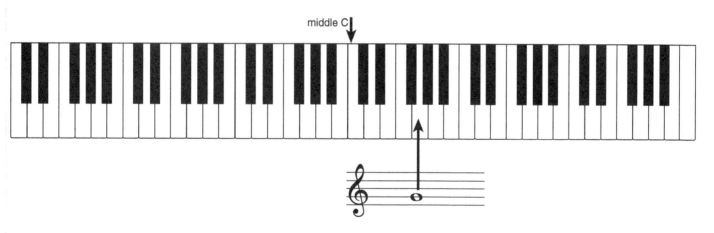

As you move upward in the staff, move forward in the musical alphabet, alternating lines and spaces. The next note up from G is a space, called A, followed by a line, B, and so forth. Moving downward on the staff moves backward through the musical alphabet: The note just below G is a space, F, and below that is a line, E, and so forth. Here are the names of all the lines and spaces in treble clef:

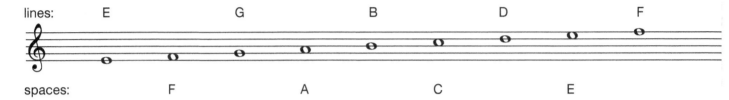

You might want to use a mnemonic device to remember these. The spaces are easy because they spell a word. For the lines, a perennial favorite is Every Good Boy Does Fine, but other possibilities range from ornithological (Every Good Bird Does Fly), to humanitarian (Every Good Boy Deserves Fudge), culinary (Every Good Burger Deserves Fries), zoological (Elephants Get Big Dirty Feet), music-historical (Elvis's Guitar Broke Down Friday), legal (Every Good Barrister Deplores Fraud), biblical (Eden Grows Beautiful Dainty Flowers), and weird (Electric Garbanzo Beans Don't Float). Can you think of other ones?

The staff can also be extended up or down by **ledger lines**:

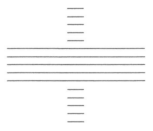

Ledger lines are equally spaced, the same distance apart as the lines in the staff. The musical alphabet continues for notes on or between ledger lines just it does within the staff:

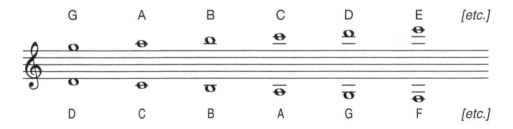

Notes that sit above the top line of the staff, or below the bottom line, or above or below a ledger line, don't need an extra ledger line on the outside:

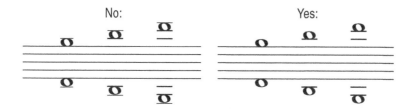

Here, then, is a summary of the notes typically used in treble clef:

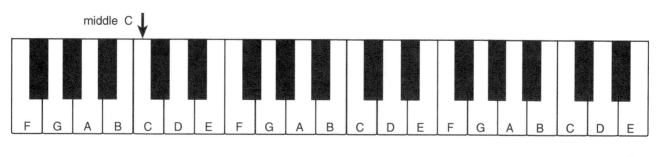

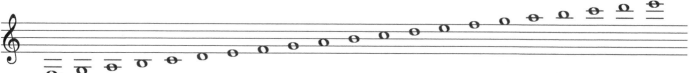

Notes higher than these may be notated using an **octave symbol**, which shifts a note up by one octave:

The octave symbol is useful for reading high notes without having to stop and count ledger lines. After an octave shift ends, you may see the word "loco," which tells you to return to normal notation.

5.2   BASS CLEF

Notes lower than treble clef may be notated in a different clef. In piano music, notes
on the lower part of the keyboard are notated in **bass clef**, also known as **F clef**
because it situates two dots on either side of the F that lies a few steps below middle C:

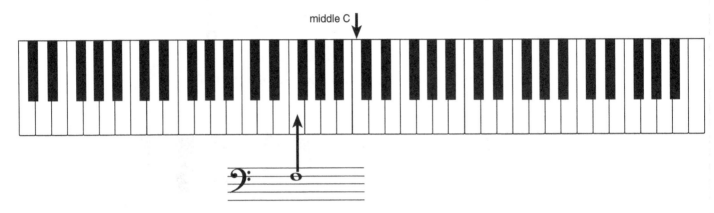

Deduce the names of the other lines and spaces just as we did for treble clef, by moving forward and backward in the musical alphabet:

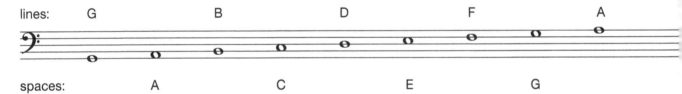

Again, mnemonic devices may come in handy. For the lines, one possibility is Great
Big Dogs Fight Animals, but perhaps you'd prefer something less violent (Grizzly
Bears Don't Fly Airplanes, Good Boys Do Fine [Deserve Fudge] Always), or even
pacifistic (Good Boys Don't Fight Anyone). For the spaces, try All Cows Eat Grass
or All Cars Eat Gas, or some other thing-or-animal-starting-with-C having a meal of
something-delectable-starting-with-G (All Crocodiles Eat Goldfish? All Californians
Eat Guacamole?).

Ledger lines work the same in bass clef as for treble clef:

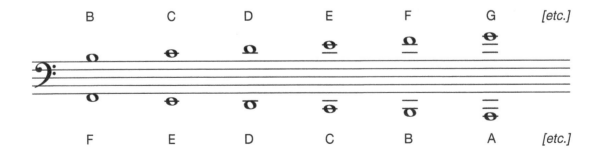

Here, then, is a summary of the notes typically found in bass clef:

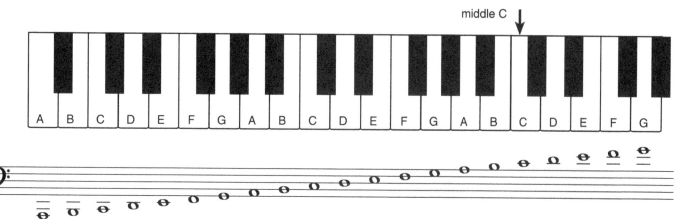

Notes lower than these may be notated with the **8va basso** symbol:

5.3   THE GRAND STAFF

You've probably noticed that the clefs overlap. Middle C, for example, is notated on the first ledger line below the treble clef or the first ledger line above the bass clef. Other notes in the general area just above and just below middle C can also be, and often are, notated in either clef. Notators usually have good reasons for choosing one clef over another for the notes surrounding middle C. The notation may help a pianist know which notes are to be played by the right hand and which by the left. If any of these notes appear in violin music, they would always be notated in treble clef, because violin music is always notated in treble clef. The tenor voices in choral music often sing these notes, but in that case they would be notated in bass clef, because the tenor part in choral music is customarily notated in bass clef.

It's easy to see the overlapping when we bring together the notes in both clefs:

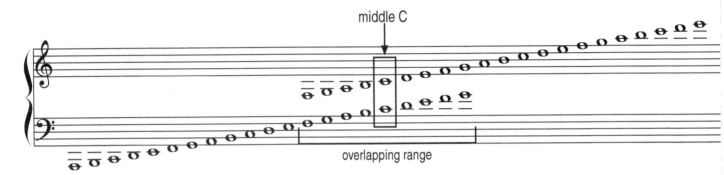

middle C

overlapping range

The pairing of a treble clef staff with a bass clef staff in this manner is known as the **grand staff**. Middle C is a useful point of orientation within the grand staff, because of its placement in the center of the overlapping range and at similar positions below the treble staff and above the bass staff. This is another sense in which that note is in the "middle" of something.

5.4   OCTAVE DESIGNATIONS

When discussing a passage of music, or writing about music for a project or assignment, you may need to be very specific about a particular pitch. You may want to refer to a specific E, not just any E. That's just like what we do when we say "middle C"—referring not just to any C, but specifically to the one white key named C that's roughly in the center of the piano keyboard, and between staffs in the grand staff.

One way to be pitch-specific is to use the staff as a point of reference: "the E on the top space of the treble clef" or "the E notated one ledger line below the bass clef," and so forth. But that approach can get old fast.

A more efficient method divides the range of human hearing into octaves, each starting on some C and including all the notes up to the next B. The lowest octave is the "0" octave; this includes some of the lowest notes on the piano. The middle range, starting on middle C, is the "4" octave. The highest key on the piano is the beginning of the "8" octave. To refer to a specific pitch, use its octave designation as a subscript. Here's what that looks like for the entire span of white keys on the piano:

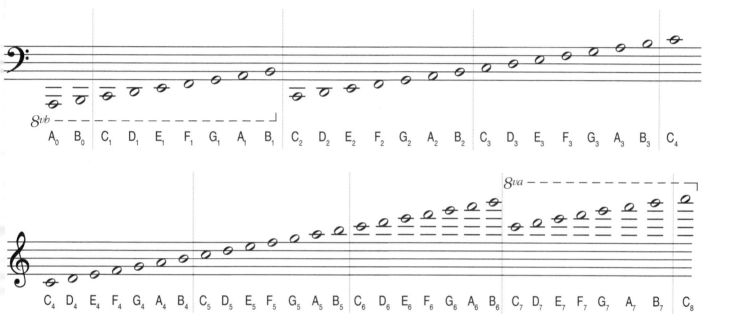

This notation is sometimes called the "**ASA Standard**" because it originated with the Acoustical Society of America.

So, instead of "E on the top space of the treble clef," you can just say or write "E_5." Instead of "E one ledger line below the bass clef," "E_2." Notes with accidentals are identified the same way:

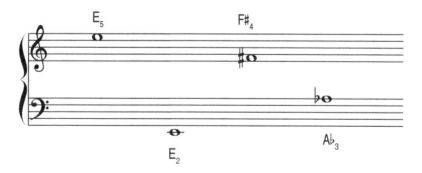

5.5   C CLEFS

Treble and bass are by far the most common clefs you'll find in printed music. All piano music, for example, is notated using these two clefs exclusively. Music for violin or flute is notated exclusively in treble clef, and music for double bass or tuba is notated exclusively in bass clef.

The music for some other instruments, however, uses different clef signs, either primarily or in certain circumstances. Viola music, for example, is notated primarily in **alto clef**, which situates middle C on the middle line of the staff:

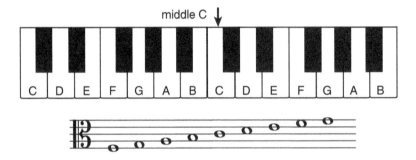

This symbol is known as a **C clef** because it is oriented around middle C. If you move the C clef symbol up two steps you have **tenor clef**, which situates middle C on the fourth line of the staff:

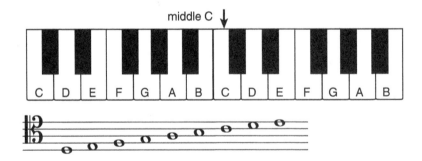

Cello, bassoon, and trombone music is primarily notated in bass clef but sometimes shifts to tenor clef for notes in the upper register of the instruments.

 For suggestions for further listening and online exercises and drills, go to www.oup.com/us/lambert

▶ STUDY QUESTIONS FOR LESSON 5

1. Define these terms:
   alto clef
   ASA standard
   bass clef
   C clef
   clef sign
   F clef
   G clef
   grand staff
   ledger line
   octave symbol
   staff
   tenor clef
   treble clef

2. What are the names of the lines and spaces in treble, alto, tenor, and bass clefs?

3. What note is in the center of the "overlapping range" on the grand staff?

4. What is the purpose of the octave symbol?

5. Give the ASA standard notation for these pitches:
   middle C
   an octave lower than middle C
   two octaves higher than middle C
   the E notated one ledger line below the bass clef
   the fourth line of the treble clef
   the lowest key on the piano
   the highest key on the piano

▶ **EXERCISES FOR LESSON 5**

To draw a treble clef symbol, (1) start below the staff and draw a curving line up through the staff; (2) make a loop at the top and curve back down, crossing over your earlier line at the fourth staff line and then bulge out to the left; (3) cross your earlier line again at the bottom line of the staff and curl around the second staff line:

A. Practice drawing treble clef symbols.

To draw a bass clef symbol, (1) make a tight clockwise curl around the fourth staff line and touch the top staff line; (2) continue the clockwise curl in the upper part of the staff and then straighten out the line as you reach the bottom staff line; (3) add two dots to the right, like a "colon" symbol, on either side of the fourth staff line:

B. Practice drawing bass clef symbols.

When you first learn treble and bass clefs (Lessons 5.1 and 5.2), mnemonic devices can help you remember the lines and spaces separately (EGBDF vs. FACE, GBDFA vs. ACEG). Our goal, however, is to recognize notes immediately by sight, without gimmicks.

Notes involving ledger lines can take even longer to learn. Move forward in the musical alphabet to identify notes above the staff, backward to identify notes below the staff. But eventually, learn to recognize these too by sight.

C. Above or below each note, write its name.

Optional: Label pitches in their specific octaves, as explained in Lesson 5.3 (the first one is B$_4$).

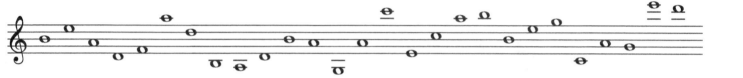

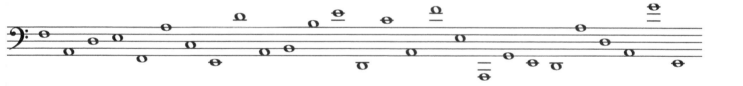

Middle C is situated in the center of the "grand staff" (Lesson 5.3). You can figure out the notation of any other key on the keyboard by knowing its relationship to middle C. The C that lies one octave lower than middle C, for example, is the next C down from middle C in bass clef:

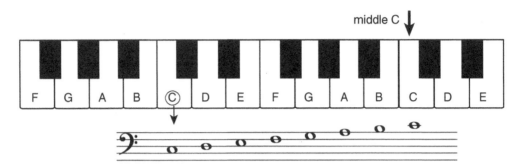

Notes in the overlapping range can be notated in either treble or bass clef:

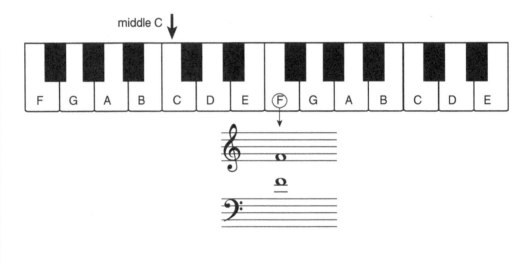

D. Find each numbered note on the keyboard diagram. On the staffs below, write that note underneath the corresponding number. (The first one is done for you, showing the location of middle C on the diagram.) If the note is in the overlapping range on the grand staff (as middle C is), write it in both treble and bass clefs.

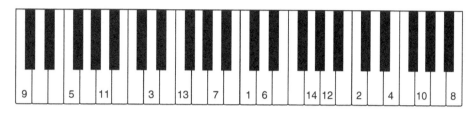

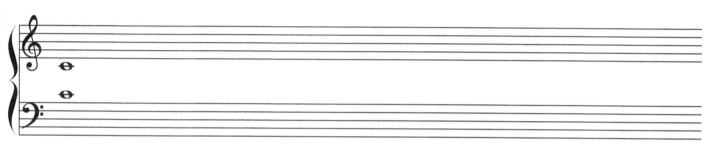

Because a white-key scale (Lesson 1.2) steps through the musical alphabet, it's notated on a staff with notes on alternating lines and spaces.

E. Notate all the white-key scales as a series of whole notes in treble and bass clefs.

C:

D:

E:

F:

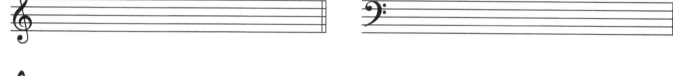

Name: _____

G:

A:

B:

F. Underneath each letter of each word, notate the corresponding musical pitch as a whole note on the staff, <u>without using ledger lines</u>. If a letter appears twice in the same word, use a different octave for the second occurrence (still, without using ledger lines).

1. F A C E   2. G A G   3. B E A D E D

4. D E C A F   5. B A G G E D   6. F E D

For the letters in words 7–10, write the corresponding pitches <u>above</u> or <u>below</u> the staff. (Most will require ledger lines.) As before, notate repeating letters within the same word as pitches in different octaves (but still <u>above</u> or <u>below</u> the staff).

7. D E C A D E   8. B A D G E

9. F E E D B A G   10. C A G E D

LESSON 5: STAFFS AND CLEFS

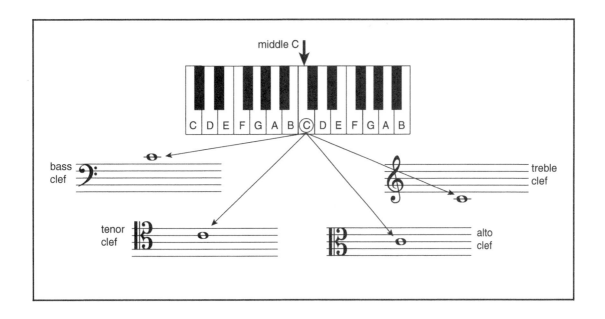

G. Above or below each note, write its name.

Optional: label pitches in their specific octaves, as explained in Lesson 5.3 (the first one is C$_4$).

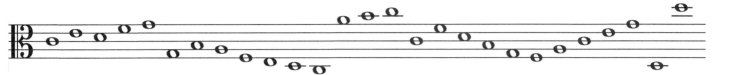

H. Underneath each letter of each word, notate the corresponding musical pitch as a whole note on the staff, <u>without using ledger lines</u>. If a letter appears twice in the same word, use a different octave for the second occurrence (still, without using ledger lines).

1. F   A   C   E   2. G   A   G   3. F   E   E   D   B   A   G

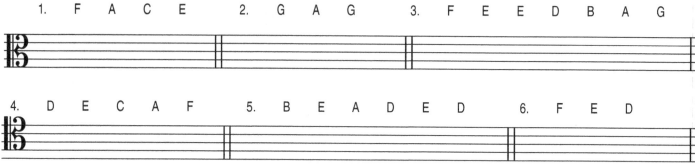

4. D   E   C   A   F   5. B   E   A   D   E   D   6. F   E   D

For the letters in words 7–10, write the corresponding pitches <u>above</u> or <u>below</u> the staff. (Most will require ledger lines.) As before, notate repeating letters within the same word as pitches in different octaves (but still <u>above</u> or <u>below</u> the staff).

7.   D   E   C   A   D   E   8.   B   A   D   G   E

9. B   A   G   G   E   D   10. C   A   G   E   D

✑ create!

Play note sequences on the piano that spell words on the staff (such as those in sections F and H of the Lesson 5 exercises). Think of different ways to develop these note sequences into music:

• Improvise melodies based on the note sequences.

• Use a note sequence as a repeating pattern in your left hand while you improvise a melody using some of the same notes in your right hand (or vice versa).

• Do the same but use only black keys in your improvised melody.

• Play the notes at the same time rather than in sequence. Which words make harmonious combinations and which ones don't? Use some of these combinations as the basis for an accompaniment and improvisation.

LESSON **6**
MORE RHYTHM AND METER

6.1 STRESS PATTERNS AND METER

Sing the opening of the song known in England as "God Save the Queen," better known in the United States as "America":

My coun-try 'tis of thee, sweet land of lib-er-ty, of thee I sing . . .

Let's figure out how to notate the rhythm of this phrase. We start by determining the meter, by finding the beat groupings. To do that, we need to listen for a stress pattern, for emphasized words or syllables. The stress pattern in this melody begins on the first word:

My coun-try **'tis** of thee, **sweet** land of **lib**-er-ty, **of** thee I **sing** . . .

By keeping a steady beat, and placing each stressed word or syllable at the beginning of a measure, we can make a three-beat grouping:

1	2	3	1	2	3	1	2	3	1	2	3	1	2	3	1	2	3 . . .
My	coun-	try	**'tis**		of thee,	**sweet**	land	of	**lib**	-	er- ty,	**of**	thee	I	**sing** . . .		

As we learned in Lesson 4, this is triple meter, three beats per measure. In other words, the top number of the meter signature will be "3." That's determined by the music.

The bottom number, indicating which note type is defined as the beat, is determined by the notator. In common practice we use the quarter note as the beat here; we would expect to find "4" as the bottom number of the meter signature. That's the notation that most musicians know best and expect. As you know from Lesson 4, however, melodies can be notated using several different beat units: only custom and pragmatism, not any principle of notation, prevents us from defining the beat as an eighth note or half note.

6.2　DOTTED NOTES

So we'll notate "America" in $\frac{3}{4}$ meter. To determine exactly what the complete rhythm will look like, start by singing or playing the song while listening carefully to the beat. Notice, for example, that the words or syllables in measures 1, 3, and 5 occur right on the beats, and have the same duration as beats. Those notes will be notated as quarter notes.

How do we notate measures 2 and 4? In measure 2, the word "'tis" happens on the first beat of the measure, the downbeat, but the next note, on "of," happens halfway between beats 2 and 3. Similarly in measure 4, the first syllable of "lib-er-ty" falls on the downbeat, but the second syllable falls halfway between beats 2 and 3. The first notes of these measures are longer than a quarter note, but not as long as a half note; they last for 1½ beats.

To notate these notes we will use a **dotted note**. A dot placed just after a note head extends that note's duration by half:

In other words, the value of the dot is half of the value of the note that precedes it; a dotted quarter note is the equivalent of a quarter note combined with an eighth note. That's the best way to notate the first notes of measures 2 and 4.

When writing notes on the staff, a dot following a note on a space is centered in that space:

A dot following a note on a line is positioned above the line:

Dots may be added to any note value:

$$\mathbf{o} \cdot \; = \; \mathbf{o} \; + \; \text{𝅗𝅥}$$

$$\text{𝅗𝅥} \cdot \; = \; \text{𝅗𝅥} \; + \; \text{𝅘𝅥}$$

$$\text{𝅘𝅥} \cdot \; = \; \text{𝅘𝅥} \; + \; \text{𝅘𝅥𝅮}$$

$$\text{𝅘𝅥𝅮} \cdot \; = \; \text{𝅘𝅥𝅮} \; + \; \text{𝅘𝅥𝅯}$$

. . . and so forth. Occasionally dots are also added after other dots, creating **doubly dotted notes**. The second dot takes half the value of the first one. A doubly dotted quarter note, for example, is the equivalent of a quarter combined with an eighth (first dot) and a sixteenth (second dot).

$$\text{𝅘𝅥} \cdot\cdot \; = \; \text{𝅘𝅥} \; + \; \text{𝅘𝅥𝅮} \; + \; \text{𝅘𝅥𝅯}$$

But we need only some single dots to notate the rhythm of the entire first phrase of "America":

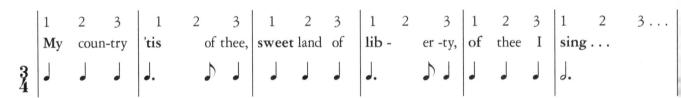

The final dotted half note has a duration of three beats: two from the half note, and one from the dot, which is the equivalent of half of a half note, or a quarter note.

A **tie** is another way of combining durations. That final dotted half note, for example, could be notated as a half note tied to a quarter note:

$$\text{𝅗𝅥} \cdot \; = \; \text{𝅗𝅥} \smile \text{𝅘𝅥}$$

But ties can also be used to combine durations that can't also be expressed using dots. Any two notes may be tied together, within or between measures.

6.3   THE ANACRUSIS

Now sing the opening of "America the Beautiful":

Oh beaut-i-ful for spa-cious skies, for am-ber waves of grain . . .

We immediately notice two big differences with the stress patterns of "America." One is that the first stressed note of "America the Beautiful" is not the first note of the melody. We sing "Oh **beaut**-i-ful for spa-cious skies," not "**Oh** beaut-i-ful for spa-cious skies. . . ." That first note ("Oh") that precedes the first stressed note is called an **upbeat** or **pickup** or **anacrusis**.

The second big difference is that the beat groupings in this song occur in fours, not threes:

	1	2	3	4	1	2	3	4	1	2	3	4	1	2	3 . . .
Oh	beaut	- i -	ful		for	spa -	cious	skies,	for	am -	ber	waves	of	grain . . .		

In other words, "America the Beautiful" is in quadruple meter. The top number of the meter signature is "4." In $\frac{4}{4}$ meter, its rhythms would look like this:

	1	2	3	4	1	2	3	4	1	2	3	4	1	2	3 . . .
Oh	beaut	- i -	ful		for	spa -	cious	skies,	for	am -	ber	waves	of	grain . . .		

The pickup note ("Oh") is notated as an incomplete first measure. By custom, the last measure of the entire song should also be incomplete, and the pickup plus the final measure should combine to form one complete measure. In this case, because the pickup measure is one beat, the last measure contains three beats:

. . . from | sea to shin- ing | sea.

The last measure always concludes with a **double bar**.

6.4   RESTS

We've been focusing on durations of *sounds*. Now let's think about durations of *silences*. Suppose, for example, that you decide not to use a dotted half note on the word "sing" at the end of the first phrase of "America." Instead, you want to notate just a half note on "sing" and then a **rest** on beat 3, to give the singer time to take a big breath before starting the next phrase. You would use a rest with the equivalent duration of a quarter note. That's called a **quarter rest**:

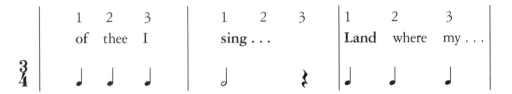
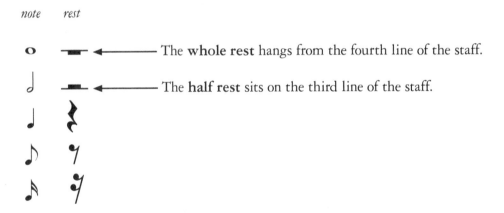

Each note has an equivalent rest:

note   *rest*

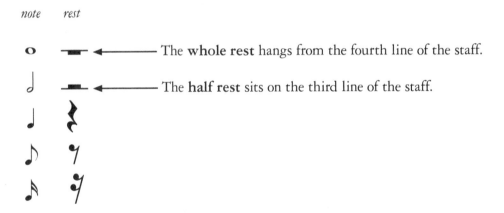

The **whole rest** hangs from the fourth line of the staff.

The **half rest** sits on the third line of the staff.

Rests may also be dotted to extend their duration by half, or doubly dotted to extend their duration by half of the first dot.

 For suggestions for further listening and online exercises and drills, go to www.oup.com/us/lambert

▶ STUDY QUESTIONS FOR LESSON 6

1. Define these terms:
   anacrusis
   dotted note (or rest)
   double bar
   doubly dotted note (or rest)
   eighth rest
   half rest
   pickup
   quarter rest
   rest
   sixteenth rest
   tie
   upbeat
   whole rest

2. What information is used to determine the meter of a melody?

3. Describe the difference in appearance of these pairs of rests:
   half rest and whole rest
   eighth rest and sixteen rest

4. Describe the mathematical proportion between these pairs of notes or rests:
   quarter and half
   dotted quarter and dotted half
   dotted quarter and dotted eighth
   dotted half and whole
   doubly dotted quarter and doubly dotted half

5. How does the notation of an upbeat affect the notation of the final measure?

6. True or false:
   A dotted note increases the number of beats per measure.
   A tie may connect notes in different measures.
   Rests may not be dotted.

RHYTHM READING

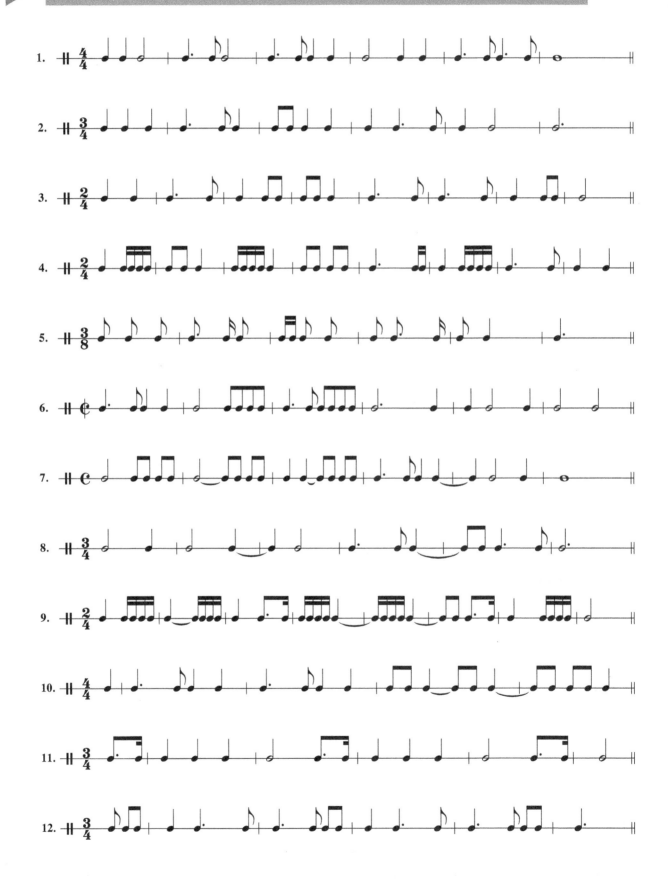

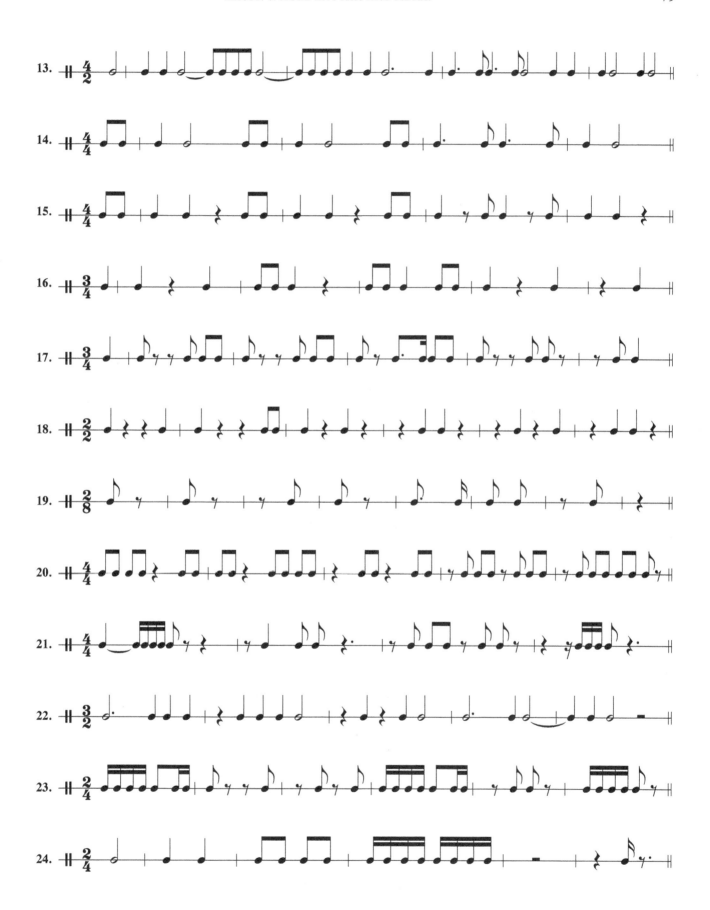

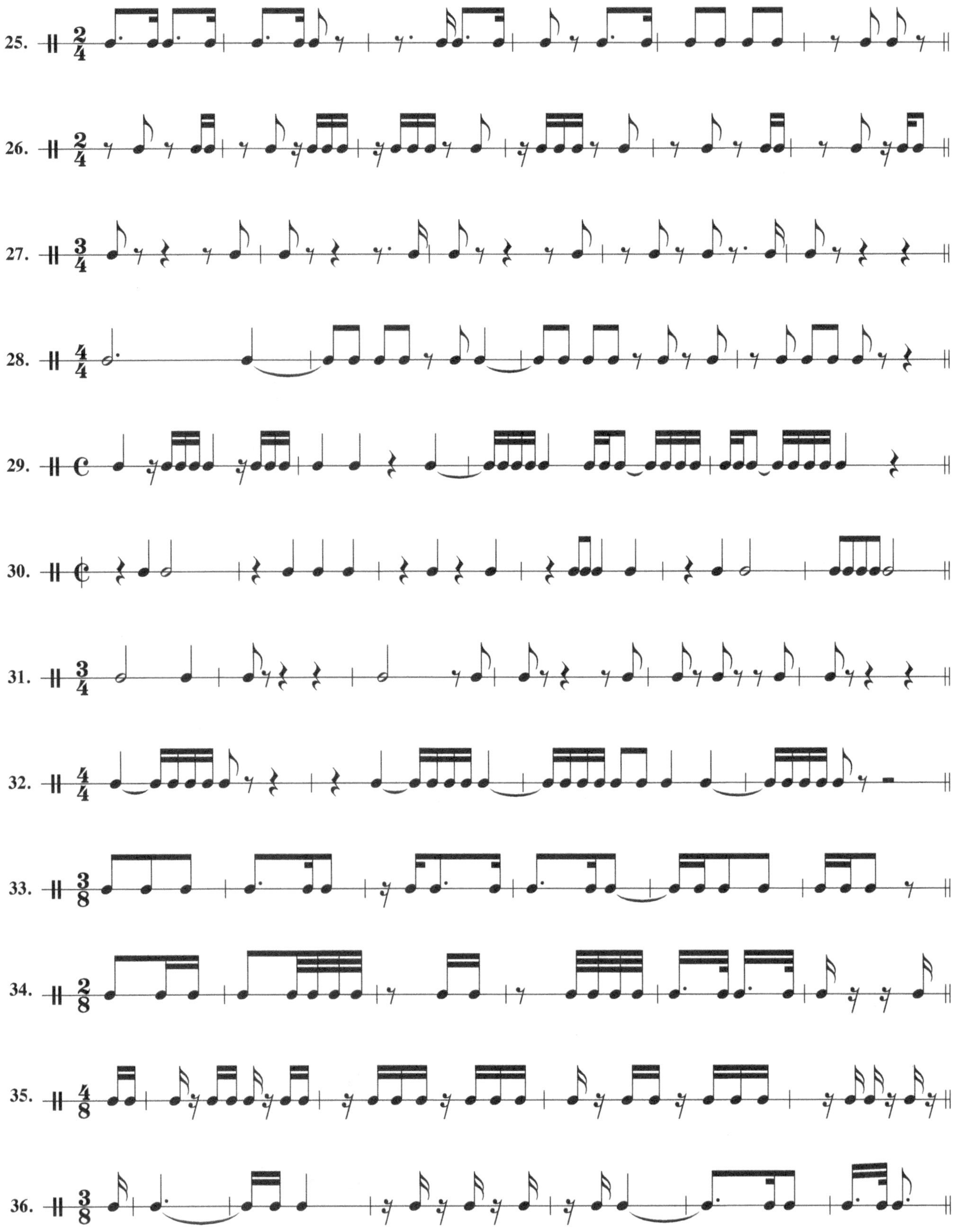
25.
26.
27.
28.
29.
30.
31.
32.
33.
34.
35.
36.

▶ EXERCISES FOR LESSON 6

Here are the commonly used rhythmic values and their equivalent rests, in order from shortest to longest:

A. Write one note in each blank to complete the equation.

1. ♩ + ♩ = _____

2. ♩ + ♪ = _____

3. ♪. + ♬ = _____

4. ♩ + ♪ + ♪ + ♩. + ♪ = _____

5. ♩. + ♩. = _____

6. ♬ + ♬ + _____ = ♪.

7. ♪ + ♩. + ♩ + _____ = o.

8. ♩ + ♩ + _____ = ♩..

B. Write one rest in each blank to complete the equation.

1. 𝄾 + 𝄾 = _____

2. 𝄼 + 𝄼 = _____

3. 𝄽 + _____ = 𝄽.

4. 𝄿 + 𝄿 + 𝄿 + 𝄿 = _____

5. 𝄽. + 𝄾 = _____

6. 𝄾 + 𝄾 + 𝄿 + 𝄿 = _____

To insert missing bar lines, make beat groupings determined by the meter signature as in the Lesson 4 exercises. Ties may connect notes in the same measure or in different measures:

C. Insert bar lines in the proper places.

1.

2.

3.

4.

5.

6.

To determine which note or rest is needed to make a measure complete, find the difference between what's there and what's required (as indicated by the meter signature). In $\frac{4}{4}$ meter, for example, determine how much more is needed to make the equivalent of four quarter notes:

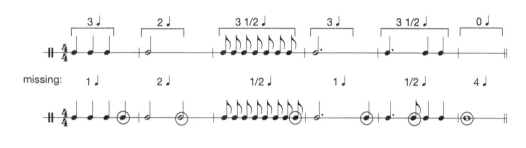

D. Add one <u>note</u> to each measure to make it complete in the prevailing meter.

E. Add one <u>rest</u> to each measure to make it complete in the prevailing meter.

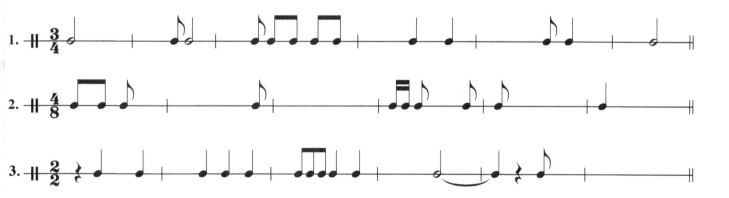

✑ create!

Take a short rhythm from one of the rhythm exercises, or create one of your own using dotted rhythms, and repeat it over and over using your feet and/or hands and/or a repeating note on an instrument.

- Make a recording of yourself repeating the rhythm. Play it back and improvise different rhythmic patterns to go with it, or improvise unpatterned rhythms.

- Continue a repeating rhythmic pattern while a friend improvises a complementary pattern or unpatterned rhythm to go with it. Try different sounds, such as foot-tapping, knee-slapping, hand-clapping, finger-snapping, and so forth.

- Use a repeating rhythmic pattern as the background for an improvised melody, on the white or black keys of the piano or on any instrument.

LESSON 7
THE NOTATIONAL SYSTEM

7.1   PITCH RESOURCES

In Lesson 6 we figured out the rhythm and meter of the first phrase of "America." Now we're ready to use what we know about pitch notation from Lesson 5 and specify both the rhythm and the pitches of the tune, by situating each notehead of the rhythm on a particular line or space of a musical staff. But what pitch do we start on, and how do we know which pitches to use?

Actually, we could start on any pitch and make it work. The choice of starting note might be influenced by a number of factors, such as the instruments we're writing for and the ability level of the musicians who will be performing. If we're notating the melody to be sung, we will want to make sure the pitches sit comfortably in the vocal ranges of the singers.

Let's see (and hear) what happens if we use C as a starting pitch for "America." The C repeats on the first word "My" and on the first syllable of "country." After that the melody moves up for the second syllable in "country." Use your ear to find the pitch it moves to, D. Then the melody jumps down on " 'tis." Listen for the difference between this note and the starting C: it's B, a half step lower. After that we hear a series of notes taken from a white-key scale, C–D–E, on the words "of thee, Sweet." Continue listening and experimenting until you've found all the notes in the first phrase of the melody, up through the final D–C–B–C on "Of thee I sing."

To notate the melody completely we take those notes and express them in the proper rhythms, in treble or bass clef:

7-1

or

By starting on C we were able to use only white keys for the melody. In fact, starting on C is the *only* way to use exclusively white keys for this melody. If we start on any other note, we'll need to use at least one black key to make it sound right.

Try starting on D, for example. Right after the first three notes, D–D–E ("My coun–try"), if you try jumping down to another white key for "'tis," you can hear that something's wrong. The only way to make it sound right is to jump down to C♯. Shortly after that, on "Sweet land" in measure 3, you need an F♯. You need F♯ again in measure 4 ("lib-") and C♯ again in measure 5 ("I"). So when we notate the melody starting on D, we'll need to use sharp signs to alter the Fs and Cs:

7-2

or

Place accidentals directly in front of notes they modify. The opening in the center of the symbol should be about the same size as a notehead, and should be positioned similarly on the line or space. Notice that the symbol doesn't need to be repeated in the same measure: once an F has been sharped, all subsequent occurrences of an F on the same line or space in that measure are automatically sharped. That's why no sharp sign appears on beat 2 of measure 3, on "land." After the next bar line, however, the alteration is canceled—that's why the sharp reappears on the first beat of measure 4 ("lib-").

If we start "America" on any other note, we will need a unique supply of accidentals to make the melody sound right. When we start on F, we'll use mostly white keys, but we'll need to use a B♭ on the word "of":

or

. . . and so forth. Our system of musical notation accommodates any starting pitch for "America," each calling for a unique combination of white and black keys.

7.2   STEPS ON THE STAFF

Let's think more about pitches and their notation, starting with a return to the chromatic scale (Lesson 1.3, 2.1). Here's one way to write chromatic scales on the grand staff:

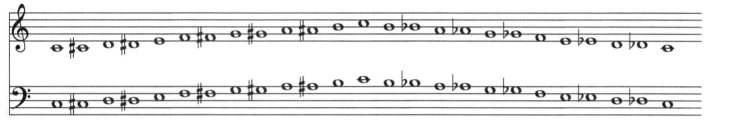

As we learned in Lesson 2, we have choices when notating black keys (between two enharmonic equivalences), and here we've notated black keys as sharps when going up the scale, flats when coming back down.

Looking at this notation of a chromatic scale also helps us see what half and whole steps look like on the staff (Lesson 3). *Chromatic* half steps stay on the same line or space, while *diatonic* half steps occupy neighboring lines and spaces:

At the two places where white keys aren't separated by a black key (E–F, B–C), we find two diatonic half steps right next to each other (D♯–E, E–F; A♯–B, B–C).

The steps formed between alternate notes in a chromatic scale are whole steps: <C (skip C♯) D>, <C♯ (skip D) D♯>, and so forth. But remember that whole steps, like diatonic half steps, must also be spelled with adjacent letters in the musical alphabet (Lesson 3.2). In other words, they must also occupy neighboring lines and spaces. That means that not all of the whole steps inherent in the spelling of the chromatic scale shown above are spelled correctly. Look at <D♯ (skip E) F>, for example. D♯ and F are not adjacent letters; they are on adjacent spaces, not on a neighboring line and space. (The problem recurs at the end, between A♯ and C.)

To fix this problem, all we have to do is respell the C♯ as D♭ and D♯ as E♭. That will alter the original arrangement of chromatic and diatonic half steps, but it will allow us to form correctly spelled whole steps between alternate notes:

The beams connecting whole steps formed by alternate notes in the chromatic scale help us visualize a chromatic scale as an interlocking of two whole-tone scales (Lesson 3.3).

► STUDY QUESTIONS FOR LESSON 7

1. Define these terms:
   chromatic half step
   chromatic scale
   diatonic half step
   whole step
   whole-tone scale

2. In a notation of "America" that uses only white keys, what is the starting note?

3. In the notation of "America" starting on D, which notes are sharped?

4. In a notation of "America" that uses white keys except for B♭, what is the starting note?

5. In a notation of a chromatic scale in the treble clef, where on the staff would you find consecutive notes without accidentals?

6. In a notation of a chromatic scale in the bass clef, where on the staff would you find natural notes (white keys) that are both preceded and followed by notes with accidentals?

7. After a sharp or flat has been applied to a note, how does that affect other occurrences of that same note in the same measure? In the next measure?

8. What would be incorrect about the spelling of the whole-tone scale shown below?
   C♯ D♯ F G A B

 For suggestions for further listening and online exercises and drills, go to www.oup.com/us/lambert

▶ EXERCISES FOR LESSON 7

When writing accidentals, the space in the center of the symbol should be about the same size as a notehead, and should be similarly situated on the line or space, **preceding** the notes they modify:

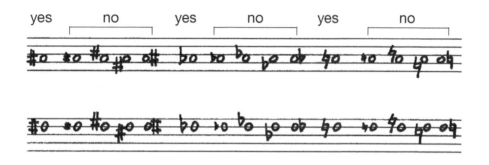

A. Notate two of the specified notes (one octave apart) in both clefs. In each measure, notate an accidental for <u>each</u> note (♯ ♭ or ♮), demonstrating their correct size and placement on the staff. The first one is done for you.

1. D♯   2. G♯   3. A♭   4. D♭   5. F♮   6. E♮   7. C♯   8. B♭

Because notes in chromatic half steps are spelled with the same letter (Lesson 3), they're notated on the same line or space in the staff:

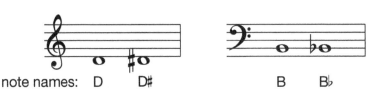

note names: D   D♯   B   B♭

B. In the staff next to each given note, write a note that is one chromatic half step <u>higher</u>. Below the staff, write the names of both notes.

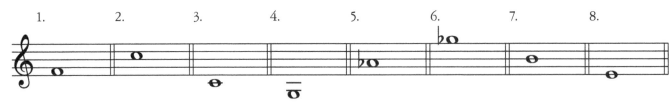

note
names: ____ ____ ____ ____ ____ ____ ____ ____ ____ ____ ____ ____ ____ ____ ____ ____

C. In the staff next to each given note, write a note that is one chromatic half step <u>lower</u>. Below the staff, write the names of both notes.

note
names: ____ ____ ____ ____ ____ ____ ____ ____ ____ ____ ____ ____ ____ ____ ____ ____

Name: _____

Because notes in diatonic half steps are spelled with adjacent letters (Lesson 3), they're notated on adjacent lines and spaces in the staff:

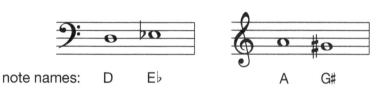

note names:　　　D　　E♭　　　　　A　　G#

D. In the staff next to each given note, write a note that is one diatonic half step <u>higher</u>. Below the staff, write the names of both notes.

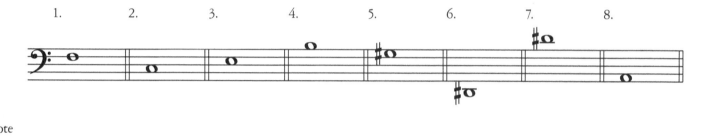

1.　　2.　　3.　　4.　　5.　　6.　　7.　　8.

note names: ___ ___　___ ___　___ ___　___ ___　___ ___　___ ___　___ ___　___ ___

E. In the staff next to each given note, write a note that is one diatonic half step <u>lower</u>. Below the staff, write the names of both notes.

1.　　2.　　3.　　4.　　5.　　6.　　7.　　8.

note names: ___ ___　___ ___　___ ___　___ ___　___ ___　___ ___　___ ___　___ ___

Name: _____

Because notes in whole steps are spelled with adjacent letters (Lesson 3), they're notated on adjacent lines and spaces in the staff:

note names: A   B   G   F

F. In the staff next to each given note, write a note that is one whole step <u>higher</u>. Below the staff, write the names of both notes.

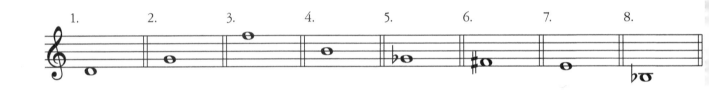

note
names: ____ ____   ____ ____   ____ ____   ____ ____   ____ ____   ____ ____   ____ ____   ____ ____

G. In the staff next to each given note, write a note that is one whole step <u>lower</u>. Below the staff, write the names of both notes.

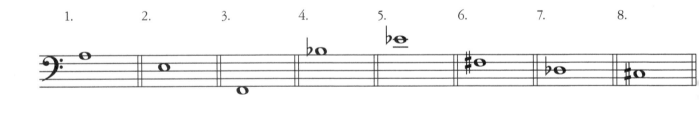

note
names: ____ ____   ____ ____   ____ ____   ____ ____   ____ ____   ____ ____   ____ ____   ____ ____

Different spellings of the same note ("enharmonics," Lesson 2) appear on adjacent lines and spaces in the staff:

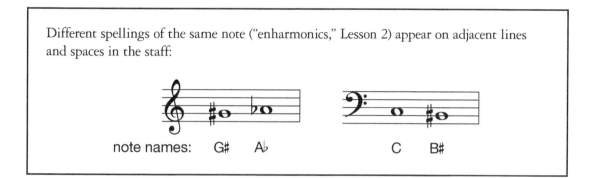

note names: G♯   A♭   C   B♯

H. In the staff next to each note, write its enharmonic equivalent. Below the staff, write the names of both notes.

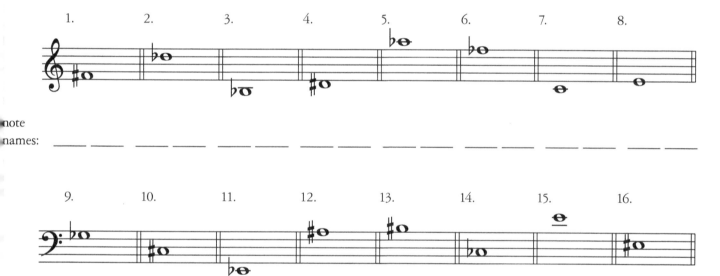

note
names: ____ ____   ____ ____   ____ ____   ____ ____   ____ ____   ____ ____   ____ ____   ____ ____

note
names: ____ ____   ____ ____   ____ ____   ____ ____   ____ ____   ____ ____   ____ ____   ____ ____

A scale of all half steps, the chromatic scale (Lessons 1.3, 2.1, 7.2), contains twelve differ-ent notes (excluding the repetition of the first note at the end): seven white keys and five black keys. When you're notating consecutive half steps to form a chromatic scale, make sure you write seven notes without accidentals (white keys) and five notes with accidentals (black keys). The black keys can all be notated as sharped notes:

. . . or the black keys can all be notated as flatted notes:

In either case, the scale alternates natural notes with sharped or flatted notes except for the two places in the octave where white keys aren't separated by a black key: between E and F, and between B and C. At those places (bracketed above), make sure you notate two natural notes in a row.

I. Write chromatic scales starting on the given notes. Spell black keys using sharps or flats as specified.

1. *(sharps for black keys)*

2. *(flats for black keys)*

3. *(sharps for black keys)*

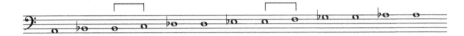

4. *(sharps for black keys)*

5. *(flats for black keys)*

6. *(flats for black keys)*

7. *(sharps for black keys)*

✍️ create!

Take a look at Etude in the Fifteen Character Pieces (www.oup.com/us/lambert). Notice that:

- The music in each hand stays within a single collection of notes, all of which are different from the collection in the other hand.

- The hands sometimes work in dialogue, other times in tandem.

- The rhythms are very basic, mostly quarter notes with a few halves and wholes.

Write a short piano piece modeled on Etude.

- Establish a certain pitch collection for each hand. These collections may or may not be the same as the ones in Etude.

- Start by improvising on the notes in these collections, going back and forth between the hands. Find the sounds and tone combinations that you would like to incorporate into your composition.

- The meter and rhythm are your choice.

- Notate your piece in the standard two-stave format for piano music (as in Etude). Check over your notation to make sure that your symbols are clear, noteheads are correctly placed, and measures contain the proper number of beats.

LESSON **8**
THE MAJOR MODE

8.1	**KEY AND TONIC**

Let's think more about the "America" melody. In Lesson 7 we noticed that if we start this melody on C, we use only white keys throughout the first phrase:

8-1

> My coun –try 'tis of thee, Sweet land of lib – er –ty, Of thee I sing.

To be more specific, the first phrase uses the white keys B, C, D, E, and F. Notice what happens in the rest of the song:

8-2

> Land where my fa – thers died, Land of the pil – grims' pride,
>
> From ev – ery moun – – tain - side, Let free - dom ring!

Immediately the second phrase begins with a note we haven't heard yet, G. We continue to hear more G's, along with other notes we've heard before, and then near the end, starting the dramatic final flourish, on the word "Let," we hear one last new note, A. With the arrival of the A we can confirm that we've heard all seven of the white-key notes at some point in the melody—that we've completed the musical alphabet.

We can say, then, that the white keys of the piano are the primary resource for the starting-on-C version of "America." As we learned in Lesson 1, however, there are seven different white-key scales, seven different orderings of the musical alphabet: ABCDEFG, BCDEFGA, CDEFGAB, DEFGABC, EFGABCD, FGABCDE, and GABCDEF. Which of these do you think *best* represents the pitch content of "America"?

Unlike the citizens of the democracy the song exalts, the notes of the starting-on-C version of "America" are not all created equal. We hear C not only at the beginning but also at the end of the first phrase (on the words "My" and "sing"). Most importantly, it's the song's final sound ("ring!"). C is more important than any of the other six white keys in this version of the song. C is the **key** of the music. We say that the song is *in* the key of C, that C is its **tonic** pitch, from C to shining C.

We can apply these same principles to determine the key of any piece of tonal music:

- First decide what its most important notes are. You may be able simply to collect together all the notes in the melody, although be aware that sometimes melodies use notes from outside the main collection as decorations or deviations.

- Look at the melody's final note. In most cases, this will be the tonic. You should also find this same note elsewhere in the melody, at crucial places such as phrase endings, and playing a primary role in the accompaniment. A melody's first note is generally *not* a reliable indicator of a song's tonic pitch: tonal melodies *don't* always start on the tonic pitch, but they usually do end on tonic.

- Put the notes in order, as a scale, starting on the tonic pitch.

8.2   THE DIATONIC MODES

When we choose the C scale over the other six white-key scales as a representation of the primary pitch material of the starting-on-C version of "America," we've made an important observation about the way the music sounds. If we came across other music using only white keys, but with a tonic of A, or D, or any of the other white keys, we would hear a big difference. Each of the seven white-key scales has its own sonic personality, its own means of distinguishing itself from the others.

For this reason, they have received separate attention and have been explored by composers in different ways. The seven white-key scales are also known as the **diatonic modes**. Each mode has its own traditional name:

> C white-key scale (CDEFGAB): **Ionian**
> D white-key scale (DEFGABC): **Dorian**
> E white-key scale (EFGABCD): **Phrygian**
> F white-key scale (FGABCDE): **Lydian**
> G white-key scale (GABCDEF): **Mixolydian**
> A white-key scale (ABCDEFG): **Aeolian**
> B white-key scale (BCDEFGA): **Locrian**

The Ionian mode, or C white-key scale, is more commonly known as **major**. If we sing "America" starting on C, we're singing in the key of C major.

8.3   STRUCTURE OF THE MAJOR SCALE

In a later lesson we'll study the Aeolian mode, also known as **minor**. For now, let's focus on major. Here again is the C white-key scale, which we now call the C major scale:

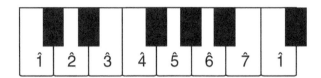

It helps to number the scale tones, repeating the first number when the octave is completed at the end. The rooftop (caret) over the numbers indicates **scale degree**. "$\hat{5}$" means "scale degree five."

As we noticed in Lesson 3, the C major scale is constructed mostly of whole steps between consecutive notes, but half steps between E and F ($\hat{3}$ and $\hat{4}$) and between B and the C octave ($\hat{7}$ and $\hat{1}$). It's easy to see this on a keyboard, because the notes you're skipping over when you form whole steps are the black keys:

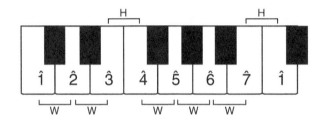

In other words, to construct a C major scale from the twelve notes of the chromatic scale, just pull out the seven white keys and leave the five black keys alone. Here's how that looks on the staff:

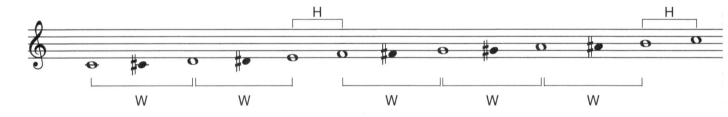

We'll use the whole- and half-step sequence as a primary definition: a **major scale** is formed by the sequence of two whole steps and a diatonic half step followed by three whole steps and a diatonic half step. Not just the C major scale, but any major scale—starting on any white or black key—can be formed using this same sequence of whole and half steps. Here, for example, is the major scale with D as its tonic:

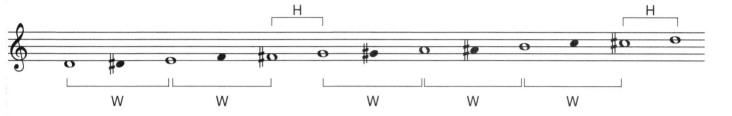

Out of the twelve notes of the chromatic scale on D, we select the seven notes forming the sequence WWHWWWH:

The two sharped notes here, F and C, are the two alterations we used to notate "America" starting on D in Lesson 7. That version of the song is in the key of D major; its primary pitch content is the D major scale.

In Lesson 7 we also looked at "America" starting on F, which uses one accidental, B♭. Here's the scale for that version:

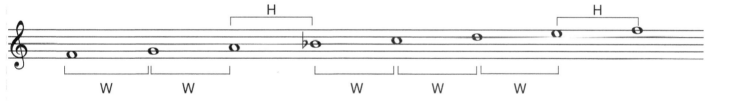

In summary,

- All major scales have the same sequence of whole and half steps, WWHWWWH. That is, they're constructed mostly of whole steps but have diatonic half steps between $\hat{3}$ and $\hat{4}$ and between $\hat{7}$ and the upper $\hat{1}$.

- The notation of major scales uses all seven letters of the musical alphabet, without skipping or repeating.

- Notated on the staff, major scales fill up an octave alternating lines and spaces without skipping or repeating.

- Notes with accidentals are either all sharps or all flats; a major scale never contains some of both.

8.4   SCALE CONSTRUCTION

To write a major scale:

1. Fill in an octave with notes on alternating lines and spaces, without skipping or repeating. If this is done correctly, each letter in the musical alphabet will be used once, up until the tonic returns at the end.

2. Add accidentals to form whole steps between all the notes except for the diatonic half steps between $\hat{3}$ and $\hat{4}$ and between $\hat{7}$ and the upper $\hat{1}$. To calculate the whole steps, think of the notes you're skipping in the chromatic scale.

To write a G major scale, for example, first write all the notes between one G and another:

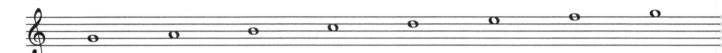

Calculate the scale tones by referring to a chromatic scale starting on G:

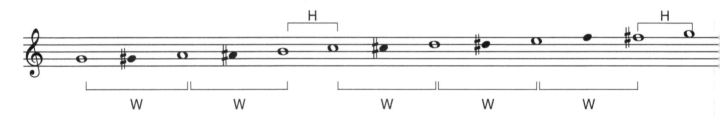

This shows that we need to add only one accidental, F♯:

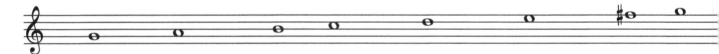

Suppose the tonic note is E♭. Begin as before, by filling in an octave without skipping or repeating:

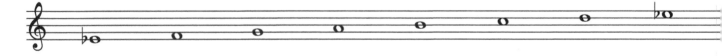

To use the chromatic scale as a point of reference when the scale begins on a flatted note, use only flats when you write (or visualize) the chromatic scale:

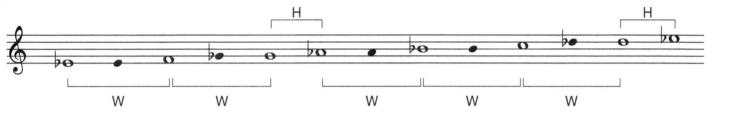

From this we can conclude that E♭ major has two flatted notes in addition to the tonic:

8.5   THE MAJOR SCALES

Every major scale has a unique number of sharps or flats. Because there are seven different notes in the scale, there are seven different possible combinations of sharps, and seven different possible combinations of flats.

Let's look at the entire inventory. We start with C major, then write the scale with one sharp (G), then the scale with two sharps (D), and so forth. Notice that the fifth degree of each scale is always the tonic of the next one.

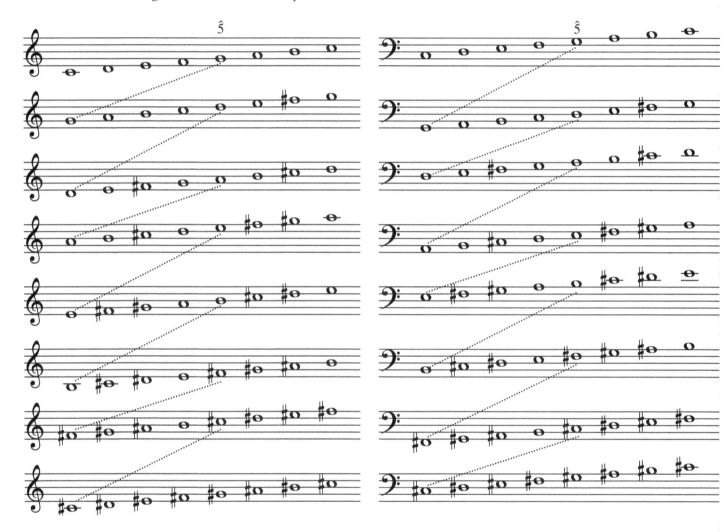

For the flat-key scales, the fourth degree becomes the next tonic.

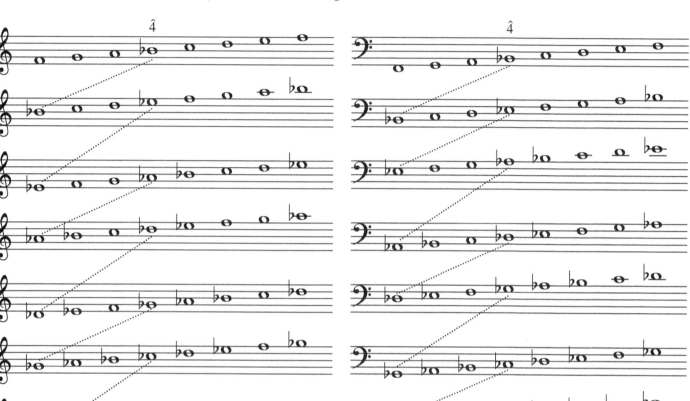

That makes a total of fifteen possibilities—C major plus seven scales with different numbers of sharps and seven with different numbers of flats. Any music in a major key is based on one of these fifteen scales.

We have fifteen possibilities, even though there are only twelve notes in the chromatic scale, because three scales appear in both lists, notated with sharps in one and with enharmonically equivalent flats in the other. The three enharmonic pairs are:

sharp-key scale		*flat-key scale*
B (5 sharps)	=	C♭ (7 flats)
F♯ (6 sharps)	=	G♭ (6 flats)
C♯ (7 sharps)	=	D♭ (5 flats)

Composers and other notators have choices when writing music in one of these keys. Whenever possible they choose the key with fewer accidentals; B and D♭ are much more common than C♯ and C♭. F♯ and G♭ are about equally common.

These are the *only* instances where we have choices between enharmonic equivalents for scales. If we want our tonic to be the second black key in a group of two on the piano keyboard, we use the E♭ major scale; we don't have an option of D#. Likewise, there is no such thing as G# major, or A# major, or F♭ major.

8.6   SCALE DEGREE NAMES

Not just tonic, but all the notes in the scale have special names. The next-most-important scale degree after $\hat{1}$ is $\hat{5}$, known as the **dominant**. The dominant is five steps *up* from tonic ($\hat{1}$–$\hat{2}$–$\hat{3}$–$\hat{4}$–$\hat{5}$), and $\hat{4}$ is called **subdominant** because it's five steps in the other direction ($\hat{1}$–$\hat{7}$–$\hat{6}$–$\hat{5}$–$\hat{4}$):

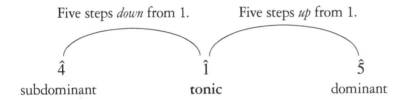

$\hat{3}$ is called **mediant** because it's halfway between tonic and dominant, and $\hat{6}$ is **submediant** because it lies the same distance below tonic as the mediant lies above:

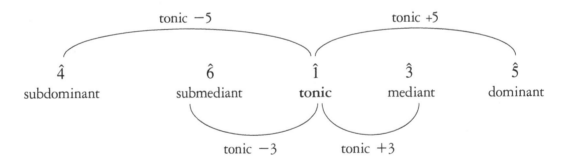

The remaining two scale degrees, $\hat{2}$ and $\hat{7}$, also have names that reflect their relationship to tonic. $\hat{2}$ is **supertonic** because it's just above tonic, and $\hat{7}$ is known as the **leading tone** because it progresses strongly toward the tonic note.

Here are the scale degree names as they're ordered in the scale:

$\hat{1}$ tonic
$\hat{2}$ supertonic
$\hat{3}$ mediant
$\hat{4}$ subdominant
$\hat{5}$ dominant
$\hat{6}$ submediant
$\hat{7}$ leading tone

Another naming system, known as *solfège*, is useful for learning the sounds of the scale tones and using them to build melodies. Each scale degree has its own simple syllable:

scale degree number:	$\hat{1}$	$\hat{2}$	$\hat{3}$	$\hat{4}$	$\hat{5}$	$\hat{6}$	$\hat{7}$
solfège symbol:	do	re	mi	fa	sol	la	ti

You can become intimately familiar with the tone relationships within the scale by singing these scale tones in various patterns and combinations.

8.7   TRANSPOSITION

In tonal music, **transposition** is key change. When tonal music is transposed, it's rewritten in a different key. What's preserved during transposition is the scale-degree arrangement and (usually) the rhythm. What changes is the key.

Suppose, for example, that you play a C major scale and then a D major scale. You've essentially transposed the major scale from the key of C to the key of D. You began with a certain sequence of scale degrees, the scale tones in order from first to last in C major, and then you restated that same sequence of scale degrees—the scale tones in order from first to last—in D major. Any other major scale could likewise be considered just another transposition of that same scale-degree sequence.

A transposition of some other arrangement of scale degrees—a tonal melody, for instance—works the same way. To transpose, simply determine the ordering of scale degrees as they appear in the melody and present that same scale-degree sequence in a different key. In most cases you'll also preserve the original rhythm.

Suppose we want to transpose the first phrase of "America" to a different key, as we did when we compared versions of this phrase in C major, D major, and F major in Lesson 7.1. To start, become familiar with the scale degrees in the key that we're starting in, C major. Assign numbers or *solfège* symbols to each degree:

C major							
scale degree:	$\hat{1}$	$\hat{2}$	$\hat{3}$	$\hat{4}$	$\hat{5}$	$\hat{6}$	$\hat{7}$	$\hat{1}$
solfège symbol:	do	re	mi	fa	sol	la	ti	do

Next, determine the particular ordering of these scale degrees in the melody. "America" begins with the first scale degree (do) repeated on the first two beats, followed by a step up to $\hat{2}$ (re) on the last beat of the first measure, then a jump down to $\hat{7}$ (ti) on the downbeat of measure 2, and so forth:

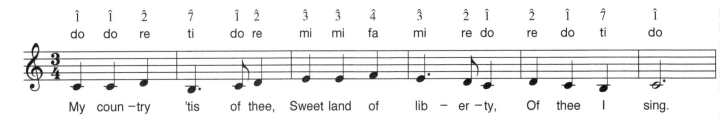

Let's say we want to transpose this phrase to G major. First, become familiar with the scale degrees in the G major scale:

Then simply rewrite the melody, preserving the original rhythm and scale-degree pattern but using scale degrees from the G major scale instead of C major:

As long as you know the rhythm and scale degrees of a tonal melody, you can transpose it to any other key.

8.8 TRANSPOSITION OF THE DIATONIC MODES

Here again are the white-key scales and their modal names (Lesson 8.2):

C white-key scale (CDEFGAB): Ionian
D white-key scale (DEFGABC): Dorian
E white-key scale (EFGABCD): Phrygian
F white-key scale (FGABCDE): Lydian
G white-key scale (GABCDEF): Mixolydian
A white-key scale (ABCDEFG): Aeolian
B white-key scale (BCDEFGA): Locrian

Think of each successive scale as a one-step rotation of the one before it. To produce the D white-key scale (Dorian), for example, take the first note of the C white-key scale (Ionian) and rotate it to the end:

C Ionian:	C	D	E	F	G	A	B	
D Dorian:		D	E	F	G	A	B	C

To produce the next scale on the list, the E white-key scale (Phrygian), rotate the first note of the D scale to the end:

D Dorian:	D	E	F	G	A	B	C	
E Phrygian:		E	F	G	A	B	C	D

. . . and so forth. The process continues until each of the seven tones has rotated into the starting position:

C Ionian:	C	D	E	F	G	A	B			
D Dorian:		D	E	F	G	A	B	C		
E Phrygian:			E	F	G	A	B	C	D	
F Lydian:				F	G	A	B	C	D	E
G Mixolydian:					G	A	B	C	D	E	F
A Aeolian:						A	B	C	D	E	F	G
B Locrian:							B	C	D	E	F	G	A

Now let's take this idea a step further. As we know from this lesson, a major scale can start on any note on the keyboard, not just C. Likewise, we can apply modal concepts to any major scale, not just C. G major can also be called G Ionian. B♭ major can also be known as B♭ Ionian. And so forth.

We can therefore use any major scale as a starting point for a family of modal rotations. Here, for example, is the family of scales derivable from the rotations of G major:

G Ionian:	G	A	B	C	D	E	F♯					
A Dorian:		A	B	C	D	E	F♯	G				
B Phrygian:			B	C	D	E	F♯	G	A			
C Lydian:				C	D	E	F♯	G	A	B		
D Mixolydian:					D	E	F♯	G	A	B	C	
E Aeolian:						E	F♯	G	A	B	C	D
F♯ Locrian:							F♯	G	A	B	C	D	E

In effect, this G major family is a transposition of the C major family (white-key scales) to the key of G. Any other family of rotations could be viewed as a transposition to some other key.

 For suggestions for further listening and online exercises and drills, go to www.oup.com/us/lambert

STUDY QUESTIONS FOR LESSON 8

1. **Define these terms:**
   diatonic modes
   dominant
   Ionian mode
   key
   leading tone
   major mode
   major scale
   mediant
   minor mode
   scale degree
   solfège
   subdominant
   submediant
   supertonic
   tonic
   transposition

2. Where can you usually find the tonic pitch of a melody?

3. What is a more common name for the Ionian mode?

4. In the major scale, between what scale degrees do half steps occur?

5. When you write a major scale, how many notes in the chromatic scale do you skip over to form whole steps?

6. What do all major scales have in common?

7. When you transpose a tonal melody, what changes and what stays the same?

► EXERCISES FOR LESSON 8

To construct a major scale by selecting certain notes from a chromatic scale, as in Lessons 8.3 and 8.4, first write an ascending chromatic scale. If the starting note is tonic for a scale that uses sharps, spell the five black keys in the scale as sharped notes. If the starting note is tonic for a scale that uses flats, spell the five black keys as flatted notes.

Here's how we would begin if the starting note is A:

Extract notes from this chromatic scale to follow the standard pattern of whole- (W) and half- (H) steps: WWHWWWH. For whole steps, make sure you're skipping over one note in the chromatic scale. For half steps, make sure you're *not* skipping over any notes in the chromatic scale:

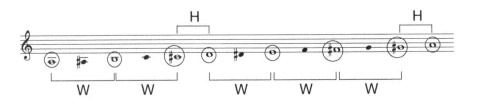

A. Write an ascending chromatic scale starting on the given note. If the given note is a white key, spell the five black keys in the scale using sharped notes. If the given note is a flatted note, spell the five black keys in the scale using flatted notes. Then <u>circle</u> the notes of the major scale within that chromatic scale, assuming that the given note is 1̂.

1.
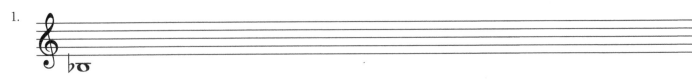

2.

3.

4.

5.

If we can rearrange the notes of a melody to form a major scale, we say that the melody is based on that scale, even if the actual scale tones don't appear in that order in the melody. To demonstrate the scale on which a melody is based, start on the tonic, which is usually the melody's final note, and write all the notes of the melody in scale order.

Suppose we want to find the scale source for this melody:

Collect all the notes together and write them as a scale, using the final note of the melody as the tonic pitch:

The key of the melody is G major.

B. Take all the notes in each melody and re-order them as an ascending scale on the lower staff. Circle and label the tonic note and indicate the key.

1.

KEY: _____

Name: _____

8-4

2.   Schumann

KEY: _____

8-5

3.   Schubert

KEY: _____

8-6

4.   Handel

KEY: _____

Any note is a member of seven different major scales. (Some are in more if you count en-harmonics separately.) The note G, for example, is $\hat{1}$ in the G major scale (GABCDEF#G), $\hat{2}$ in the F major scale (FGAB♭CDEF), $\hat{3}$ in the E♭ major scale (E♭FGA♭B♭CDE♭), and so forth.

If you know the scale degree number (other than $\hat{1}$) of a certain note in some scale, you can find $\hat{1}$ by counting down or up to tonic. If you know, for example, that G is $\hat{6}$, you can find $\hat{1}$ by counting from $\hat{6}$ down to $\hat{1}$ . . .

. . . or from $\hat{6}$ up to $\hat{1}$ . . .

G is $\hat{6}$ in B♭ major. When you are locating tonic, remember to move within the actual major *scale*, not just within the musical alphabet. G is $\hat{6}$ in *B♭* major, not *B* major; in B major, $\hat{6}$ is *G♯*.

C. Write major scales to show how the given notes can be reinterpreted as different scale degrees in different major scales. Use the given notes as they appear (don't change the accidental).

1.

2.

LESSON 8: THE MAJOR MODE

3.

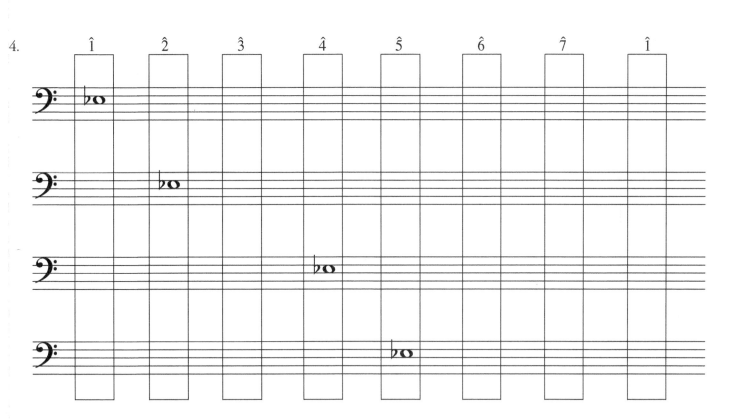

4.

Name: _____

To transpose a melody, replicate its rhythm and scale degrees in a different key (Lesson 8.7). Suppose we want to transpose this melody:

J. S. Bach

Start by determining the key. Because it ends on F, and uses the notes F, G, A, B♭, C, and D, we can say that it's in the key of F major. We can make that assertion even though the complete scale isn't represented in the melody ($\hat{7}$ [E] is absent).

Write out the scale to identify its scale degrees:

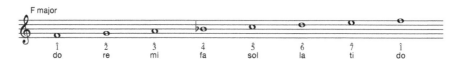

Now label the notes of the melody with their scale degree numbers in F major:

To transpose the melody to G major, first identify the degrees in that scale:

Then rewrite the melody using identical rhythms and scale degrees, but in G major instead of F:

D. Follow the instructions to transpose the melodies.

1.

8-7

J. S. Bach

Write the C major scale:

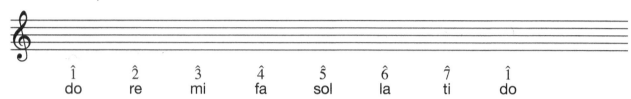

$\hat{1}$	$\hat{2}$	$\hat{3}$	$\hat{4}$	$\hat{5}$	$\hat{6}$	$\hat{7}$	$\hat{1}$
do	re	mi	fa	sol	la	ti	do

Transpose the melody to C major:

2.

8-9

Haydn

Identify the key of the melody and write the scale:

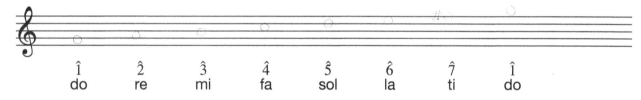

$\hat{1}$	$\hat{2}$	$\hat{3}$	$\hat{4}$	$\hat{5}$	$\hat{6}$	$\hat{7}$	$\hat{1}$
do	re	mi	fa	sol	la	ti	do

Next to the notes of the original melody, write the scale degree numbers.

Write the D major scale:

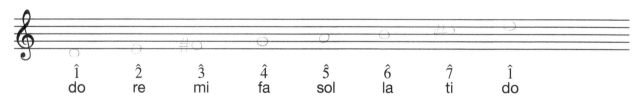

$\hat{1}$	$\hat{2}$	$\hat{3}$	$\hat{4}$	$\hat{5}$	$\hat{6}$	$\hat{7}$	$\hat{1}$
do	re	mi	fa	sol	la	ti	do

Transpose the melody to D major:

3.

\ Schubert

8-3

Identify the key of the melody and write the scale:

E♭ M

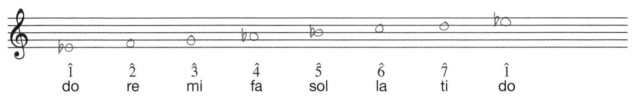

1̂	2̂	3̂	4̂	5̂	6̂	7̂	1̂
do	re	mi	fa	sol	la	ti	do

Next to the notes of the original melody, write the scale degree numbers.

Write the A major scale:

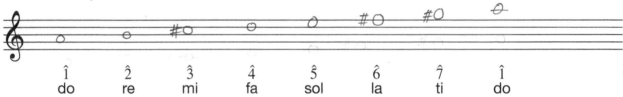

1̂	2̂	3̂	4̂	5̂	6̂	7̂	1̂
do	re	mi	fa	sol	la	ti	do

Transpose the melody to A major:

✎ create!

1. Get to know one of the melodies in the exercises from this lesson. Write an eight-measure melody of your own in the same key and meter, using the existing melody as an inspiration. End on tonic. Your melody should sound different from the existing melody, but it might replicate some of its rhythms or scale-degree combinations.

2. Write an eight-measure melody in any key and meter, not inspired by an existing melody. End on tonic. Include several instances of a short rhythm or scale-degree combination that you've devised.

LESSON 9
MAJOR KEY SIGNATURES

9.1   THE KEY SIGNATURE

One of the versions of the first phrase of "America" that we looked at in Lesson 7 started on D:

As we learned in Lesson 8, this version of the song is in the key of D major. Its primary pitch material can be summarized by the D major scale:

Throughout this version of the song, the melody uses only the notes of this scale, and D is the most important one, the tonic.

    There's more. Our system of notation takes the accidentals of this scale and collects them together at the left margin, just after the clef sign. That's called the **key signature**:

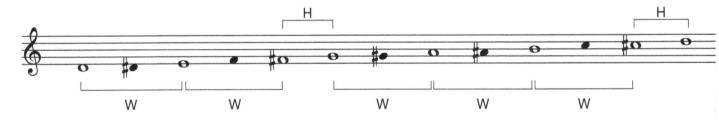

The key signature tell us which notes will always be sharped or flatted, every time they appear, even though you don't see the actual accidental on the staff. In this case, the C in measure 2, the two Fs in measure 3, the F in measure 4, and the C in measure 5 are all sharped, because the key signature makes it so. If for some reason you wanted them not to be, you would need to add natural signs within the staff (which would remain in effect only until the end of the measure where they occur).

You find a key signature at the beginning of every line of music, just after the clef sign and before any meter signature. We could go back and renotate several of our previous demonstrations and exercises using key signatures instead of individual accidentals as needed. Here, for example, is the first phrase of "America" starting on F, in the key of F major (Lesson 7):

The B in the third measure is actually B♭, even though you don't see a flat symbol in front of that note on the staff.

9.2 FORMATTING KEY SIGNATURES

Because each of the fifteen major keys has a unique number of sharps or flats, each also has a unique key signature. This means, among other things, that a performer is able to glance at a key signature and learn a great deal of information right away about the music that follows, even before looking at the actual notes and rhythms.

To make the notation as clear as possible, key signatures always follow a standard format. The process of writing a key signature is more than just collecting the sharps or flats and then writing them down at the beginning of the line. The accidentals always appear in a standard order and on specific lines and spaces.

The key signature for D major in treble clef, for example, must always appear as we saw it earlier in this lesson, with a sharp on the top line followed by a sharp in the third space. Any other arrangement, such as these, would be incorrect:

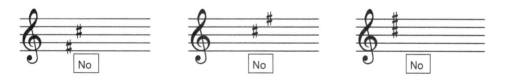

In bass clef the sharps of course fall on different lines and spaces from those in treble clef, but they must be in the same order:

As you move down the list of major scales in Lesson 8.5, each new scale retains accidentals from the previous scale and adds one new one. G major has one sharp, F. The next scale, D, has that same F plus C. The next scale, A, has the F and C from the previous scale plus G. This continues until each of the seven letters in the musical alphabet has been represented once. The resulting key signatures look like this:

The order in which sharps are added, F–C–G–D–A–E–B, follows a count-5 pattern reminiscent of the relationships between tonics of scales we noticed in Lesson 8.5. Think of stepping through the musical alphabet starting with F as "1." Count five letters to arrive at the second sharp on the list:

count:	1	2	3	4	5
	F	G	A	B	C

Now start with C and count five more letters to arrive at the third sharp on the list:

count:	1	2	3	4	5
	C	D	E	F	G

This continues until you've accumulated all seven:

F G A B C
        C D E F G
              G A B C D
                    D E F G A
                          A B C D E
                              E F G A B

The order in which flats are accumulated is the reverse of the sharps list, B–E–A–
D–G–C–F. Like the sharps, the flats must always appear on specific lines or spaces
and in the standard order:

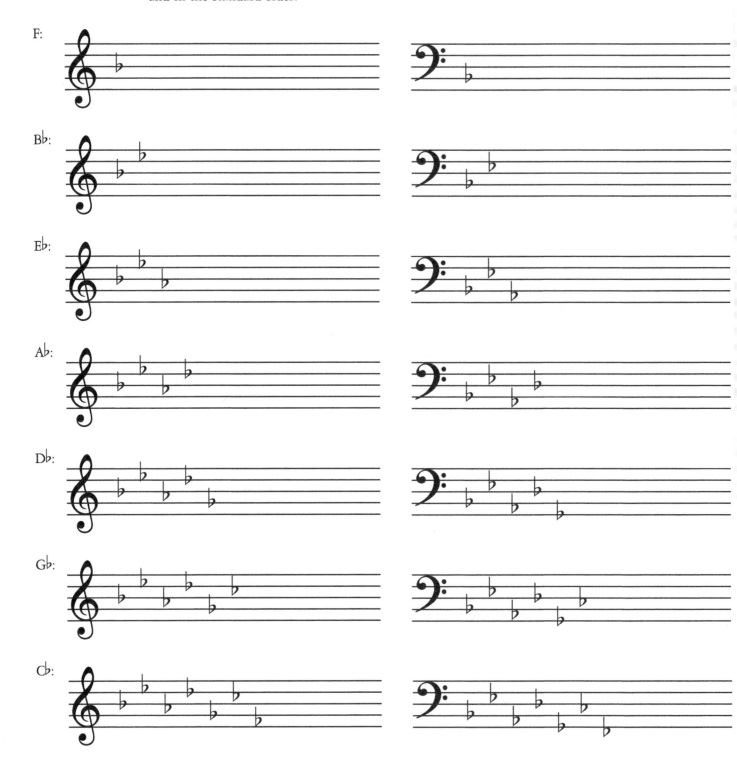

You can list the flats by following a count-4 pattern:

B C D E
         E F G A
                  A B C D
                           D E F G
                                    G A B C
                                             C D E F

To remember what any key signature looks like, simply remember the signatures in which everything is sharped or flatted, the keys of C♯ and C♭ (in both clefs). All the other key signatures are subsets of these. To write a key signature of four sharps (E major), for example, write the first four sharps of C♯ major:

To write a key signature of three flats (E♭ major), write the first three flats of C♭ major:

. . . and so forth. If you can write the key signatures for C♯ major and C♭ major, you can write all the others.

If you're looking at a key signature and not sure what key it indicates, there are separate tricks for sharps and flats:

- For sharp keys, the tonic is one diatonic half step above the last sharp in the key signature.

- For flat keys, the tonic note is the penultimate flat in the key signature.

- There's no trick for F and C; you just have to remember those.

9.3   THE CIRCLE OF KEYS

Another way to organize the keys and key signatures is called the **circle of keys**. Imagine an analog clock face with key names rather than hours every five minutes. Start with C major at twelve o'clock, then progress clockwise to the one-sharp key, G, at one o'clock. Continue to the two-sharp major key, D, at two o'clock, the three-sharp key, A, at three o'clock, and so forth. The progression of sharps ends with C♯ major at seven o'clock.

As we noticed in Lesson 8.5, scale-degree $\hat{5}$ of C is the tonic note of G, and $\hat{5}$ of G is $\hat{1}$ of D. As you move clockwise around the circle, the fifth degree of a given key is the same note as the first degree of the next one. For this reason, the circle of keys is sometimes known as the **circle of fifths**.

To derive the flat keys, move counter-clockwise from C and go to the fourth scale degree (or count backwards five degrees, from $\hat{1}$ down to $\hat{4}$). At eleven o'clock is the one-flat key, F ($\hat{4}$ of C). From there progress to the two-flat key, B♭ ($\hat{4}$ of F), at ten o'clock, the three-flat key, E♭ ($\hat{4}$ of B♭) at nine o'clock, and so forth, until finally arriving at C♭ major at five o'clock. The enharmonic keys overlap at seven o'clock (D♭ and C#), six o'clock (G♭ and F#), and five o'clock (C♭ and B).

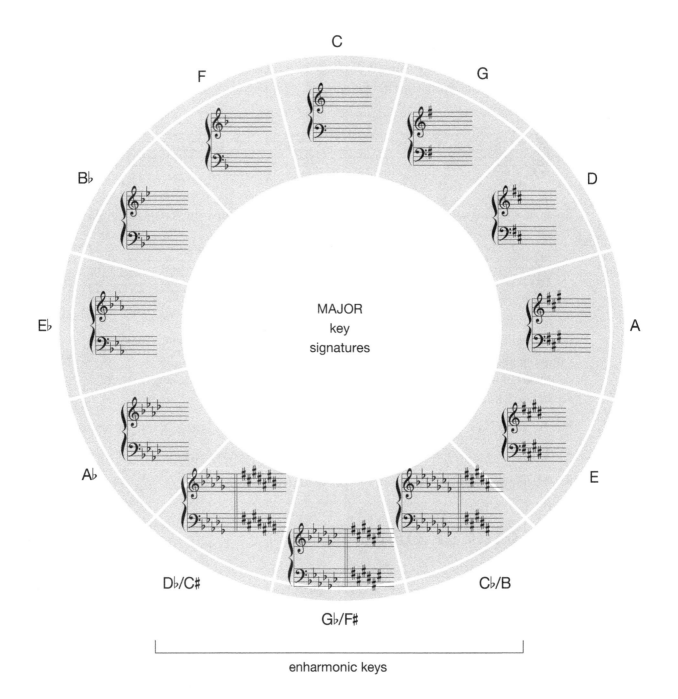

enharmonic keys

The order of sharps in key signatures, F-C-G-D-A-E-B, is shown in the key names on the outside of the circle, clockwise from eleven o'clock (F) to five o'clock (B). This means, of course, that the order of flats, B-E-A-D-G-C-F, is displayed between these same points in a counter-clockwise direction.

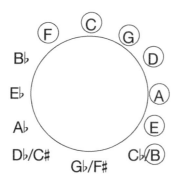

 For suggestions for further listening and online exercises and drills, go to www.oup.com/us/lambert

▶ STUDY QUESTIONS FOR LESSON 9

1. Define these terms:
    circle of keys
    key signature

2. Where do you expect to find the key signature in printed music?

3. In the standard notation of key signatures, how is the ordering of sharps related to the ordering of flats?

4. In the standard notation of key signatures, how is the placement of sharps on the staff similar to the placement of flats, and how is it different?

5. What is another name for the circle of keys, and why does it make sense?

6. On the circle of keys, why are pairs of keys listed together at five o'clock, six o'clock, and seven o'clock?

Name: _____

▶ EXERCISES FOR LESSON 9

Key signatures follow standard rules of placement and ordering (Lesson 9.2). If accidentals appear in some nonstandard ordering, or on the wrong lines or spaces, the key signature is malformed.

When writing accidentals on the staff, remember the notational guidelines shown with the Lesson 7 exercises.

A. Practice writing major key signatures on the staffs below.

G:

D:

A:

E:

B:

F♯

LESSON 9: MAJOR KEY SIGNATURES   127

C#:

F:

B♭:

E♭:

A♭:

D♭:

G♭:

C♭:

LESSON 9: MAJOR KEY SIGNATURES

A key signature is placed at the beginning of each line of music, just after the clef sign (and before the meter signature). It determines which notes are to be read as sharped or flatted throughout, or until the key signature changes.

A melody notated with accidentals appearing directly in front of notes as needed . . .

Handel

. . . can be renotated by placing a key signature at the beginning of the line and then removing the individual accidentals:

Handel

B. Renotate these melodies from Exercise 8B, using key signatures rather than as-needed accidentals.

1.

Schubert

2.

Schumann

3.

Schubert

If you know all the major scales by heart, then you can easily figure out their key signatures by playing (or imagining) a scale and then counting the number of accidentals.

To identify a particular key signature without consulting a memorized scale or reference table, we learned this method in Lesson 9.2:

→   For sharp keys, the tonic is one diatonic half step above the last sharp in the key signature.
→   For flat keys, the tonic note is the penultimate flat in the key signature.
→   There's no trick for F and C; you just have to remember those.

C. In the staff following each major key signature (in both clefs), write the tonic note. The first one is done for you.

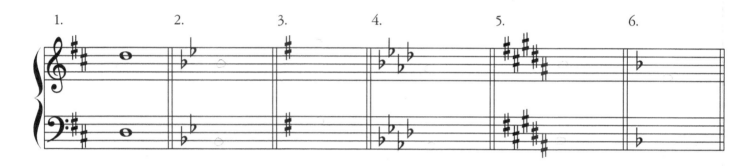

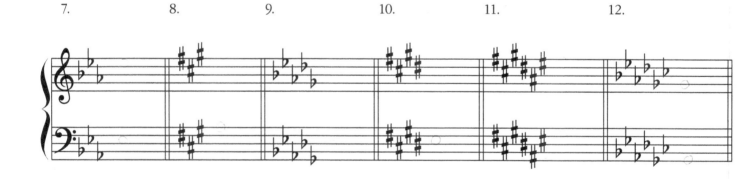

✑ create!

1. Take a look at Invention in the Fifteen Character Pieces (www.oup.com/us/lambert). Notice that:

    • Each hand plays only five notes—the first five scale degrees in the D major scale.

    • The hands trade figures in the first sixteen measures, first a stepwise figure, then a figure outlining triads. After a contrasting middle section based on the end of the first section, material from the beginning returns.

    • One source of contrast in the middle section (measures 17–26) is the changing roles of the hands. At the beginning of the piece the hands relate more as equals, while in the middle section, the right hand presents a melody while the left hand stays in the background as accompaniment.

    • The rhythms are active but never complex.

2. Study other piano music with the same title, or with similar underlying compositional strategies. For example:

    • J. S. Bach, Two-Part Inventions

    • Igor Stravinsky, *Le cinq doigts*

    • Béla Bartók, *Mikrokosmos*:

        • "Imitation and Counterpoint" (book 1, no. 22)

        • "Imitation and Inversion (1)" (book 1, no. 23)

        • "Imitation and Inversion (2)" (book 1, no. 25)

        • "Five-Tone Scale" (book 3, no. 78)

3. Write a short piano piece modeled on Invention.

    • Start by deciding on a key. Place the fingers of both hands on the first five scale degrees of the scale of that key. Restrict yourself to those notes.

    • Think of a little musical idea ("motive") you would like to explore in your piece. Figure out how to notate it.

    • Improvise, then write down, different ways of combining and developing your idea.

    • Notate your piece in the standard two-stave format for piano music. Use key signatures, not individual accidentals as needed. Check over your notation to make sure that your symbols are clear, noteheads are correctly placed, and measures contain the proper number of beats.

LESSON 9: MAJOR KEY SIGNATURES

LESSON **10**
COMPOUND METER

10.1 THE THREE-PART DIVISION OF THE BEAT

The meters we've studied thus far (Lesson 4.3), all divide the beat into two or four parts. In $\frac{4}{4}$ or $\frac{3}{4}$, for example, the quarter-note beat is divided into two eighths or subdivided into four sixteenths. In $\frac{4}{2}$ or $\frac{3}{2}$ the half-note beat is divided into two quarters or subdivided into four eighths. In $\frac{4}{8}$ or $\frac{3}{8}$ the eighth note beat is divided into two sixteenths or subdivided into four thirty-seconds. The two-part division of the beat is known as **simple meter**.

In **compound meter** the beat is divided into three parts. It's usually notated with an 8 as the bottom number in the meter signature, as in this melody by Haydn:

As the tempo marking indicates, this music is played "very fast." At this tempo, we hear the beat as two dotted-quarter-notes per measure, each divided into three eighth notes. The meter signature here does not indicate six eighth-note beats per measure. In a compound meter signature, the top number divided by three is the number of beats per measure. The musical note represented by the bottom number, grouped in threes, is the duration of one beat.

$\frac{6}{8}$ ← ÷ 3 = number of beats per measure
← note value grouped in threes to represent one beat

When 8 is the bottom number in a compound meter signature, beams can help display the metric divisions. In Haydn's first measure, for example, the last three eighth notes are beamed together because they all occur within the second beat, separate from the preceding eighth note, which is part of the first beat. You would never beam all four of these eighth notes together, crossing over beat boundaries:

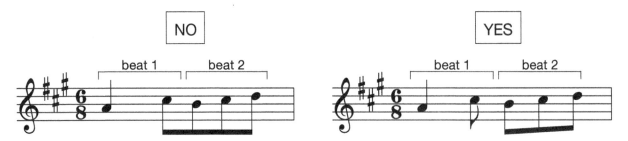

Only at slower tempos does $^6_8$ actually indicate six eighth-note beats per measure. Such music does exist, but $^6_8$ is more commonly used with moderate or faster tempos, organized into two dotted-quarter-note beats per measure.

Don't confuse beat *divisions*, which can be either simple or compound, with beat *groupings*, which can be either duple, triple, or quadruple (Lesson 4.2). $^6_8$ has compound divisions and a duple grouping: it's a *compound duple* meter. $^2_4$ is also a duple meter but with simple divisions; it's *simple duple*.

Any of the most common numbers of beats per measure—two, three, or four—can have simple or compound beat divisions. The top numbers of compound meter signatures are all multiples of three. A triple meter with compound divisions is most commonly notated in $^9_8$. Compound quadruple is usually notated in $^{12}_8$.

It's also possible to notate compound meters using quarter notes as the beat divisions. A meter signature of $^6_4$ indicates two dotted-half-note beats per measure, or compound duple. $^9_4$ is compound triple, and $^{12}_4$ is compound quadruple (but this is rarely used). Essentially, any time the top number in a meter signature is 6, 9, or 12, and the tempo is moderate or faster, the meter is compound. The bottom number is usually 8 but sometimes 4 (and very rarely 16).

Here's a summary and classification of the most common meter signatures:

	simple			*compound*	
duple	$^2_8$	$^2_4$	$^2_2$	$^6_8$	$^6_4$
triple	$^3_8$	$^3_4$	$^3_2$	$^9_8$	$^9_4$
quadruple	$^4_8$	$^4_4$	$^4_2$	$^{12}_8$	$^{12}_4$

Notice that only the top number helps indicate whether a meter is simple or compound: 2, 3, and 4 are always simple; 6, 9, and 12 are usually compound (depending on the tempo). A bottom number of 4 or 8 can be either simple or compound, although 4 most commonly indicates simple and 8 most commonly indicates compound.

Relationships between meter signatures can be tricky. To the untrained eye, $\frac{6}{8}$ and $\frac{3}{4}$ might seem to be different notations of the same thing; a measure filled with six eighth notes may seem durationally equivalent to a measure filled with three quarter notes. But the musical context makes all the difference. In $\frac{6}{8}$ the six eighth notes are musically grouped into two groups of three, creating the compound division of two beats. $\frac{3}{4}$ can also be divided into six eighth notes, but in that case it's three groups of two, the simple division of three beats.

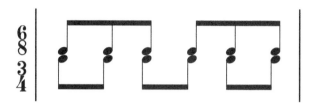

That's why $\frac{6}{8}$ is compound duple but $\frac{3}{4}$ is simple triple. Similar confusion can arise between other related signatures, especially $\frac{6}{4}$ (compound duple) and $\frac{3}{2}$ (simple triple).

It's also fairly common to find music notated in simple triple meter (most likely $\frac{3}{8}$ or $\frac{3}{4}$) but played so fast that each measure begins to represent one beat ("in one"). Even though the meter signature appears to indicate a simple meter, the experience of the music is the same as for compound meters.

10.2   COUNTING COMPOUND METER

The counting systems we learned in Lesson 4.5 are designed for two-part beat divisions and therefore won't work for compound meter. For three-part beat divisions, a common alternative adds "la-li" after each beat number:

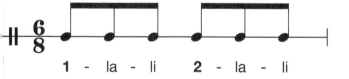

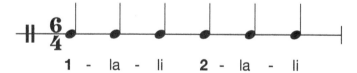

To subdivide the beats further, insert "ta":

Here's how these syllables would be used for one of the rhythm exercises at the end of this lesson:

3.

1- la- li 2   1- la- li 2 - li   1- li 2-la-li   1 - li 2-ta-la-ta-li-ta   1- la - li 2 - li   1   (2)

10.3   FLUCTUATING BEAT DIVISIONS

Occasionally it's necessary to mix simple and compound beat divisions in the same melody or piece. Let's say you're writing a song about your trip to the supermarket and want to list some of your acquisitions, with the first syllable of each word always falling on a quarter-note beat. It might go something like:

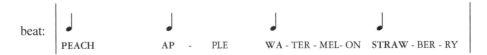

beat:

PEACH   AP - PLE   WA - TER - MEL- ON   STRAW - BER - RY

"Peach" is one syllable and so equals one beat, but the other words have multiple syllables and divide the beat differently. Assuming the syllables of each word divide the beats equally, we would notate "ap-ple" as eighth notes, and "wa-ter-mel-on" as sixteenth notes, but we would need a way to notate the compound, three-part division of "straw-ber-ry." That's called a **triplet**:

PEACH   AP - PLE   WAT - ER - MEL - ON   STRAW - BER - RY

An eighth-note triplet divides a quarter-note beat into three equal parts. Other beat units are divided by other triplet values. For example, a quarter-note triplet divides a half-note beat into three equal parts:

PEACH   AP - PLE   WAT - ER - MEL - ON STRAW - BER - RY

Triplets can divide any duration:

PINE - AP - PLE   CHEESE - CAKE

The possibilities are endless. We can also divide durations into units other than three:

The divisions shown here are: **triplet, quintuplet, septuplet,** and regular sixteenth notes.

 For suggestions for further listening and online exercises and drills, go to www.oup.com/us/lambert

► STUDY QUESTIONS FOR LESSON 10

1. Define these terms:
   compound meter
   quintuplet
   septuplet
   simple meter
   triplet

2. What is the difference between simple meter and compound meter?

3. What are the usual top numbers for compound meter signatures?

4. Does the bottom number 8 in a meter signature most likely indicate compound meter or simple meter? What about 4?

5. What is the top number of the meter signature for music "in one"?

6. If you find a triplet on only one beat of a $\frac{4}{4}$ measure, would you say that the meter of the measure is primarily simple or primarily compound?

RHYTHM READING

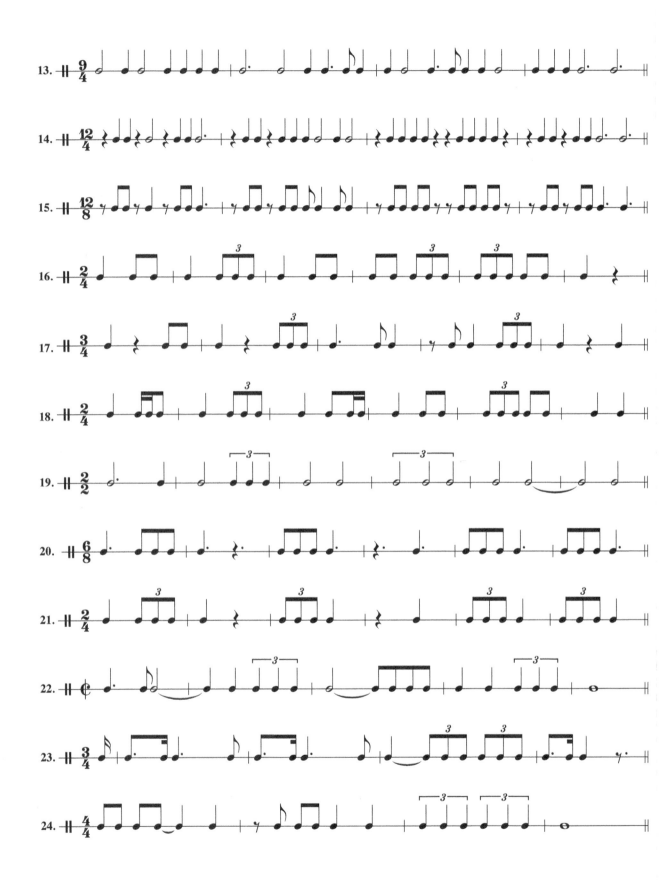

► EXERCISES FOR LESSON 10

As we learned in Lesson 10.1, meter signatures with the upper numbers 6, 9, or 12, when played at a moderate tempo or faster, usually have beats divided into three parts ("compound meter"). In these instances, the top number of the meter signature divided by three equals the number of beats per measure. The bottom number, as a rhythmic value, grouped in threes is the duration of one beat:

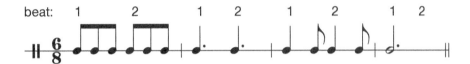

When the bottom number of a compound meter signature is 8, three eighth notes (one dotted quarter note) equal one beat.

In an exercise to replace flags with beams, find flagged notes within the same beat and beam them together. If you encounter this rhythm, for example . . .

. . . beam together the last three eight notes because they all occur within the second beat:

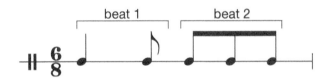

Some other beaming that crosses over beat boundaries is incorrect:

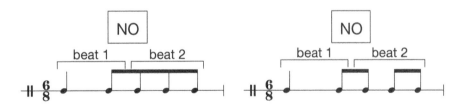

A. Rewrite the given rhythms in the space provided, adding beams and bar lines in appropriate places. Remember that beams may only group together notes within the same beat.

1.

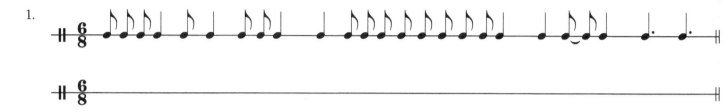

2.

3.

4.

5.

LESSON 10: COMPOUND METER

In compound meter signatures with 4 as the bottom number, it's usually not possible to use beams to indicate beat groupings. But the principle is the same as for compound meter signatures with 8 as the bottom number: the bottom number indicates the note value grouped in threes to make one beat. So, 4 as the bottom number of a compound meter indicates that three quarter notes, or a dotted half note, equal one beat.

B. Circle the note or rest that occurs exactly on each beat of each measure, assuming a moderate tempo or faster. Add bar lines in the appropriate places.

1.

2.

3.

C. Add exactly one <u>note</u> to each measure to make the measure complete in the prevailing meter.

1.

2.

D. Add exactly one <u>rest</u> to each measure to make the measure complete in the prevailing meter.

1.

2.

A triplet can be a temporary shift from simple to compound meter (Lesson 10.3). In $\frac{4}{4}$, for example, an eighth-note triplet divides one beat into three parts (compound) while the surrounding beats may retain two-part (simple) divisions:

E. Rewrite the rhythms in the space provided, adding beams and bar lines in appropriate places. Remember that beams may only group together notes within the same beat. Because the exercises in this section are notated in simple meter, the bottom number of the meter signature indicates the duration of the beat (Lesson 4).

1.

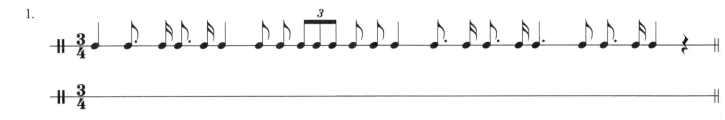

2.

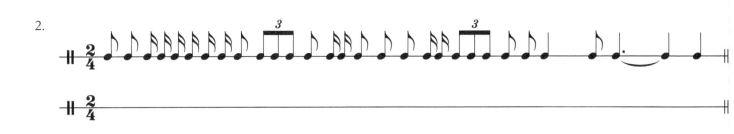

✑ create!

Take a short rhythm from one of the rhythm exercises, or create one of your own using compound meter, and repeat it over and over using your feet and/or hands and/or a repeating note on an instrument.

- Make a recording of yourself repeating the rhythm. Play it back and improvise different rhythmic patterns to go with it, or improvise unpatterned rhythms.

- Continue a repeating rhythmic pattern while a friend improvises a complementary pattern or unpatterned rhythm to go with it. Try different sounds, such as foot-tapping, knee-slapping, hand-clapping, finger-snapping, and so forth.

- Use a repeating rhythmic pattern as the background for an improvised melody, on the white or black keys of the piano or on any instrument.

LESSON **11**
THE MINOR MODE

11.1 STRUCTURE OF THE MINOR SCALE

In Lesson 1 we learned the white-key scales, and since Lesson 8 we've been studying one of them, Ionian, also known as major. Now we explore the white-key scale on A, named the Aeolian mode, also known as **minor**.

As we've learned, each of the modes has its own unique version of the sequence of five whole steps and two half steps. The C white-key scale, known as the C major scale (Lesson 8.3), places one half step between $\hat{3}$ and $\hat{4}$ and the other between $\hat{7}$ and the upper $\hat{1}$:

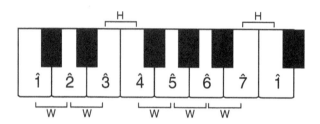

When we play the A white-key scale, the half steps fall between $\hat{2}$ and $\hat{3}$ and between $\hat{5}$ and $\hat{6}$:

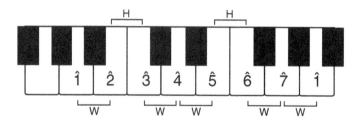

146

As with C major, it's easy to see the step sequence on the keyboard because the whole steps occur at those five places where a black key intrudes between two white keys, and half steps happen at the two places where one white key immediately follows another. Here's what that looks like on the staff:

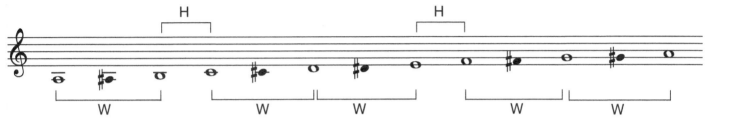

This is the A minor scale. Music based on this scale is said to be "in" the key of A minor.

We can construct any other minor scale by unfolding this same sequence of whole and half steps, WHWWHWW. Here's what it looks like if you start on E:

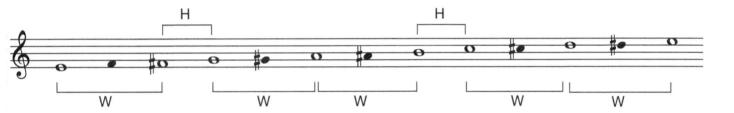

And here's just the scale, without the five notes we skip to make whole steps:

The scale degree names we learned for major scales in Lesson 8.6 are also valid for minor scales, with one exception. Scale degree $\hat{1}$ is still tonic, $\hat{2}$ is still supertonic, $\hat{3}$ is still mediant, and so forth, but $\hat{7}$ is a different story. Because of the whole step between $\hat{7}$ and upper $\hat{1}$ in minor scales, the $\hat{7}$ in minor doesn't have the same upward momentum that the $\hat{7}$ has in a major scale. Instead of "leading tone," the seventh degree in a minor scale is known as **subtonic**.

11.2   SCALE FAMILIES

All modes belong to **families**. C major and A minor are part of the family of **white-key scales**. All the scales in this family consist of different orderings of the white keys on the piano: CDEFGAB, DEFGABC, EFGABCD, and so forth. In Lesson 8.2 we also recognized the traditional names for these scales: Ionian, Dorian, Phrygian, Lydian, Mixolydian, Aeolian, and Locrian.

The E minor scale is one of the modal rotations of G major (Lesson 8.7). They're both members of the family of modes that all have one sharp—the one-sharp family. Here again is the complete list of modal rotations of G major:

G Ionian:	G	A	B	C	D	E	F♯				
A Dorian:		A	B	C	D	E	F♯	G			
B Phrygian:			B	C	D	E	F♯	G	A		
C Lydian:				C	D	E	F♯	G	A	B	
D Mixolydian:					D	E	F♯	G	A	B	C
E Aeolian:						E	F♯	G	A	B	C	D
F♯ Locrian:							F♯	G	A	B	C	D	E

But most of these family members are rarely used. We're going to focus only on the two that are most familiar from the vast variety of tonal music, the one starting on G, which we call G major, and the one starting on E, which we call E minor. Because they're members of the same family, let's call them **relatives**. G major and E minor are *relative* keys. G is the relative major of E minor. E is the relative minor of G major.

C is the relative major of A minor. A is the relative minor of C major. Every major scale has a minor partner from the same scale family, with a different ordering of exactly the same notes.

The difference between relatives is which note they start on. Here's how any relative scale can be derived from its partner:

- To find the starting note for a relative minor scale, go to $\hat{6}$ of major. A is $\hat{6}$ in C major. E is $\hat{6}$ in G major.

- To find the starting note for a relative major scale, go to $\hat{3}$ of minor. C is $\hat{3}$ in A minor. G is $\hat{3}$ in E minor.

11.3   THE MINOR SCALES

Let's look at the entire range of possibilities. Because every minor scale is simply a different ordering of its relative major, our listing can follow the same logic that we used to list major scales in Lesson 8.5. We start with the white-key minor scale, A minor, then go to the scale with one sharp, E minor, followed by the scales with two sharps, three sharps, and so on, until we get to the minor scale in which every note is sharped. Then we'll make a similar listing of all minor scales that use flats. As with major, in the scales with sharps, the fifth degree of each scale is the tonic note of the next scale on the list, while for the scales with flats it's the fourth degree that becomes the first degree of the next scale. Compare this listing to the list of all major scales in Lesson 8.5.

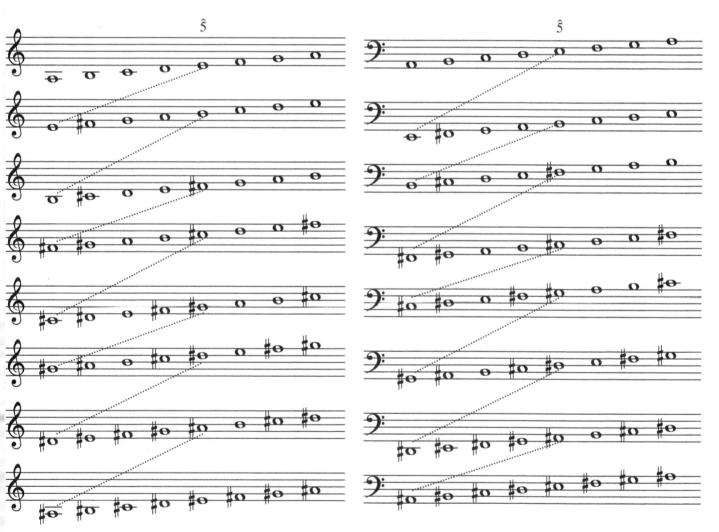

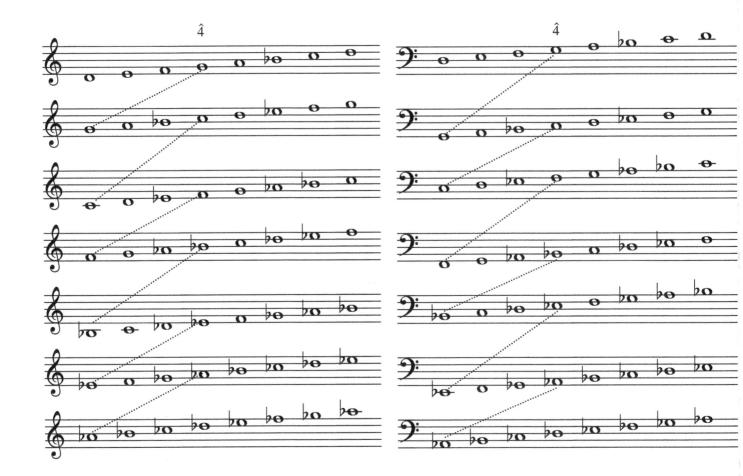

Any music in a minor key is based on one of these fifteen scales.

Enharmonics work in minor just like they do in major. The scales with five, six, or seven sharps or flats have enharmonic equivalents elsewhere on the list. The three enharmonic pairs are:

sharp-key scale		flat-key scale
G♯ (5 sharps)	=	A♭ (7 flats)
D♯ (6 sharps)	=	E♭ (6 flats)
A♯ (7 sharps)	=	B♭ (5 flats)

G♯ minor and B♭ minor are much more common than A♭ minor and A♯ minor. D♯ minor and E♭ minor are about equally common.

11.4 MINOR SCALE CONSTRUCTION

Because of the familial bond between major and relative minor, we have options when constructing minor scales. One way of writing a minor scale is just to produce the relative major and then reorder. To create an A minor scale, rearrange C major to start on $\hat{6}$. To create E minor, rearrange G major to start on $\hat{6}$. And so forth.

Or we can think of minor independently of its relative and focus just on the step sequence. Let's say we want to notate the B minor scale. Start by placing notes on all the lines and spaces between one B and another:

This ensures that all the notes of the scale will be properly placed in the staff. As with major, any minor scale is notated using all the letters in the musical alphabet, alternating lines and spaces without skipping or repeating.

Now determine which notes need accidentals to create the step sequence WHWWHWW, using the chromatic scale for reference:

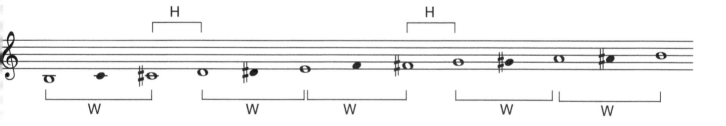

B minor has two sharped notes, F and C, just like its relative, D major:

If you're constructing a flat-key minor scale and using the chromatic scale for reference, use only flats for notating the five black keys. G minor, for example:

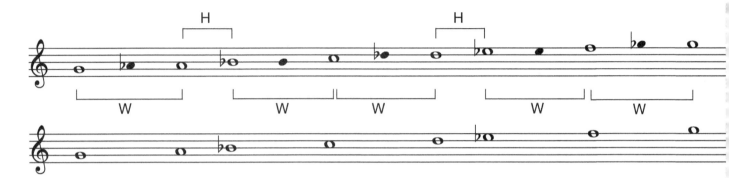

G minor uses two flats, B and E, just like its relative, B♭ major.

11.5   THE SOUND OF MINOR

Music based on minor scales usually sounds substantially different from music based on major. Listen, for example, to this melody by Handel:

The pitch content of this melody may be summarized by the D minor scale:

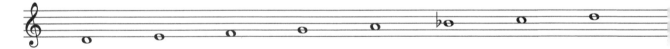

In fact, the melody ends by stepping down the scale starting on $\hat{6}$, the B♭ in the penultimate measure.

Music in minor generally has a darker, mellower sound than major. It may carry a sense of mystery or melancholy. Words like "dark" or "sad" may not be the best ways to characterize it, but at least they might help develop a deeper sense of what it means to be in minor. Some music, like the first movement of Beethoven's Fifth Symphony (in C minor), derives much of its power and drama from the minor mode. The minor mode can also be found in popular music and jazz.

Actually, composers have many tricks for counteracting these tendencies—for brightening the sound of minor or darkening the sound of major, in the way they use rhythm, tempo, instruments, style, and other factors. For the most part, however, the major mode does tend to have a sunnier disposition than minor.

 For suggestions for further listening and online exercises and drills, go to www.oup.com/us/lambert

▶ STUDY QUESTIONS FOR LESSON 11

1. Define these terms:
    Aeolian mode
    family of scales
    minor mode
    relative keys
    subtonic

2. In the minor scale, between what scale degrees do half steps occur?

3. When you write a minor scale, how many notes in the chromatic scale do you skip over to form whole steps?

4. What do all minor scales have in common?

5. Where in a major scale do you find the starting note of the relative minor?

6. Where in a minor scale do you find the starting note of the relative major?

7. In many cases, how can you tell whether music is in major or minor, just by listening?

► EXERCISES FOR LESSON 11

To construct a minor scale by selecting certain notes from a chromatic scale, as in Lessons 11.1 and 11.4, first write an ascending chromatic scale. Here's how we would begin if the starting note is D:

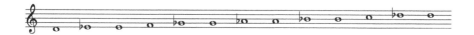

Extract notes from this chromatic scale to follow the standard pattern of whole- (W) and half- (H) steps: WHWWHWW. For whole steps, make sure you're skipping over one note in the chromatic scale. For half steps, make sure you're *not* skipping over any notes in the chromatic scale:

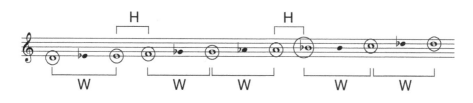

A. Write an ascending chromatic scale starting on the given note. If the given note is a natural or flatted note, spell the five black keys in the scale using flatted notes. If the given note is a sharped note, spell the five black keys using sharped notes. Then <u>circle</u> the notes of the minor scale within that chromatic scale, assuming that the given note is 1̂.

1.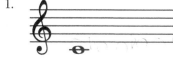

2.

3.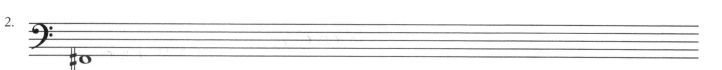

4.

5.

Any note is a member of seven different minor scales. (Some are in more if you count en-harmonics separately.) The note E, for example, is $\hat{1}$ in the E minor scale (EF♯GABCDE), $\hat{2}$ in the D minor scale (DEFGAB♭CD), $\hat{3}$ in the C♯ minor scale (C♯D♯EF♯G♯ABC♯), and so forth.

   If you know the scale degree number (other than $\hat{1}$) of a certain note in some scale, you can find $\hat{1}$ by counting down or up to tonic. If you know, for example, that E is $\hat{6}$, you can find $\hat{1}$ by counting from $\hat{6}$ down to $\hat{1}$ . . .

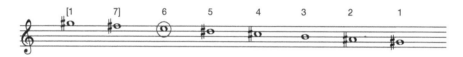

. . . or from $\hat{6}$ up to $\hat{1}$ . . .

E is $\hat{6}$ in G♯ minor. When you are locating tonic, remember to move within the actual minor *scale*, not just within the musical alphabet. E is $\hat{6}$ in *G♯* minor, not *G* minor; in G minor, $\hat{6}$ is *E♭*.

Name: _____

B. Write minor scales to show how the given notes can be reinterpreted as different scale degrees in different minor scales. Use the given notes as they appear (don't change the accidental).

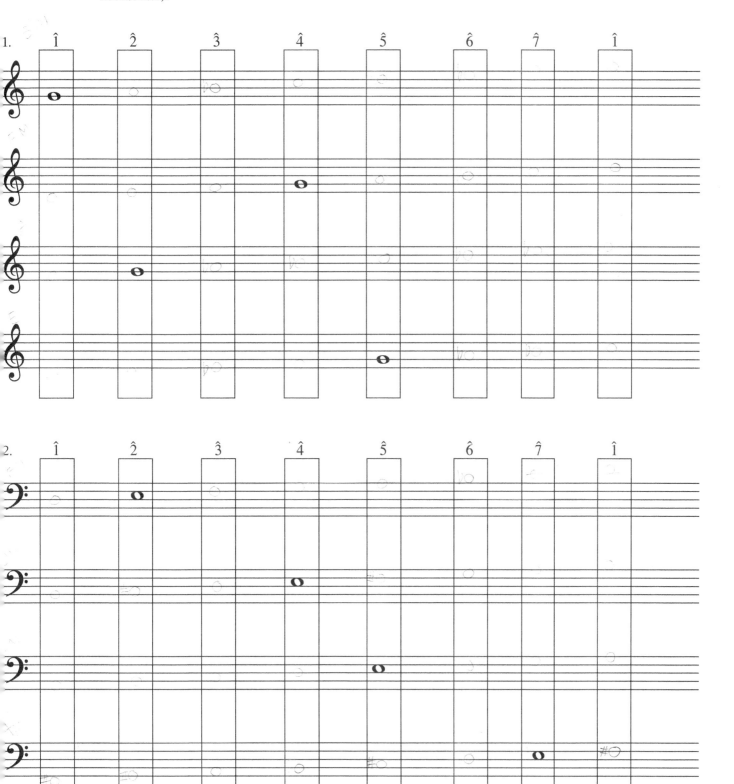

3.

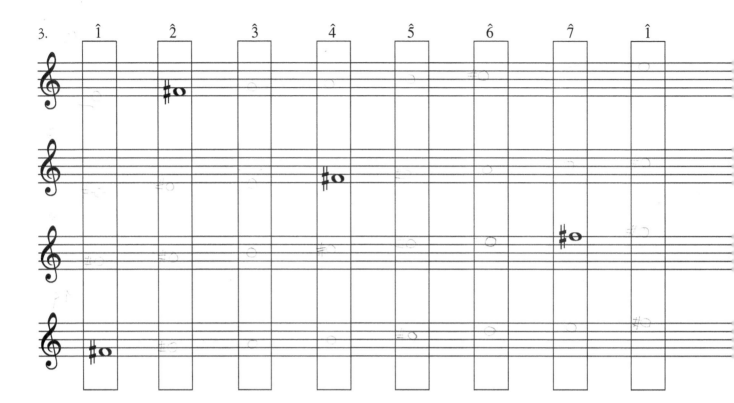

✑ create!

1. Listen to or play the first fourteen measures of Folk Song in the Fifteen Character Pieces (www.oup.com/us/lambert). Repeat this same accompaniment pattern (the left hand in the first two measures) while improvising a different melody in your right hand. Try the same exercise in different minor keys.

2. Invent your own short, repeating accompaniment pattern in a minor key, inspired by Folk Song or something similar. Improvise a melody in your right hand to go with it.

LESSON 12
MINOR KEY SIGNATURES

12.1   RELATIVE KEY SIGNATURES

Because every minor scale can be partnered with a major scale that has exactly the same notes in it, every minor key signature can be partnered with a major key signature that has exactly the same accidentals in it. In other words, every key signature that we learned for major keys in Lesson 9 is also the key signature for its relative minor.

The principles we learned for major key signatures in Lesson 9 continue to apply. The order and placement of accidentals follow the same formatting standards. The key signature appears at the beginning of every line of music, just after the clef sign and before any meter signature.

Let's think about what this means. It means, among other things, that a quick glance at a key signature of a piece of music will not automatically reveal its key. The key signature narrows it down to two relatives, but we can't know which is the actual key until we get to know the music. Take a look, for example, at this melody by Gabriel Fauré:

12-1

Molto adagio

The three-flat key signature tells us that the key is either E♭ major or its relative minor, C. The accompaniment would provide important clues, but let's restrict ourselves just to the melody. It starts on E♭, which might lead you to suspect that it's in E♭ major, but don't let that throw you. Look instead at the last note, C. The last note, not the first note, is usually a better indicator of tonic. This melody is in the key of C minor, not E♭ major.

160

12.2 ALL MINOR KEY SIGNATURES

To list all the minor key signatures, all we have to do is add the relative minor key labels to the lists of major key signatures in Lesson 9.2. Now we have two possible tonics for each signature, using uppercase to indicate major and lowercase to indicate minor:

G or e:

D or b:

A or f#:

E or c#:

B or g#:

F# or d#:

C# or a#:

F or d:

B♭ or g:

E♭ or c:

A♭ or f:

D♭ or b♭:

G♭ or e♭:

C♭ or a♭:

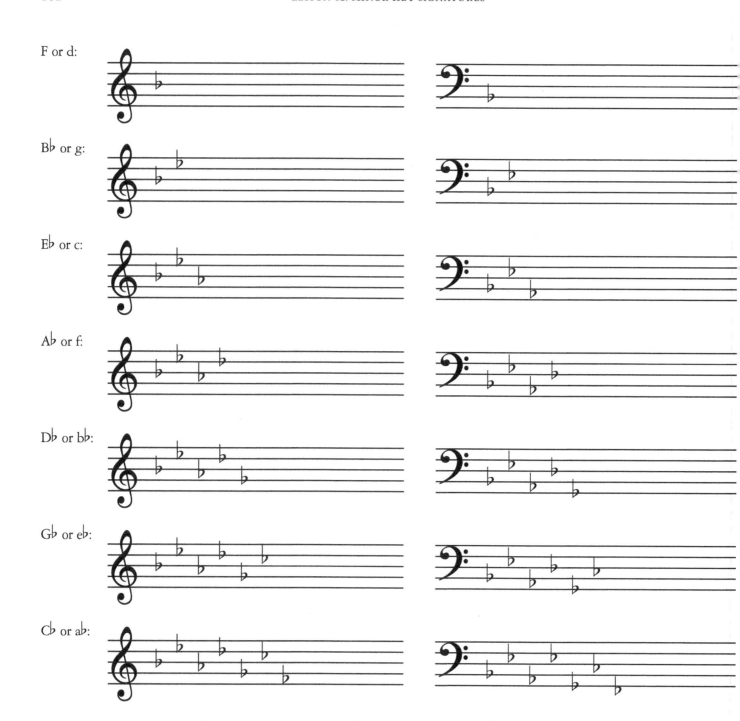

Remember that the sixth degree of any major scale is the first degree of its relative minor. If you know the major key indicated by a particular signature, you can find its relative minor by counting up (or down) to $\hat{6}$.

In a major scale, $\hat{6}$ is only three half steps below $\hat{1}$. One fast way to find a relative minor is to count back three half steps from the major tonic. If you use this method, just remember to spell the sixth degree correctly. If you're thinking about the B major scale, for example, and counting down three half steps, you arrive at a black key that indicates the key of g♯, not a♭.

You can recognize minor key signatures by associating them with their relative majors, or you can use little tricks, similar to those we learned for major key signatures (Lesson 9.2):

- For sharp keys, the minor tonic is one whole step below the last sharp in the key signature.

- For flat keys, the minor tonic is two whole steps above the last flat in the key signature.

12.3 CIRCLE OF KEYS FOR MAJOR AND MINOR

We can now update the circle of keys (Lesson 9.3) to include the relative minors:

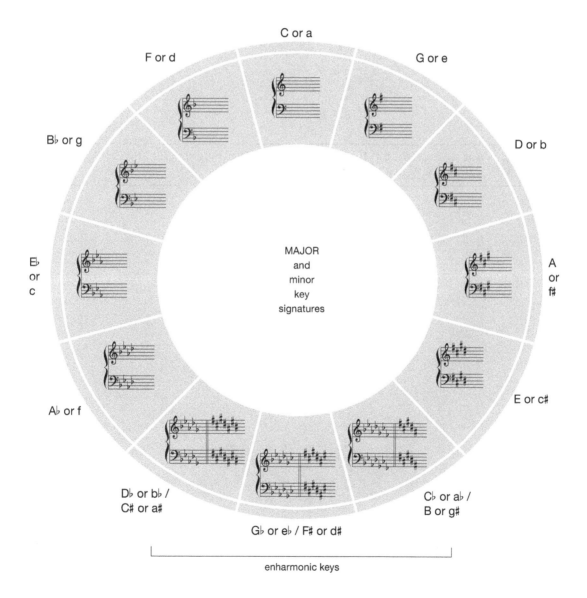

Now we have four possibilities at five o'clock, six o'clock, and seven o'clock: two enharmonic keys and their relatives.

We could also make a circle of keys consisting only of minor keys, starting with the key of a alone at twelve o'clock, moving clockwise to the key of e at one o'clock, b at two o'clock, and so forth. The principle is the same as the major circle: as you move clockwise, the fifth degree of a given key becomes the first degree of the next; as you move counterclockwise, the fourth degree of the current key becomes the first degree of the next. You can see these relationships very clearly in the lists of minor scales in Lesson 11.3.

 For suggestions for further listening and online exercises and drills, go to www.oup.com/us/lambert

▶ STUDY QUESTIONS FOR LESSON 12

1. Define these terms:
    circle of keys for major and minor
    key signature

2. How are the key signatures for minor keys related to the key signatures for major keys?

3. What are the tricks for identifying minor key signatures?

4. Where do you find relatives on the circle of keys?

5. On the circle of keys for major and minor, how many different keys are indicated at five o'clock, six o'clock, and seven o'clock?

EXERCISES FOR LESSON 12

As we learned in Lesson 9.2, key signatures must follow standard rules of placement and ordering. If accidentals appear in some nonstandard ordering, or on the wrong lines or spaces, the key signature is malformed.

When writing accidentals on the staff, remember the notational guidelines shown with the Lesson 7 exercises.

A. Practice writing key signatures for minor keys on the staffs below.

  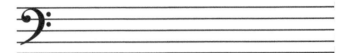

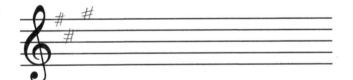 

 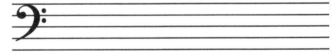

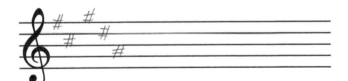 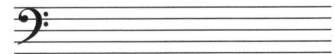

b♭:

g: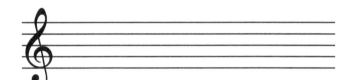

In Lesson 9.2 we learned this method for identifying **major** key signatures without consulting a memorized scale or reference table:

→ For sharp keys, the tonic is one diatonic half step above the last sharp in the key signature.
→ For flat keys, the tonic note is the penultimate flat in the key signature.
→ There's no trick for F and C; you just have to remember those.

And in Lesson 12.2 we learned this method for identifying **minor** key signatures:

→ For sharp keys, the tonic is one whole step below the last sharp in the key signature.
→ For flat keys, the tonic is two whole steps above the last flat in the key signature.

To move back and forth between relative keys, you might find it helpful to use some combination of both of these methods. Or remember what we learned about relative scales in Lesson 11.2:

→ To find the starting note for a relative minor scale, go to $\hat{6}$ of major.
→ To find the starting note for a relative major scale, go to $\hat{3}$ of minor.

If you know, for example, that a key signature of two sharps indicates D major, find $\hat{6}$ of that scale to identify its relative minor, B. If you know that a key signature of two sharps indicates B minor, find $\hat{3}$ of that scale to identify its relative major, D.

B. In the staff following each key signature (in both clefs), write the tonic notes of the major and relative minor keys. The first one is done for you.

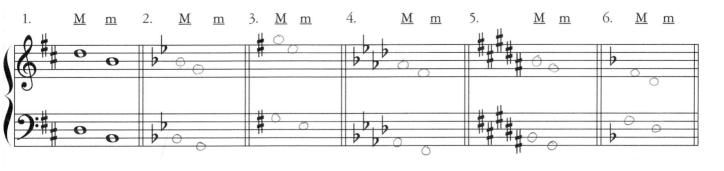

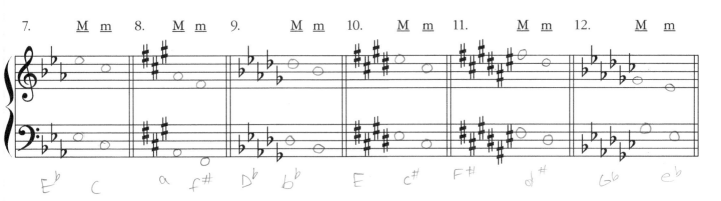

The last note of a melody is usually the tonic note of the scale on which it's based. Well before the last note arrives, the mode (major or minor) of a melody can be clearly established, by rhythmic emphasis and scale patterns and other things. Even if all seven notes of a scale aren't represented in a melody, it's still possible to determine a source scale, by looking at the last note and listening to the melodic gestures.

C. In the spaces provided on the next page, name the key and mode (major or minor) of each melody and write its key signature and tonic note (in both clefs).

12-2

1.

Wolf-Ferrari

12-3

2.

traditional

3.

Schubert

12-4

4.

Italian folk song

12-5

5.

Massenet

12-6

ANSWERS:

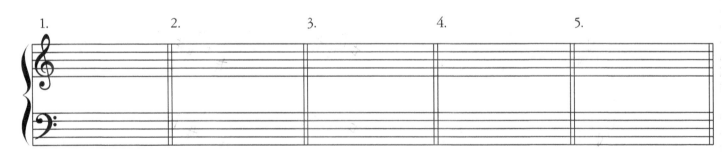

1.　　　　2.　　　　3.　　　　4.　　　　5.

key: _____　_____　_____　_____　_____

　　LESSON 12: MINOR KEY SIGNATURES

 create!

1. Get to know one of the minor melodies in the exercises or text from this lesson or the previous one. Write an eight-measure melody of your own in the same key and meter, using the existing melody as an inspiration. End on tonic. Your melody should sound different from the existing melody, but it might replicate some of its rhythms or scale-degree combinations.

2. Write an eight-measure melody in any minor key and meter, not inspired by an existing melody. End on tonic. Include several instances of a short rhythm or scale-degree combination that you've devised.

LESSON **13**
MORE ABOUT MINOR

13.1 PARALLEL MAJOR AND MINOR

So far we've learned about major and minor keys that have the same key signatures but different tonics—*relatives*. Now let's think about major and minor keys that have the same tonics but different key signatures. C major and C minor, for example:

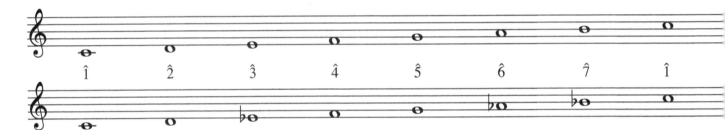

Major and minor keys with the same tonics are known as **parallel** keys. C major is the parallel major of C minor. C minor is the parallel minor of C major.

Parallel scales differ at three places, degrees $\hat{3}$, $\hat{6}$, and $\hat{7}$. The other scale degrees are the same. Because parallel scales have three different accidentals, they're three places apart on the circle of keys (see Lesson 12.3).

Knowing about parallels gives you one more method of constructing a minor scale. Rather than calculating whole and half steps, or reordering the relative major, in some instances it might be easiest to construct a minor scale by first spelling its parallel major, then lowering that scale's third, sixth, and seventh degrees. To convert C major to C minor, for example, lower E ($\hat{3}$) to E♭, A ($\hat{6}$) to A♭, and B ($\hat{7}$) to B♭.

If you use the parallel conversion method, just be sure to keep the note on the same line or space when you're making the alteration. In other words, lower the note by a *chromatic*, not a *diatonic*, half step (Lesson 3.1). When you lower $\hat{3}$ in C major, for example, E becomes E♭, not D♯.

Of course you can also use the principle of parallel modes to move in the opposite direction, to convert minor to parallel major by *raising* $\hat{3}$, $\hat{6}$, and $\hat{7}$ (again, making sure to keep the note on the same line or space). To construct A major, for example, you could start with its parallel, A minor (the relative of C major, no sharps or flats) and raise C ($\hat{3}$) to C♯, F ($\hat{6}$) to F♯, and G ($\hat{7}$) to G♯.

172

13.2 HARMONIC MINOR

Thinking about the relationships between $\hat{6}$ and $\hat{7}$ in parallel keys raises another issue for the study of minor: these scale degrees, especially $\hat{7}$, are often altered.

For example, listen to this melody by Schubert:

The mode is clearly minor, and the tonic is clearly C, but every time $\hat{7}$ occurs, Schubert adds an accidental to make it B♮, not B♭. The best way to summarize the pitch content of Schubert's melody is to write a C minor scale with B♮, not B♭, as the seventh degree:

Many pieces in minor keys, in a variety of styles and representing diverse traditions throughout music history, include this same alteration of $\hat{7}$. In fact, raising the seventh scale degree is more common than leaving it as it is. The examples of minor melodies with no altered tones in Lessons 11.5 (Handel) and 12.1 (Fauré) are actually in the minority.

Because the minor scale with raised $\hat{7}$ is so common, it deserves special attention, and a special name: **harmonic minor**. Without alteration the scale is known as **natural minor**. These are both **forms** of the minor scale. In previous lessons (11, 12) we studied only the natural form. Now we explore the harmonic form.

To write a minor scale in its harmonic form, start by writing the natural form. After you're sure that your notation is correct—that you have notes on all the lines and spaces within an octave, with the correct accidentals—find the seventh degree and raise it by one chromatic half step. In other words, make the change without moving the note to a different line or space.

If the seventh degree of the natural form is a flatted note, as we've just seen in the C natural minor scale, the change for harmonic minor makes it natural. If the seventh degree in the natural form is a white key, the change for harmonic minor makes it a sharped note:

A harmonic minor

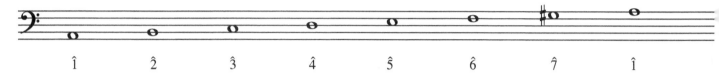

In some rare cases, such as G harmonic minor, the alteration results in a scale that mixes sharps and flats:

G harmonic minor

Mixing flats and sharps never happens in natural minor scales, or in major scales.

For minor scales with seventh degrees that are already sharped in the natural form . . .

G# natural minor

. . . you'll need to use a **double sharp** to convert it to harmonic minor:

G# harmonic minor

A double sharp symbol looks like an "x" in a bold font. It raises a sharped note by a chromatic half step. In other words, a double sharped note is two half steps higher than a white key.

Think about the impact of the raised seventh scale degree in harmonic minor. For one thing, the alteration creates an unusually large gap, three half steps, between $\hat{6}$ and $\hat{7}$. This is the only instance, in all the scales we've studied, of a distance between scale degrees that's not a half or whole step.

The altered $\hat{7}$ also requires a name change. Recall that in Lesson 11.1 we named the seventh step "subtonic" because of its whole-step relationship with tonic. With the raised $\hat{7}$ of harmonic minor we've created a half step from $\hat{7}$ up to 1, just like major. So in harmonic minor we use the same name for $\hat{7}$ that we use for major, "leading tone." In other words, we have two names for the seventh degree in a minor scale, depending on the form: *subtonic* in the natural form, and *leading tone* in the harmonic form. All the other scale degree names are the same as they are for major (Lesson 8.6).

13.3   MELODIC MINOR

Listen to this melody by Tchaikovsky:

A summary of the pitch content of this melody looks like this:

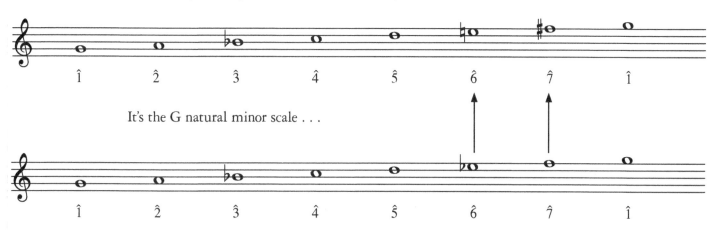

It's the G natural minor scale . . .

. . . with both the sixth and seventh degrees raised by a chromatic half step. This is the third form of minor, known as **melodic**.

The raised $\hat{6}$ and $\hat{7}$ heighten the tendency of those tones to pull upward toward the tonic octave. For this reason, the melodic form of minor is often used in the ascending direction. When musicians practice melodic minor scales, they usually play them only going up the scale and then revert to the natural form on the way back down.

The upward pull of the raised $\hat{7}$ indicates the same renaming we used for $\hat{7}$ in harmonic minor: "leading tone," not "subtonic," for the seventh degree of a melodic minor scale. Further, the raised $\hat{6}$ also makes the minor scale sound more like major. Compare, for example, C major and C melodic minor:

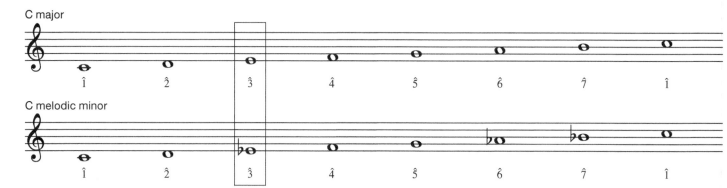

Parallel major and natural minor differ on three degrees, but melodic minor removes two of those differences, leaving just $\hat{3}$ to distinguish between major and parallel melodic minor.

And we no longer have any unusual gaps, as we do between $\hat{6}$ and $\hat{7}$ in harmonic minor. The distances between scale degrees in melodic minor, and in natural minor and in major, are all either whole or half steps.

13.4   SUMMARY OF THE FORMS OF MINOR

The unaltered *natural* form of minor is a rearrangement of the notes of its relative major; both keys have the same key signature. To convert the natural form to the *harmonic* form, raise $\hat{7}$ by one chromatic half step. To convert the natural form to the *melodic* form, raise both $\hat{6}$ and $\hat{7}$ by one chromatic half step:

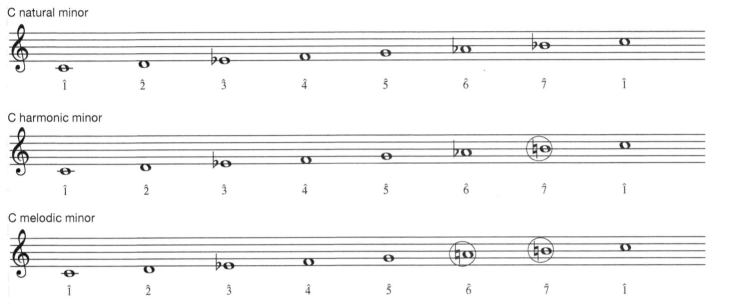

For suggestions for further listening and online exercises and drills, go to www.oup.com/us/lambert

▶ STUDY QUESTIONS FOR LESSON 13

1. Define these terms:
    double sharp
    forms of minor
    harmonic minor
    melodic minor
    natural minor
    parallel keys

2. What is the difference between parallel keys and relative keys?

3. On what scale degrees do parallel major and natural minor scales differ?

4. How is the natural minor scale converted to the harmonic form?

5. How is the natural minor scale converted to the melodic form?

6. What is the difference between harmonic and melodic minor scales?

7. What is the difference between a melodic minor scale and its parallel major?

8. What are the different names for scale degree $\hat{7}$ in the natural and harmonic minor scales?

► EXERCISES FOR LESSON 13

When notating the harmonic and melodic forms of minor, always work from the natural form (Lesson 13.4). After you're sure that the natural form is correct, you can change it to harmonic by raising $\hat{7}$ one chromatic half step (i.e., raise it a half step without moving it to a different line or space):

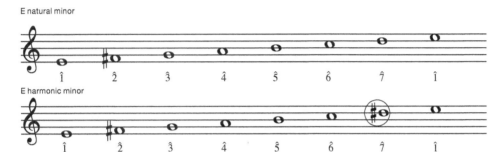

You can change natural to melodic by raising both $\hat{6}$ and $\hat{7}$ one chromatic half step:

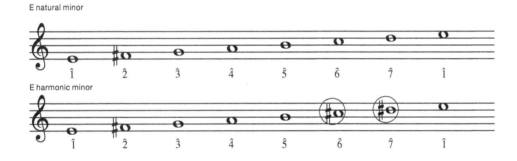

Notes that are already natural (white keys) become sharp when altered. Notes that are already flat become natural. Notes that are already sharp become double sharps.

A. Write a natural minor scale with the given note as tonic. Use accidentals as needed, not a key signature. Then notate the scale again but change the form to harmonic. Beneath that, write the melodic form of the same scale. Line up the scale degrees in the boxes.

1.

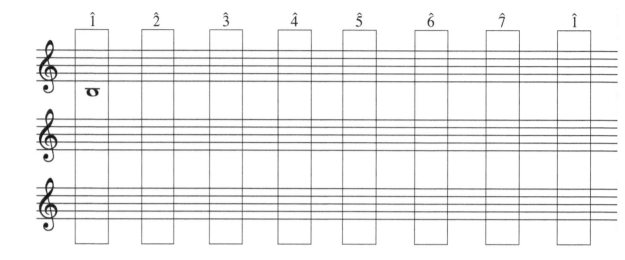

natural

harmonic

melodic

2.

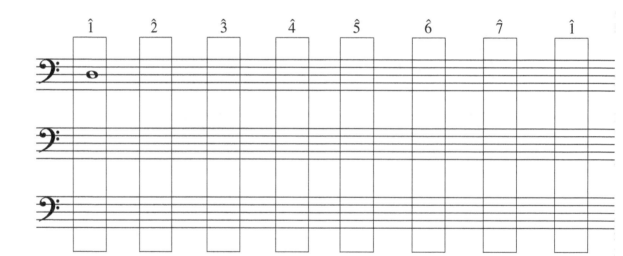

natural

harmonic

melodic

3.

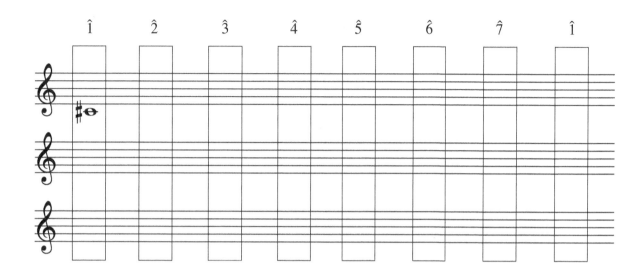

natural

harmonic

melodic

4.

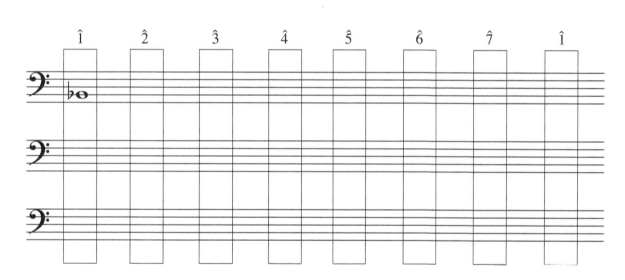

natural

harmonic

melodic

5.

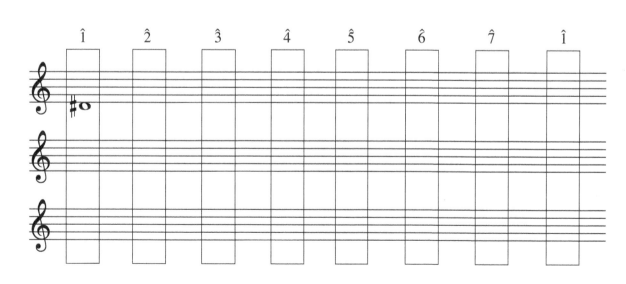

natural

harmonic

melodic

Name: _____

Relative major and natural minor have different tonics but the same pitch content (Lessons 11.2, 12.1). *Parallel* major and natural minor have the same tonic but differ at $\hat{3}$, $\hat{6}$, and $\hat{7}$ (Lesson 13.1). Work out the parallel and relative relationships first, before making any adjustments for harmonic or melodic forms.

Let's say we want to notate the parallel minor of E major, harmonic form. First determine the tonic and then write the natural form of the scale. The tonic is E; parallel modes have the same starting pitch. So begin by writing E natural minor:

After you're sure this is correct, raise $\hat{7}$ to create the harmonic form:

B. Notate the indicated scales. Don't use key signatures (add accidentals as needed).

1. G minor, harmonic form

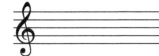

2. A minor, melodic form

3. G♯ minor, melodic form

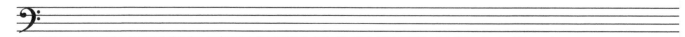

4. Eb minor, melodic form

5. The parallel minor of D major, natural form

6. The parallel minor of F major, harmonic form

7. The parallel minor of B major, melodic form

8. The relative minor of A major, natural form

9. The relative minor of G major, harmonic form

10. The relative minor of Ab major, melodic form

When you reorganize the notes of a melody in the form of a scale, start on the tonic, even if the tonic note isn't the lowest note in the melody:

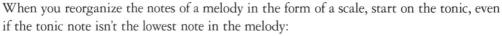

13-3

scale source:

To identify a scale type, look at the distances between scale degrees. A scale that begins with two whole steps is probably major, and a scale that begins with a whole and then a half step is probably minor. The scale above starts with C–D whole step, D–E♭ half step; it's C minor.

To distinguish between the forms of minor, focus on scale degrees $\hat{5}$–$\hat{6}$–$\hat{7}$–$\hat{1}$. The natural form will complete the whole- and half-step sequence WHWWHWW (Lesson 11.1). The raised seventh degree of the harmonic form will create a gap of three half steps between $\hat{6}$ and $\hat{7}$ (Lesson 13.2). And in the melodic form, $\hat{5}$–$\hat{6}$–$\hat{7}$–$\hat{1}$ will look exactly like those same degrees in the parallel major (Lesson 13.3). The C minor scale above has the raised $\hat{7}$ and three-half-step gap between $\hat{6}$ and $\hat{7}$ of the harmonic form.

C. Write the scale on which each melody is based and identify the scale tonic and type (major or minor). If the scale is minor, identify the form (natural, harmonic, or melodic).

1.

13-4

scale source:

scale tonic and type: _____

2.

scale source:

scale tonic and type: _____

3.

Krieger

scale source:

scale tonic and type: _____

4.

Mexican folk song

scale source:

scale tonic and type: _____

5.

Bizet

scale source:

scale tonic and type: _____

6.

Couperin

scale source:

scale tonic and type: _____

✐ create!

Convert the melodies you wrote at the end of Lesson 12 from natural minor to the harmonic or melodic form. Notate the new versions below.

LESSON 14
UNBALANCED METER

14.1   MEASURE DIVISIONS

Because the beats of duple, triple, and quadruple meters are evenly distributed throughout a measure, they are **balanced**. In quadruple, "wa-ter-" balances "mel-on." In duple, "ap-" balances "ple." In triple, "straw-" and "ry" are balanced around "ber-."

WA - TER - MEL - ON	AP - PLE	STRAW - BER - RY
2 + 2	1 + 1	1 + 1 + 1

Meters with five or seven beats per measure—**quintuple** and **septuple** meters—are **unbalanced**. Their beats are unevenly distributed:

HOT - HOUSE CU - CUM - BER	EL - E - PHANT GAR - LIC
2 + 3	3 + 2

MEX - I - CAN A - VO - CA - DO	CAL - I - FORN - IA AP - RI - COT
3 + 4	4 + 3

These are all *equal* beats, having *equivalent* durations. It's not the same as taking the same units and squeezing them into alternating simple (two-part) and compound (three-part) beats:

HOT - HOUSE   CU - CUM - BER

Here "hot-house" takes up the same space as "cu-cum-ber" (one beat). A simple division ("hot-house") gives way to a compound division ("cu-cum-ber"). The syllables in "hothouse" are slightly longer than the syllables in "cucumber," because both words are squeezed into the same amount of durational space.

In an unbalanced meter, by contrast, each syllable has the same duration. "Cucumber" takes up more space than "hothouse," because "cucumber" has more syllables than "hothouse."

14.2 NOTATIONAL ISSUES

Unbalanced meters are typically notated with eighth-note beats $\left(\frac{5}{8}, \frac{7}{8}\right)$ or quarter-note beats $\left(\frac{5}{4}, \frac{7}{4}\right)$. Beats are typically grouped as 2+3 or 3+2 for quintuple, and 3+4 (3+2+2) or 4+3 (2+2+3) for septuple. The grouping can be especially clear in $\frac{5}{8}$ (or $\frac{7}{8}$), when beamings demonstrate the rhythmic organization:

14-1

Here the beaming demonstrates the 2+3 grouping of the measures. The melodic contours and the *tenuto* marking (–) on each beginning of a 3-group help articulate these beat groupings.

In $\frac{5}{4}$, beaming not being an option for quarter notes, the rhythmic grouping can still be clearly evident from expressive markings and general musical patterning:

14-2

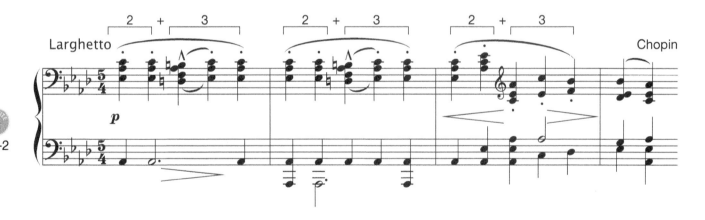

Septuple meter is perceived as alternating quadruple and triple measures, and is sometimes notated that way. When notated using a seven-beat meter signature, the measure is often divided by a broken line to facilitate reading:

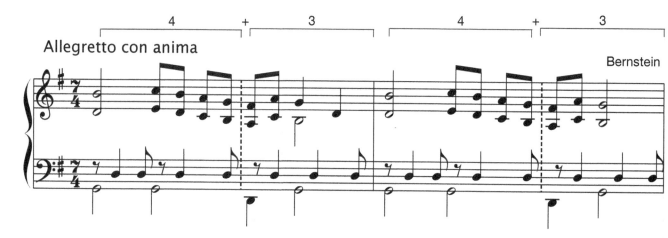

Unbalanced meters are relatively uncommon in Western concert music. They have been used more frequently in folk music in some parts of the world, especially Eastern Europe.

 For suggestions for further listening, go to www.oup.com/us/lambert

▶ **STUDY QUESTIONS FOR LESSON 14**

1. Define these terms:
   balanced meter
   quintuple meter
   septuple meter
   unbalanced meter

2. What are the possible upper numbers for unbalanced meter signatures? What are the most common lower numbers?

3. How can beaming make quintuple meters easier to read?

4. What are common groupings within measures of music in septuple meter?

▶ RHYTHM READING

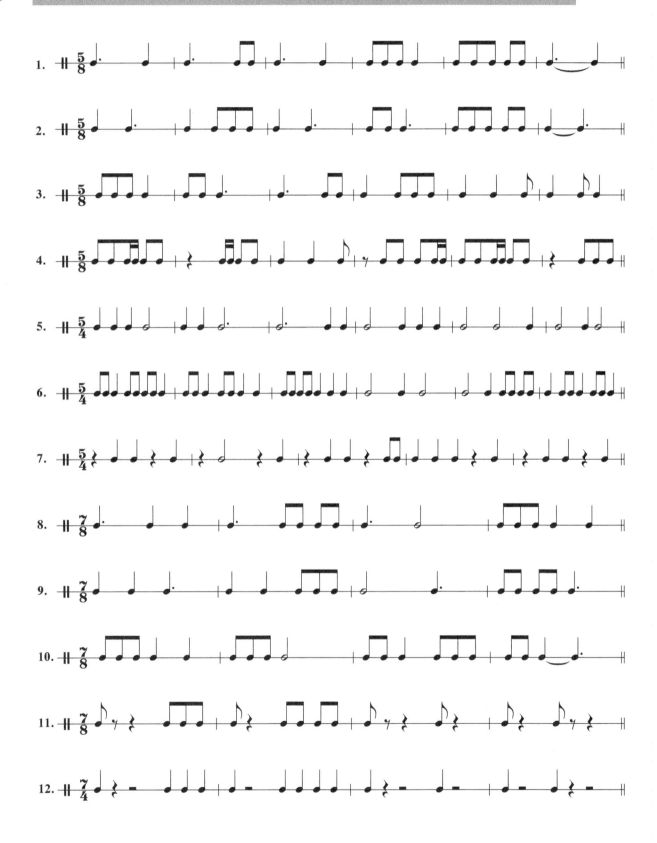

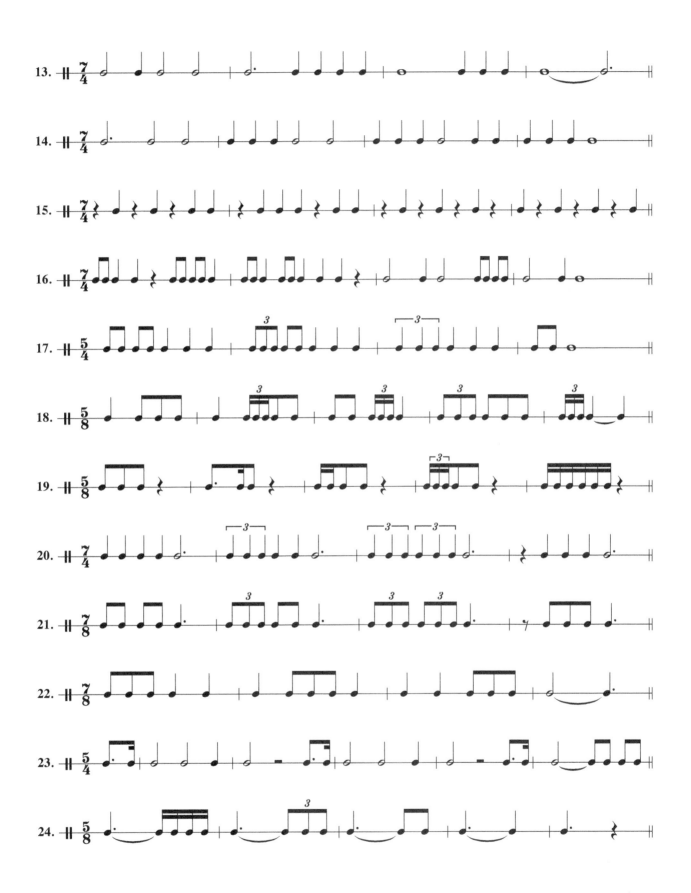

► **EXERCISES FOR LESSON 14**

A passage of music can be renotated in a different meter by redefining the beat as a different note value. The top number of the meter signature doesn't change (because the number of beats per measure doesn't change), but the bottom number does. Let's say we want to renotate this measure:

$\frac{5}{4}$ ♩   ♪   ♪   ♪   ♪   ♩ |

If we redefine the beat as the eighth note, the meter signature becomes $\frac{5}{8}$ and all the note values are halved:

$\frac{5}{8}$ ♪   ♪   ♪   ♪   ♪   ♩ |

In either notation, the measure sounds exactly the same, assuming we haven't changed the tempo.

A. Renotate each melody in the given meter on the lower staff. The newly notated version should sound exactly the same as the original.

1.

2.

Music in unbalanced meters is usually performed with regular beat groupings. Quintuple is usually grouped as 2+3 or 3+2, and septuple is usually grouped as 3+4 or 4+3 (Lesson 14.2). These groupings should be evident to the performer and listener, just in the way each measure is rhythmically and melodically organized.

In this measure, for example . . .

. . . the pattern of single note versus two notes together establishes a 3+2 grouping, which can be demonstrated by beaming:

B. Rewrite each measure, adding beams to show its most logical rhythmic organization. In quintuple meter, your beams will show either 2+3 or 3+2 groupings. In septuple meter, your beams will reveal either 3+4 or 4+3 groupings.

1.

2.

3.

4.

5.

6.

7.

⤎ create!

1. Study Dance in the Fifteen Character Pieces (www.oup.com/us/lambert). Notice that:

- The groupings are mostly 3+2. The contrasting material starting in measure 17 briefly features 2+3.

- The left hand repeats a two-measure accompaniment pattern.

- The melody is very simple, based only on the first five steps in C major. After the first two phrases are presented, we hear them again with variation (in measures 9–16, 22–27).

- Contrast in measures 17–21 arises not only from the change to 2+3 but also from the presence of dissonance when the right hand plays whole steps (F–G).

- The music playfully suggests the spirit of dancing, even if most dancers might find it hard to get in the groove of an unbalanced meter!

2. Study other short pieces in unbalanced meters listed in the *Suggestions for Listening* for Lesson 14 (www.oup.com/us/lambert), especially those by Bartók and Shostakovich.

3. Write a short piano piece modeled on Dance.

- After you've selected a key (perhaps minor?), improvise an accompaniment pattern in your left hand in quintuple or septuple meter.

- When you're satisfied with the accompaniment pattern you've created, determine what it will look like in musical notation. Do you think it looks best with the eighth note or the quarter note as the beat?

- Next, play your accompaniment pattern in your left hand and improvise a melody in your right hand to go with it. If you have limited piano skills, keep your hand(s) in the same position. Otherwise, explore a wider range for your melody, taking your right hand away from just the first five notes of the scale.

- Think of ways to present your melody with variation (as in measures 9–16 and 22–27 of Dance) and explore possibilities for contrast, perhaps by changing the beat groupings (as in measures 17–21 of Dance).

- Notate your piece in the standard two-stave format for piano music. Use key signatures, not individual accidentals as needed. Check over your notation to make sure that your symbols are clear, noteheads are correctly placed, and measures contain the proper number of beats.

LESSON 14: UNBALANCED METER

LESSON **15**

INTERVALS I

15.1   NOTE CONNECTIONS

Play or sing this melody composed by Johann Sebastian Bach:

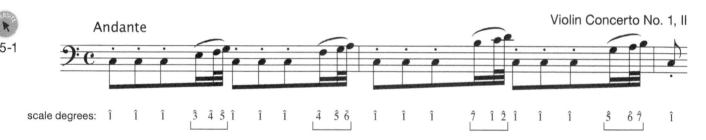

Bach's C major melody simply repeats the tonic note of the scale on staccato eighth notes, with periodic interruptions from a rhythmic "blip" of three other scale tones. At first the blip is scale degrees $\hat{3}$–$\hat{4}$–$\hat{5}$ (E–F–G), then $\hat{4}$–$\hat{5}$–$\hat{6}$ (F–G–A). In the second measure the blips are $\hat{7}$–$\hat{1}$–$\hat{2}$ (B–C–D) and $\hat{5}$–$\hat{6}$–$\hat{7}$ (G–A–B). As the melody continues to return to C after each blip, Bach draws our attention to the changing relationships between the tonic and the other scale tones.

One way to summarize these relationships would be to organize the entire scale as a series of note pairs between tonic and every other note in the scale:

Our array of pairs begins with C paired with itself, followed by C paired with $\hat{2}$ (D), C paired with $\hat{3}$ (E), and so forth, up through C paired with its octave. Bach's melody highlights different parts of the array at different times, but it generally begins, in measure 1, with blipped notes that are closer to tonic, and moves in measure 2 to blipped notes that are farther away from tonic. Eventually we hear each note of the scale as part of a blip, making us aware of each note's relationship with the repeating tonic.

15.2   INTERVAL DISTANCE

The spans between notes on display in Bach's melody are known as **intervals**. Spans between notes in a melody—that is, between notes in succession—are **melodic intervals**. Spans between notes happening at the same time—as when you play only the note pairs above—are **harmonic intervals**.

Whether melodic or harmonic, every interval has a name, a means of distinguishing one from another and drawing comparisons. We've already done some of this in earlier lessons, when we used terms like "octave" and "half step" and "whole step." Now we'll establish labels for other tone combinations.

An interval's name has two components: **quality** and **distance**. We'll also recognize a third aspect of each interval, its size in half steps. Let's take each element one at a time.

First, distance. Here again are the note pairs from tonic in C major, now in treble clef:

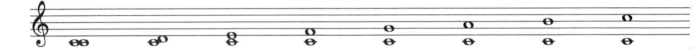

To specify the distance, simply assume that the lower note is the tonic note of the scale, in this case C major, and count scale degrees as you move upwards in the scale. The distance is the scale-degree number of the higher note. The first one, the combination of C with itself, is distance 1, also known as the **unison**. Next comes C–D, distance 2 (or a "second") because D is $\hat{2}$. Then, C–E is distance 3 ("third") because E is $\hat{3}$. And so forth:

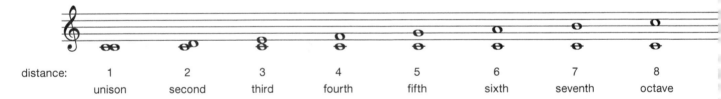

As long as you are counting scale degrees accurately, alternating lines and spaces, progressing through the musical alphabet without skipping or repeating, you'll find it easy to determine the distance.

You'll also notice some useful identifying features of the distances. For the intervals with odd-numbered distances, for example, the two notes are always notated both on lines or both on spaces:

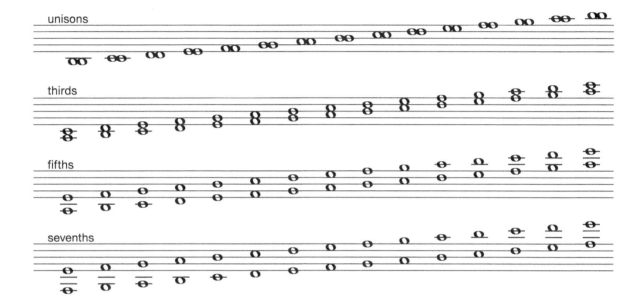

For the intervals with even-numbered distances, one note is notated on a line, the other on a space:

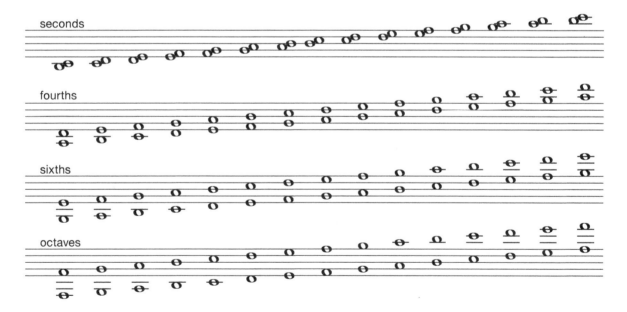

15.3   QUALITY

The quality of an interval helps make distinctions between different distances. Intervals between tonic of a major scale and any other note have two possible qualities, **perfect** or **major**. Distances 1, 4, 5, and 8 are perfect (abbreviated "P"). Distances 2, 3, 6, and 7 are major ("M"). The complete label for each interval combines the symbols for quality and distance:

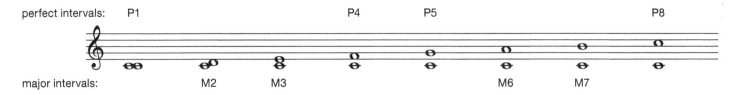

M2 ("major second") is another name for whole step. P8 is also called octave. Another name for P1 is unison.

The same labels apply to the same scale-degree combinations in any major key. Here, for example, are the intervals between tonic and the other notes in D major:

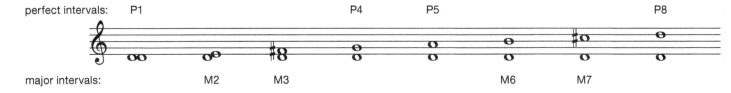

Just as in C major, the interval combining $\hat{1}$ and $\hat{3}$ is a M3 ("major third"). The interval combining $\hat{1}$ and $\hat{5}$ is a P5 ("perfect fifth"). And so forth.

15.4   SIZE IN HALF STEPS

We can also define intervals by specifying the number of half steps they span. To calculate this amount, simply situate each interval within a chromatic scale starting on the lower note:

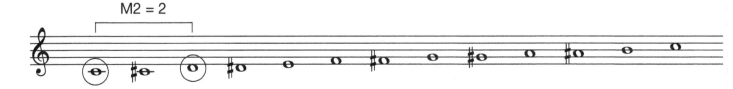

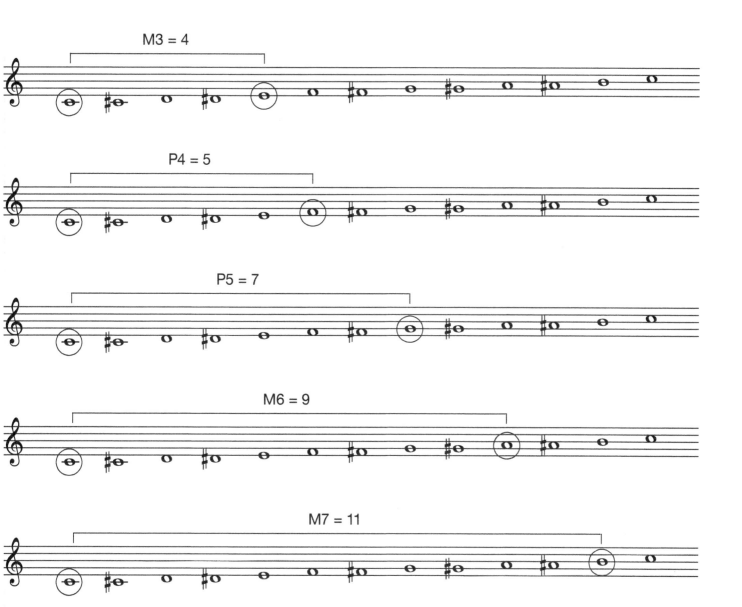

Of course, the number of half steps spanned by the P1 is 0, and by the P8, 12.

Half-step sizes are the same in any key. No matter which major scale you use as the basis of an interval, counting up two half steps from tonic will always yield a M2, counting up four from tonic will always form a M3, and so forth.

Now we can add this information, parenthetically, to our previous arrangement of interval labels starting on tonic within C major:

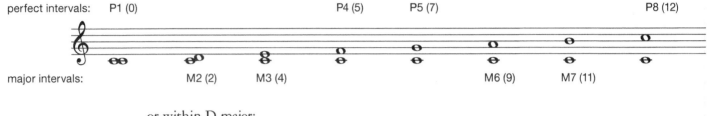

... or within D major:

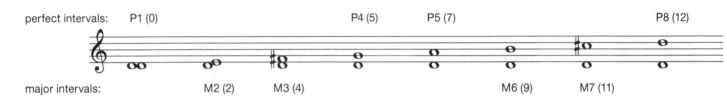

... or within any other major key. No matter what note is tonic, combining $\hat{1}$ and $\hat{4}$ will always yield an interval spanning five half steps known as the P4. $\hat{1}$ and $\hat{6}$ will combine to form a M6 spanning nine half steps. And so forth.

You can remember the half-step sizes by relating them to the step-sequence of the major scale. As you move through the list of half-step sizes, they increase by two whenever the major scale has a whole step, and by one whenever the scale has a half step:

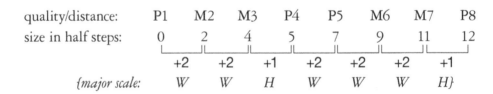

 For suggestions for further listening and online exercises and drills, go to www.oup.com/us/lambert

▶ **STUDY QUESTIONS FOR LESSON 15**

1. Define these terms:
   distance (of an interval)
   harmonic interval
   interval
   major intervals
   melodic interval
   perfect intervals
   quality (of an interval)
   unison

2. What are the three pieces of information for an interval?

3. In the list of all intervals formed from tonic of a major scale, which ones are perfect quality, and which ones are major?

4. In interval labels, which distances are never perfect, and which are never major?

5. What are the possible half-step sizes for all intervals formed from tonic of a major scale?

6. Give the interval labels for:
   unison
   octave
   whole step

7. When notated on the staff, what do all odd-numbered intervallic distances have in common? What about even-numbered distances?

Name: _____

To construct all the intervals from tonic of a major scale, make note pairs of tonic with every other note in the scale:

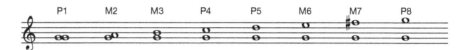

Make sure to apply any accidentals necessary to ensure that the upper notes are scale tones in the major scale starting on the lower note. The F is sharped in the M7 above because F is sharped in the key of G major.

A. Notate all perfect and major intervals within the major scales starting on the given notes. Use accidentals as needed, not key signatures.

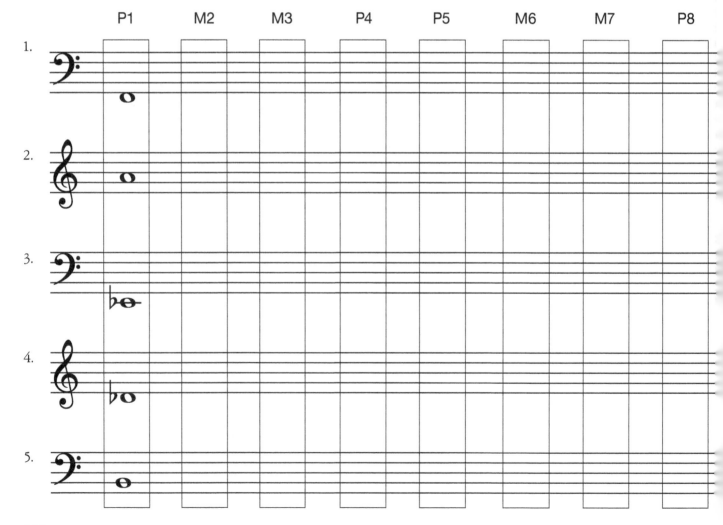

To form a certain major or perfect interval above a given note, think of the given note as the tonic of a major scale and write an upper note that's a member of that same scale. The number in the label (the "distance") will tell you which scale degree to write.

If you're given this, for example . . .

↑ M3

. . . you're looking for the third scale degree in D major. Using the whole- and half-step sequence of this scale, or drawing from your knowledge of key signatures, you can determine that the upper note is F♯:

M3

It's also possible to calculate intervals using half-step sizes. You know that the M3 spans four half steps, so to find a M3 above D, count four half steps higher than D:

If you use this method, just be sure to spell the upper note correctly. In this case, the upper note is spelled as F♯, not G♭. A note on the G line is the wrong distance above D, and G♭ is not the correct spelling of the third degree in the D major scale.

Here again are the half-step sizes of the perfect and major intervals:

P1	M2	M3	P4	P5	M6	M7	P8
0	2	4	5	7	9	11	12

B. Add a note <u>above</u> the given note to form the specified interval.

1. P5   2. P4   3. P5   4. M3   5. M7   6. M6   7. M2   8. M3

LESSON 15: INTERVALS I   207

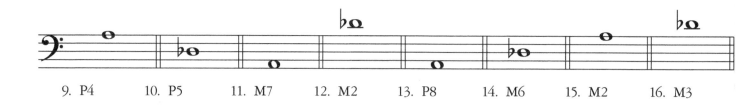

9. P4 10. P5 11. M7 12. M2 13. P8 14. M6 15. M2 16. M3

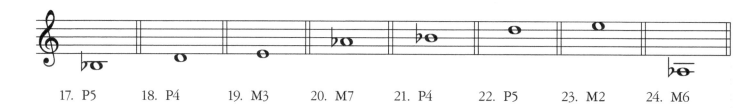

17. P5 18. P4 19. M3 20. M7 21. P4 22. P5 23. M2 24. M6

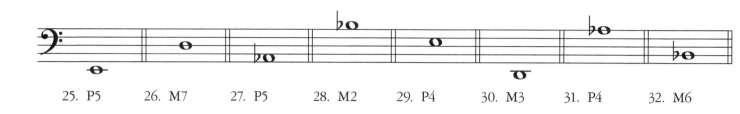

25. P5 26. M7 27. P5 28. M2 29. P4 30. M3 31. P4 32. M6

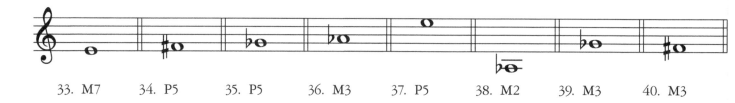

33. M7 34. P5 35. P5 36. M3 37. P5 38. M2 39. M3 40. M3

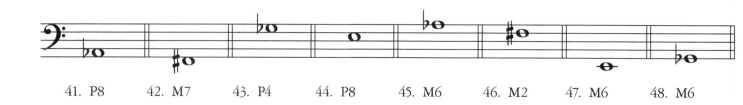

41. P8 42. M7 43. P4 44. P8 45. M6 46. M2 47. M6 48. M6

If you're given only an upper note and label and asked to provide a lower note, your task is to find the scale in which the given note is the specified scale degree. Let's say we want to find a M3 below D:

↓ M3

This asks us to provide a lower note that is tonic of a major scale in which D is $\hat{3}$. The question, essentially, is: "If D is $\hat{3}$ in a major scale, what is $\hat{1}$?" To find the answer, you can count down three on the staff (back three in the musical alphabet) to situate the note on the correct line or space, then determine whether an accidental is required. We know that distance 3 down from D is B, but we also need to know whether this B requires an accidental. It does: D is not $\hat{3}$ in B major (D♯ is) but D is $\hat{3}$ in B♭ major, so we need to flatten the B:

M3

Or using half-step counting:

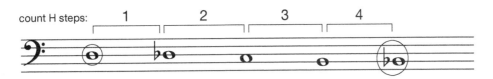

As always, if you use this method, just be sure that the spelling of the lower note is correct—B♭, not A♯.

C. Add a note <u>below</u> the given note to form the specified interval.

1. P4   2. M3   3. M7   4. M2   5. P5   6. M6   7. P4   8. M3

9. M6   10. P5   11. M7   12. P4   13. M3   14. P5   15. P5   16. P5

17. P4   18. P5   19. P4   20. M6   21. M2   22. P5   23. M6   24. P5

25. P4   26. M3   27. M3   28. P4   29. M3   30. P5   31. M6   32. P8

33. M2   34. M3   35. P4   36. P5   37. M6   38. M7   39. P8   40. M7

To find the size in half steps between two notes, write all the notes between them in the chromatic scale:

This shows that the interval D–A spans seven half steps. On the chart of half-step sizes for major and perfect intervals . . .

quality/distance:	P1	M2	M3	P4	P5	M6	M7	P8
half steps:	0	2	4	5	7	9	11	12

. . . size 7 is the perfect fifth. The interval D–A is a P5.
   To check whether this is correct, you can construct the D major scale and confirm that A is step 5.

D. Notate a series of half steps that connects the two given notes. Indicate the quality, distance, and size in half steps of the interval formed by the two given notes.

1.

      quality/distance: _____ half steps: _____

2.

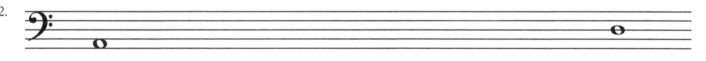

      quality/distance: _____ half steps: _____

3.

      quality/distance: _____ half steps: _____

4.

quality/distance: _____ half steps: _____

5.

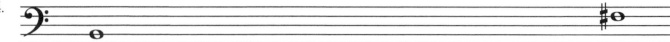

quality/distance: _____ half steps: _____

6.

quality/distance: _____ half steps: _____

7.

quality/distance: _____ half steps: _____

8.

quality/distance: _____ half steps: _____

✍ create!

Compose melodies with gradually changing interval sizes. Use the Bach melody at the beginning of this lesson, and the melodies listed in the *Suggestions for Listening*, and the melody in Minuet in the Fifteen Character Pieces (www.oup.com/us/lambert) as models. Compose only in major keys.

LESSON 16
INTERVALS II

16.1 MINOR INTERVALS

Here again are the intervals formed with the tonic of the C major scale:

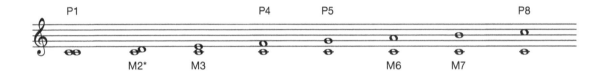

Compare these to the intervals formed with the tonic of the C minor scale:

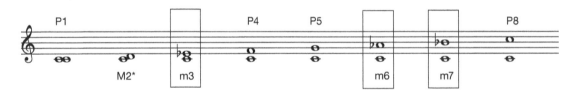

Because parallel major and minor scales differ at three places, $\hat{3}$, $\hat{6}$, and $\hat{7}$, the quality of the intervals formed at those three spots are different. Between $\hat{1}$ and $\hat{3}$ the interval is a *major* third in a major key, but in a minor key it's a *minor* third, abbreviated "m3." Similarly, the interval between $\hat{1}$ and $\hat{6}$ is a *major* sixth in a major key, but a *minor* sixth (m6) in a minor key. The interval between $\hat{1}$ and $\hat{7}$ is a *major* seventh in a major key, but a *minor* seventh (m7) in a minor key.

All the perfect intervals, 1, 4, 5, and 8, involve scale degrees that don't differ in parallel major and minor. They have the same labels in both. We can just apply what we already know about these intervals from Lesson 15.

Seconds are a special case. Scale degrees $\hat{1}$ and $\hat{2}$ are the same in major and parallel minor. In either mode, the interval from $\hat{1}$ to $\hat{2}$ is a whole step, or "major second." Even if you're thinking of forming an interval between $\hat{1}$ and $\hat{2}$ in a minor scale, you would still describe its quality as "major" (see * above). This is the only instance where an interval formed from the tonic of a minor scale is given the designation "major."

And yet the "minor second" (m2) does exist. It's not the interval formed between $\hat{1}$ and $\hat{2}$ in the minor scale but another name for the diatonic half step (Lesson 3.1), just as the major second is another name for whole step. The labels may be used interchangeably. We could, for example, describe the step patterns in major and minor scales using interval names rather than whole- and half-step labels:

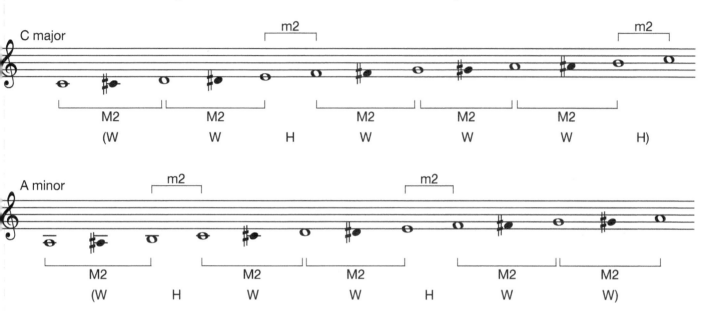

With the addition of minor intervals to our repertory, we have three new sizes of half-step spans to keep track of. The m3 is 3, the m6 is 8, and the m7 is 10:

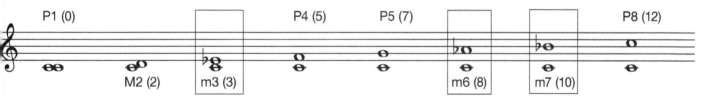

The m2 is, of course, 1. Among all perfect, major, and minor intervals, we've now seen every possible half-step size within the octave except for 6:

quality/distance:	P1	m2	M2	m3	M3	P4	?	P5	m6	M6	m7	M7	P8
size in half steps:	0	1	2	3	4	5	(6)	7	8	9	10	11	12

16.2   METHODOLOGY I

Just as you can construct a minor scale by converting its parallel major, you might also find it easier to construct minor intervals by converting major ones. To construct a minor third above C, you could first spell a major third, C–E, and then lower the E to E♭. You could also form a minor sixth above C by converting C–A to C–A♭, and a minor seventh above C by converting C–B to C–B♭. Of course, any time you make these sorts of conversions, you must be sure not to move the note to a different line or space; if you do, you change its distance.

Sometimes it's easier to calculate sevenths by reducing an octave. The major seventh is just a half step smaller than an octave. The minor seventh is a whole step smaller than an octave. So to form a major seventh above D, for example, you could first think of an octave from D to D, then lower the upper note to C♯ (of course, not spelled as D♭!). To form a minor seventh, lower it to C♮.

16.3   INTERVAL INVERSION

We also have other useful ways to think of intervals in relation to octaves. Suppose, for example, we take a perfect fifth above C, C–G, and then move the C up an octave to create a new interval, G–C:

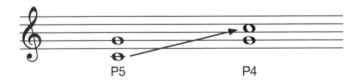

This is called interval **inversion**. It's a way of dividing up the octave into two segments, each an inversion of the other:

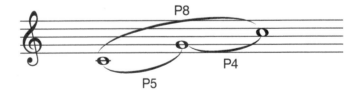

The perfect fifth inverts to the perfect fourth. The reverse is also true; the perfect fourth inverts to the perfect fifth:

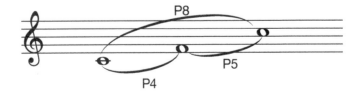

Every interval has its unique inversional partner. The major third inverts to the minor sixth:

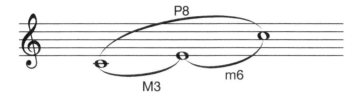

And the minor third inverts to the major sixth:

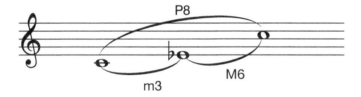

Sevenths and seconds are also inversional partners:

All interval inversions follow these same principles. After inverting, perfect intervals remain perfect. Major intervals become minor, and minor intervals become major. The distances add up to nine. The half-step sizes add up to twelve.

P1	(0)	← →	P8	(12)
m2	(1)	← →	M7	(11)
M2	(2)	← →	m7	(10)
m3	(3)	← →	M6	(9)
M3	(4)	← →	m6	(8)
P4	(5)	← →	P5	(7)

16.4   METHODOLOGY II

Knowing about inversions may be helpful when calculating intervals. Let's say, for example, that you wish to write a minor sixth above F♯. The principle of inversion says that whatever note lies a minor sixth above F♯ also lies a major third below:

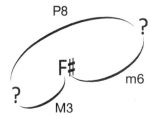

You might find it easier to calculate the major third below F♯ and then transfer that note up an octave to form a minor sixth above:

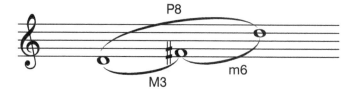

 For suggestions for further listening and online exercises and drills, go to www.oup.com/us/lambert

▶ STUDY QUESTIONS FOR LESSON 16

1. Define these terms:
   inversion (of an interval)
   minor intervals

2. In a comparison of the intervals starting on tonic of two parallel (major and minor) scales, which intervals have the same labels, and which ones are different?

3. In interval labels, which distances can be major or minor, and which cannot be either?

4. In all the intervals formed from tonic of a minor scale, what is the only instance of a quality other than perfect or minor? What is another name for this interval?

5. What are the possible half-step sizes for all intervals formed from tonic of a minor scale?

6. Give the procedure for making these interval conversions:
   M3 → m3
   M7 → m7
   m6 → M6

7. What is the difference between an octave and a major seventh? Between an octave and a minor seventh?

8. What happens to the quality, distance, and half-step size after an interval is inverted?

▶ **EXERCISES FOR LESSON 16**

To construct all the intervals from tonic of a minor scale, make note pairs of tonic with every other note in the natural form of that scale:

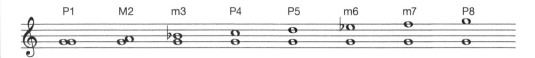

Make sure to apply any accidentals necessary to ensure that the upper notes are scale degrees in the natural minor scale starting on the lower note. The B and E are flatted in the m3 and m6 above because those notes are flatted in the G natural minor scale.

A. Notate all the intervals within the minor scales (natural form) starting on the given notes. Use accidentals as needed, not key signatures.

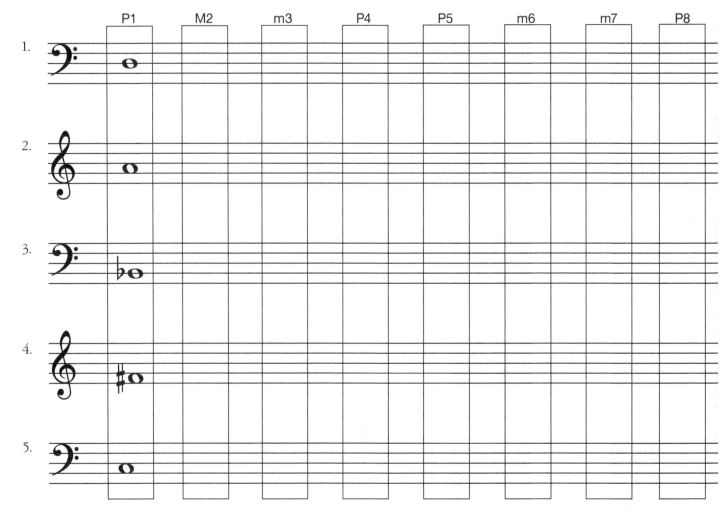

To form a certain interval above a given note, think of the given note as the tonic of a scale and use your knowledge of scales to determine the upper note.

- If the quality of the interval is perfect, you can think of the given note as tonic of either major or minor.
- If the interval's distance is 3, 6, or 7, use minor scales (natural form) to construct minor intervals and major scales to construct major intervals.
- If the distance is 2, just remember that M2 = whole step and m2 = diatonic half step (Lesson 3).

You can also calculate intervals using size in half steps (Lessons 15.4, 16.1). If you use this method, double-check to make sure your spelling is correct. Here again are the half-step sizes for the intervals we've learned:

P1	m2	M2	m3	M3	P4	P5	m6	M6	m7	M7	P8
0	1	2	3	4	5	7	8	9	10	11	12

B. Add a note <u>above</u> the given note to form the specified interval.

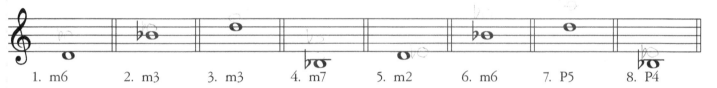

1. m6 2. m3 3. m3 4. m7 5. m2 6. m6 7. P5 8. P4

9. m3 10. m6 11. m7 12. m7 13. M2 14. m3 15. m6 16. P8

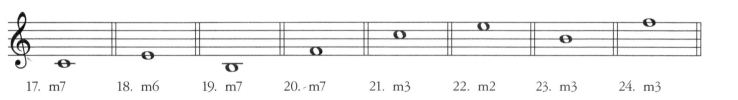

17. m7 18. m6 19. m7 20. m7 21. m3 22. m2 23. m3 24. m3

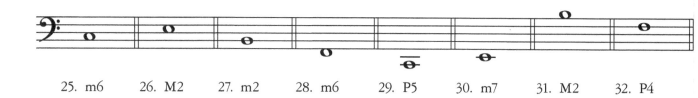

25. m6   26. M2   27. m2   28. m6   29. P5   30. m7   31. M2   32. P4

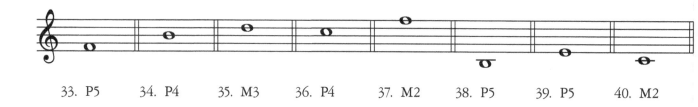

33. P5   34. P4   35. M3   36. P4   37. M2   38. P5   39. P5   40. M2

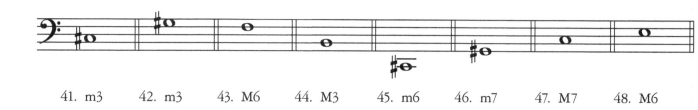

41. m3   42. m3   43. M6   44. M3   45. m6   46. m7   47. M7   48. M6

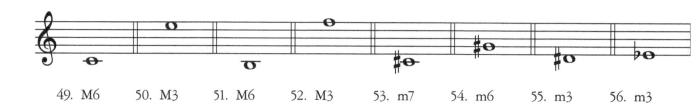

49. M6   50. M3   51. M6   52. M3   53. m7   54. m6   55. m3   56. m3

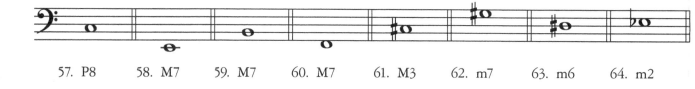

57. P8   58. M7   59. M7   60. M7   61. M3   62. m7   63. m6   64. m2

An inversion diagram (Lessons 16.3, 16.4) displays two inversionally equivalent intervals within an octave:

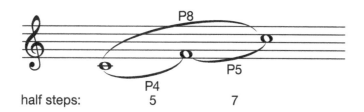

In inversional pairs, either both intervals are perfect quality or one is major and the other minor. The distances add up to nine, and the half-step sizes add up to twelve.

C. Add a note or notes and interval labels (quality/distance) to make each inversion diagram complete. In the space beneath each diagram, indicate the number of half steps spanned by the two inversionally related intervals.

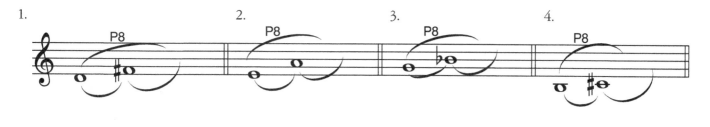

half steps: _____ _____   _____ _____   _____ _____   _____ _____

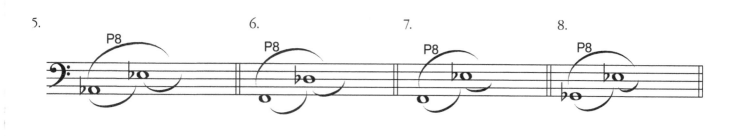

half steps: _____ _____   _____ _____   _____ _____   _____ _____

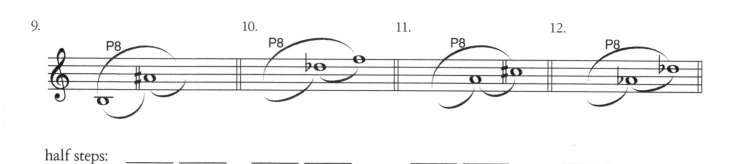

half steps: _____ _____   _____ _____   _____ _____   _____ _____

13. 14. 15. 16.

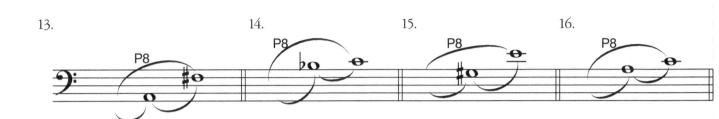

half steps: _____ _____   _____ _____   _____   _____ _____

17. 18. 19. 20.

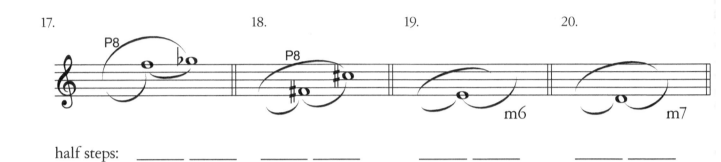

half steps: _____ _____   _____ _____   _____   _____ _____

21. 22. 23. 24.

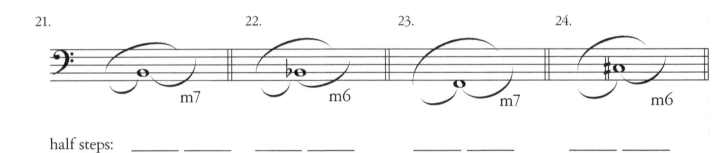

half steps: _____ _____   _____ _____   _____   _____ _____

25. 26. 27. 28.

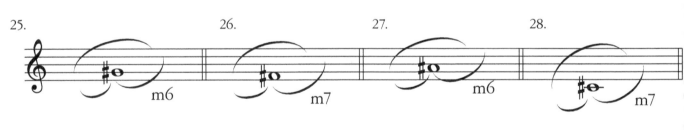

half steps: _____ _____   _____ _____   _____   _____ _____

❧ create!

Adapt the melodies you wrote at the end of Lesson 15 into parallel minor keys. The adaptation process will involve important decisions about scale degrees $\hat{6}$ and $\hat{7}$ and the forms of minor.

LESSON **17**

INTERVALS III

17.1 INTERVALS OUTSIDE OF THE KEY

In Lessons 15 and 16 we studied the vast majority of intervals that we can expect to find in music of all sorts. As we noticed in Lesson 16.2, however, there is still one half-step size we haven't yet encountered. And musical literature includes several unusual interval spellings that we haven't studied so far.

Play or sing this melody by Johannes Brahms:

Allegro giocoso Piano Trio op. 87, IV

17-1

It's in the key of C major, but it features a note, F♯, that's not part of the C major scale. Brahms draws attention to the interval between F♯ and the tonic C, first in measure 1 with an intervening E, then again in measure 2 with no other note between them.

Because the upper note of this interval is not part of the major or minor scale of the lower note, it doesn't fit any of our previous definitions. Without the sharp it would just be C–F, P4. The sharp enlarges the P4 by one half step, stretching the size from five half steps (P4) to six—this is the one half-step size not spanned by any of the perfect, major, or minor intervals we already know. When an interval is enlarged in this way, its quality becomes **augmented**. The interval from C to F♯ is an augmented fourth (A4).

Compare that example with this melody by Beethoven:

Largo assai ed espressivo Piano Trio op. 70, no. 1, II

17-2

Now we're in the key of D minor, but in measures 3 and 4 the melody jumps from the tonic D up to a note, A♭, that's not part of the D minor scale. If the A weren't flatted, the resulting interval would simply be D–A, P5. The flat reduces the P5 by one half step, shrinking the size from seven half steps (P5) to six. When a P5 is reduced in this way, its quality becomes **diminished**. The interval from D to A♭ is a diminished fifth (d5).

Notice that both the A4 in the first example and the d5 in the second example span six half steps. They're two different spellings of the same half-step size; they're enharmonically equivalent. Any A4 is simply a different spelling of a d5, and vice versa:

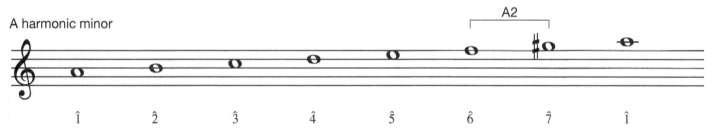

Now let's look at a different half-step size, in a melody by Mozart:

17-3

Again, without the sharp before the F we would have a routine interval, this time a M2 (whole step), E♭–F, between the second and third notes. The sharped F stretches the M2 by one half step, changing the quality from major to augmented. It's the same quality of second we find between $\hat{6}$ and $\hat{7}$ in the harmonic minor scale:

Unlike the Brahms and Beethoven examples, however, the number of half steps spanned by the A2 *isn't* unique—it's 3, the same as the m3. Again we have an enharmonic equivalence, this time between A2 and m3. And yet Mozart doesn't spell the interval as a m3 (E♭–G♭ or D♯–F♯). Nor do we spell the sixth and seventh degrees of a harmonic minor scale as a m3: they're always spelled as an A2, notated on adjacent lines and spaces. Our labels must also make distinctions between different spellings of equivalent sizes.

17.2   AUGMENTED AND DIMINISHED 1, 4, 5, AND 8

To account for any note pair we might find, let's first focus on the distances that can be "perfect" quality: 1, 4, 5, and 8. Any perfect interval enlarged by a half step, without changing its distance, becomes augmented. This can be accomplished by raising the top note, as in the Brahms melody, or by lowering the bottom note:

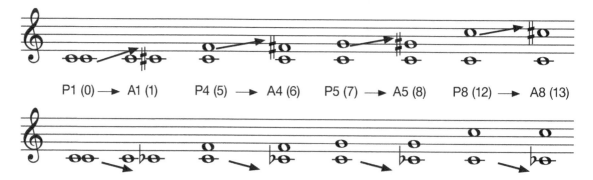

We know the A1 as the chromatic half step (Lesson 3).

When perfect fourths, fifths, and octaves are reduced by a half step, by lowering the top note or raising the bottom note without changing the distance, they become diminished. The same is *not* true of the unison (distance 1): unisons can't be diminished. It's not possible to form an interval that spans fewer than zero half steps.

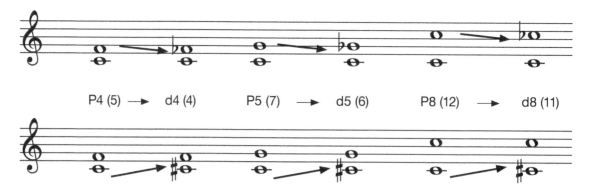

The most important of the augmented and diminished intervals is the A4 and its enharmonic equivalent d5. This interval has the only half-step size (6) that can't also be formed by an interval with perfect, major, or minor quality. It even has its own special name: because an A4 consists of three whole steps (e.g., F–G, G–A, A–B within the augmented fourth F–B), it has been called the **tritone**. In current usage the term can refer to either the A4 or d5.

17.3 AUGMENTED AND DIMINISHED 2, 3, 6, AND 7

For the distances with qualities of major and minor—2, 3, 6, and 7—the possibilities are a little more involved. Enlarging a major interval by a half step without changing the distance, as we saw in Mozart's melody, has the same result as for distances 1, 4, 5, and 8: It becomes augmented. As before, you can conceive this enlargement as an action on the upper or lower note:

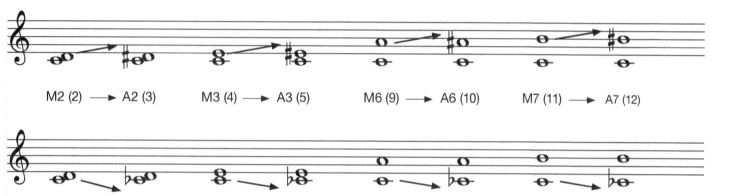

M2 (2) ⟶ A2 (3)   M3 (4) ⟶ A3 (5)   M6 (9) ⟶ A6 (10)   M7 (11) ⟶ A7 (12)

But as we know from Lesson 16, a half-step reduction of a major interval doesn't make it diminished. Reduction of a major-quality interval (as always, without changing its distance) converts its quality to minor:

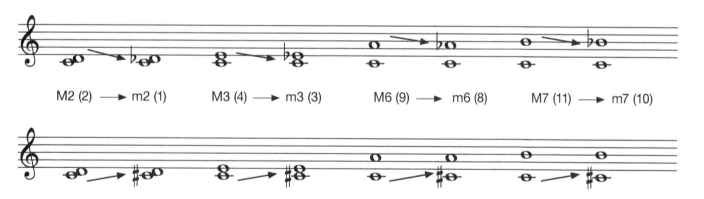

M2 (2) ⟶ m2 (1)   M3 (4) ⟶ m3 (3)   M6 (9) ⟶ m6 (8)   M7 (11) ⟶ m7 (10)

Further reducing a minor interval, without changing its distance, makes it diminished:

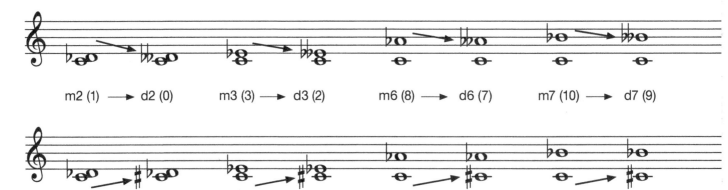

m2 (1) ⟶ d2 (0)   m3 (3) ⟶ d3 (2)   m6 (8) ⟶ d6 (7)   m7 (10) ⟶ d7 (9)

Just as raising a sharped note (without changing the interval's distance) requires a double sharp, lowering a flattened note requires a **double flat**.

17.4   SUMMARIES OF INTERVAL TYPES

As you can see in the above listings, the possibilities for overlappings and enharmonics are considerable, and can also be impractical. When, you might ask, would a notator need to use the d2 rather than the enharmonically equivalent unison? What context could possibly require the d3, which is another spelling for a whole step, or the A7, which is nothing more than a respelled octave?

Although such spellings are rare, we do need to be aware of their existence. We know not to expect to find such oddities in actual scores, but at least we'll recognize them if and when we do. And if we do come across an unusual spelling, the process of figuring out the reasoning behind the composer's notational decisions may lead us to interesting and valuable revelations about the music itself.

Here's a complete inventory of the enharmonic equivalences (lined up in the same column) and the like-named distances (all in the same row):

half steps:	0	1	2	3	4	5	6	7	8	9	10	11	12
octaves:												[d8]	P8
7ths:										d7	m7	M7	[A7]
6ths:							[d6]	m6	M6	A6			
5ths:							d5	P5	[A5]				
4ths:					[d4]	P4	A4						
3rds:			[d3]	m3	M3	[A3]							
2nds:	[d2]	m2	M2	A2									
unison:	P1	[A1]											

The bold boxes highlight intervals formed from the tonic in a major or minor scale. Labels in brackets show interval spellings that are theoretical possibilities but very uncommon.

And here's a summary of the labeling system, using the perfect and major intervals as points of reference:

	−2	−1	0	+1
1, 4, 5, 8		d	P	A
2, 3, 6, 7	d	m	M	A

As we learned earlier in this lesson, half-step enlargement of any perfect or major interval (without moving notes from their lines or spaces) changes its quality to augmented. Reduction by half step yields either diminished (1, 4, 5, 8) or minor (2, 3, 6, 7); further reduction of minor also yields diminished.

The possibility also exists for interval qualities that are **doubly augmented** and **doubly diminished**. A doubly augmented fifth, for example, is a further enlargement of a fifth that's already augmented:

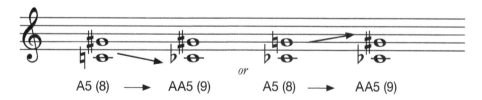

A5 (8) ⟶ AA5 (9)   A5 (8) ⟶ AA5 (9)

Likewise, a doubly diminished fifth is a further reduction of a fifth that's already diminished:

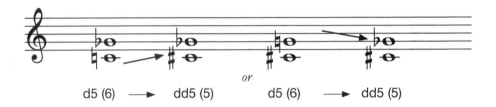

These intervals are extremely rare in musical literature. If you find one, you may feel that you should receive some sort of reward.

17.5   METHODOLOGY

Perfect fourths and perfect fifths are often easy to spell or recognize because in most cases, both notes have the same accidentals. Look, for example, at all fourths and fifths involving only white keys:

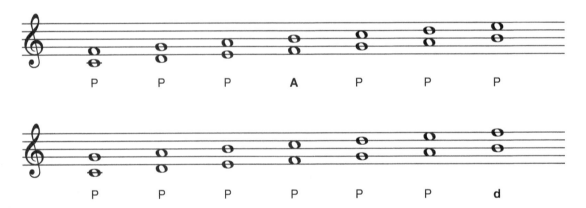

All the white-key fourths are perfect quality except the augmented fourth F–B. All the white-key fifths are perfect quality except the diminished fifth B–F. And each of these qualities will be unchanged if you apply the same accidental to both notes. Because you know that F–C is a P5, for example, you also know that F♯–C♯ and F♭–C♭ are P5s. Because you know that F–B is an A4, you also know that F♯–B♯ and F♭–B♭ are also A4s. And so forth.

Remember also that the two notes in a fourth are always situated on a line and a space, while the two notes in a fifth are either both on lines or both on spaces (Lesson 15.2).

Your knowledge of half-step sizes can help for spelling or identifying unusual intervals. Let's say, for example, that you're charged with the task of spelling a major third above F♭. We have no F♭ major (or minor) scale to use as a point of reference. But you know that a major third spans four half steps, so you can start by counting up four half steps from F♭. You arrive on the G♯/A♭ key, and then use the principle of interval distance to determine which spelling is correct: A♭, not G♯, because the letter A is distance 3 from your starting letter, F. The major third higher than F♭ is A♭.

17.6   AUGMENTED AND DIMINISHED INTERVALS UNDER INVERSION

When inverted, augmented intervals become diminished, and diminished intervals become augmented:

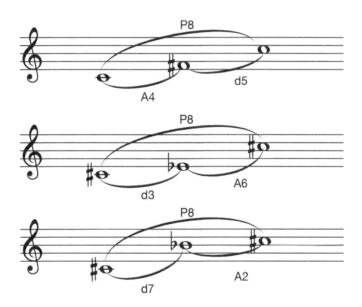

To survey all the possibilities for interval inversions, return to the chart earlier in this lesson summarizing interval types (Lesson 17.4). Inversional partners are shown in any two columns with half-step sizes that add to twelve. Intervals in the 5 column invert to intervals in the 7 column. Intervals in the 9 column invert to intervals in the 3 column. And so forth. Intervals in the 6 column (A4, d5) invert to each other.

Here's a summary of everything we've learned about what happens to an interval's quality, distance, and half-step size after inversion:

quality:

perfect	←→	perfect
major	←→	minor
augmented	←→	diminished

distance:

1	←→	8
2	←→	7
3	←→	6
4	←→	5

half steps:

0	←→	12
1	←→	11
2	←→	10
3	←→	9
4	←→	8
5	←→	7
6	←→	6

Sometimes you may find it helpful to use your knowledge of inversions to calculate particularly problematic intervals. Let's say you wanted to label a difficult interval like E♯–C. Place E♯–C at the top of an inversion diagram and calculate the lower interval first:

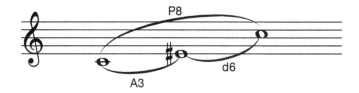

Because you know that the label for C–E♯ is A3, you know that the label for E♯–C is the A3 after inversion, d6.

STUDY QUESTIONS FOR LESSON 17

1. Define these terms:
   augmented interval
   diminished interval
   double flat
   doubly augmented interval
   doubly diminished interval
   tritone

2. Which interval qualities usually indicate the involvement of a tone from outside the major or minor scale?

3. What do you do to a perfect interval to make it augmented?

4. How are diminished intervals created?

5. Give the procedure for making these interval conversions:
   P5 → A5
   P4 → d4
   m3 → d3
   M6 → A6

6. Give three ways to describe an interval of half-step size 6.

7. Give an enharmonically equivalent label for these intervals:
   d5
   A5
   m3
   A6
   m2

8. Rearrange the intervals in each of these lists so that the half-step sizes get gradually larger, left to right:
   1) A5 d5 P5
   2) M3 m3 A3 d3
   3) A7 m7 M7 d7
   4) M2 P4 A2 M3
   5) A3 A4 d4 P5
   6) d8 d6 d7 A5 A6 A7

9. Which of the white-key fourths or fifths *isn't* perfect quality?

10. What happens to the quality of diminished and augmented intervals after inversion?

► EXERCISES FOR LESSON 17

To add appropriate accidentals to the top notes of these intervals . . .

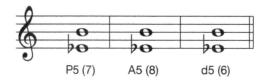

. . . start with the correct spelling of the initial P5. To do this, you need to add a flat to the B in the first measure (Lesson 15):

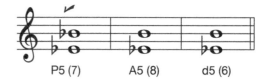

To make the second measure correct, convert P5 to A5 by raising B♭ to B♮:

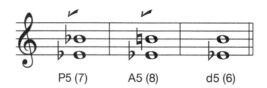

To make the third measure correct, convert P5 to d5 by lowering B♭ to B♭♭:

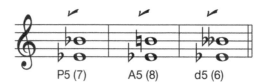

In each instance, the bottom note remains unchanged.

A. Notate an accidental (♯ or 𝄪 or ♭ or 𝄫 or ♮) for the <u>top</u> note of each interval to make the label correct. Don't add accidentals to the bottom notes.

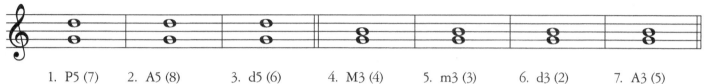

1. P5 (7)　　2. A5 (8)　　3. d5 (6)　　4. M3 (4)　　5. m3 (3)　　6. d3 (2)　　7. A3 (5)

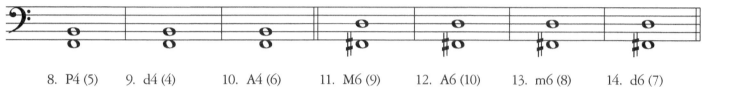

8. P4 (5)　　9. d4 (4)　　10. A4 (6)　　11. M6 (9)　　12. A6 (10)　　13. m6 (8)　　14. d6 (7)

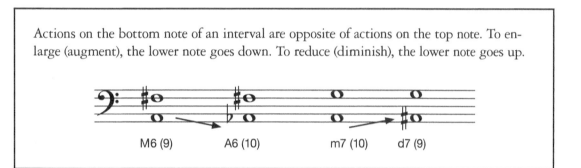

Actions on the bottom note of an interval are opposite of actions on the top note. To enlarge (augment), the lower note goes down. To reduce (diminish), the lower note goes up.

M6 (9)　　A6 (10)　　m7 (10)　　d7 (9)

B. Notate an accidental (♯ or 𝄪 or ♭ or 𝄫 or ♮) for the <u>bottom</u> note of each interval to make the label correct. Don't add accidentals to the top notes.

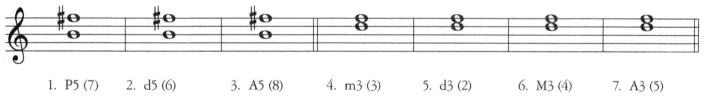

1. P5 (7)　　2. d5 (6)　　3. A5 (8)　　4. m3 (3)　　5. d3 (2)　　6. M3 (4)　　7. A3 (5)

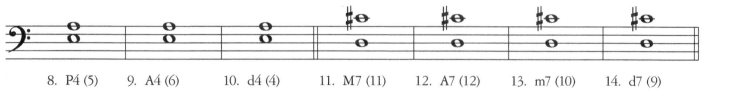

8. P4 (5)　　9. A4 (6)　　10. d4 (4)　　11. M7 (11)　　12. A7 (12)　　13. m7 (10)　　14. d7 (9)

The inversion diagram (Lessons 16.3, 17.6) brings together two inversional partners. The labels of the partners are related in predictable ways:

quality: Both are perfect; or
one is major and the other is minor; or
one is augmented and the other is diminished.

distance: The numbers add to nine.

half steps: The numbers add to twelve.

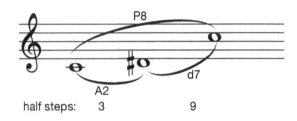

C. Add a note or notes and interval labels (quality/distance) to make each inversion diagram complete. In the space beneath each diagram, indicate the half-step size of the two inversionally related intervals. Don't change the accidental of any given note.

half steps: _____ _____   _____ _____   _____ _____   _____ _____

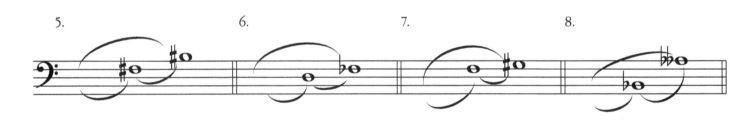

half steps: _____ _____   _____ _____   _____ _____   _____ _____

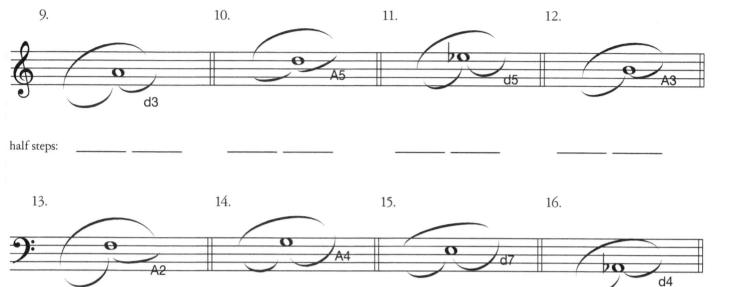

half steps: _____ _____   _____ _____   _____ _____   _____ _____

half steps: _____ _____   _____ _____   _____ _____   _____ _____

We've learned several methods for spelling intervals above a given note. If the given note is tonic of a familiar major or minor scale, it's probably easiest to use that scale as a point of reference (Lessons 15, 16). If the given note isn't tonic of a familiar major or minor scale, or if other complications arise because of the particular interval you're spelling, it might be easiest to use an inversion diagram (Lessons 16.4, 17.6) or calculate based on half-step size (Lesson 17.5). No matter which method you use, check your work with a different method.

D. Add a note <u>above</u> the given note to form the specified interval. Don't change the accidental on the given note.

1. A3   2. A4   3. d5   4. A6   5. d7   6. d3   7. A8   8. A2

9. d7   10. d5   11. A6   12. A5   13. M3   14. m7   15. m3   16. A5

17. A3   18. m2   19. P5   20. d5   21. P4   22. d3   23. d7   24. A3

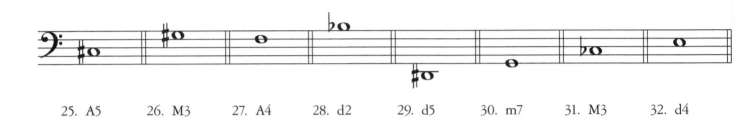

25. A5   26. M3   27. A4   28. d2   29. d5   30. m7   31. M3   32. d4

E. Add a note <u>below</u> the given note to form the specified interval. Don't change the accidental on the given note.

1. d5   2. A4   3. d5   4. P4   5. A2   6. d7   7. d4   8. A2

9. A4   10. m6   11. A5   12. d3   13. A7   14. d6   15. M3   16. d7

∽ create!

Use the given measures as the starting points for melodies, reusing musical ideas in interesting ways. For example, you might preserve the rhythm that's given but move the melody to different scale degrees. Or you might find other ways to present and develop the distinctive augmented or diminished intervals, using different pitches and rhythms.

1.

2.

3.

LESSON 18

INTERVALS IV

18.1   INTERVALS IN MUSICAL PRACTICE

Intervals are building blocks of melodies. Many melodies, like "America," are primarily built from major and minor seconds. Others are similarly saturated with other distances, or employ a variety of intervals.

Play or sing this melody by Robert Schumann:

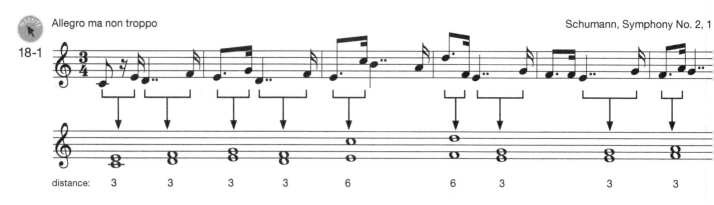

Allegro ma non troppo   Schumann, Symphony No. 2, 1

Thirds are especially prominent in Schumann's melody. The first two notes, C and E, for example, are a third apart, as are the next two notes, D and F. In two places the melody features inversions of thirds—the sixths at the beginnings of measures 3 and 4. To be specific, these two sixths are the literal inversions of the two thirds in measure 1: C–E and D–F in measure 1 recur inverted as E–C and F–D in measures 3 and 4. Overall, thirds or sixths occur nine times between consecutive notes just in these six measures.

Now play or sing this melody by Claude Debussy:

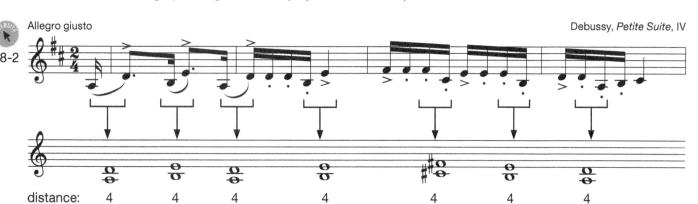

Debussy builds his melody around fourths—seven of them among consecutive notes in these four measures.

It's easy to recognize and identify the distance of intervals, to hear the presence of "thirds" and "fourths," without thinking about their qualities. You can do that just by counting within the musical alphabet, without even thinking about major or minor scales and key signatures.

But quality also matters. The qualities of the fourths in the Debussy melody are easy to determine. We know that fourths with the same accidental on both notes are perfect, except when the notes B and F are involved (Lesson 17.5). Because the notes in each of Debussy's fourths have the same accidentals, and none involves both a B and an F, we can see immediately that each one of them is perfect quality.

Identifying the qualities of the thirds in the Schumann melody may require a little more work. One method we've studied for making these identifications would involve thinking of the lower note of each interval as the tonic of a scale and then asking whether the upper note would be a scale degree in that scale: the first interval is C–E, $\hat{1}$–$\hat{3}$ in C major, so that's a M3; next is D–F, which is $\hat{1}$–$\hat{3}$ in D minor, so that's a m3; and so forth.

There's nothing inherently wrong with that approach, but you might find it faster and easier just to work with half-step sizes:

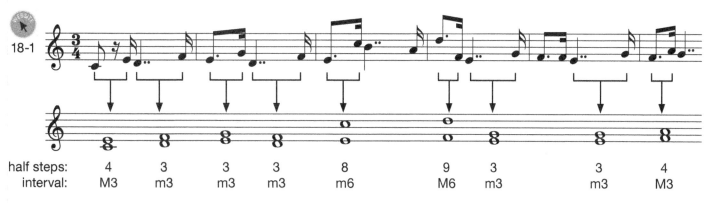

You can also use your knowledge of other aspects of intervals whenever possible. Once you have recognized, for example, that the sixth, E–C, at the beginning of the third measure is simply the inversion of the third, C–E, at the beginning of measure 1, then you can apply your knowledge of inversions to determine the quality of the sixth (M3→m6, Lesson 16.3). Likewise you can benefit from knowing the inversional relationship between the D–F (m3) in measure 1 and the F–D (M6) in measure 4.

18.2   SCALE DEGREE PAIRS

It might also help to know the full range of possibilities for combining scale degrees within a key. Let's look, for example, at all thirds we can form from the various degrees of the C major scale:

half steps:	4	3	3	4	4	3	3
interval:	M3	m3	m3	M3	M3	m3	m3
scale degrees:	$\hat{3}$ $\hat{1}$	$\hat{4}$ $\hat{2}$	$\hat{5}$ $\hat{3}$	$\hat{6}$ $\hat{4}$	$\hat{7}$ $\hat{5}$	$\hat{1}$ $\hat{6}$	$\hat{2}$ $\hat{7}$

These same scale degree combinations produce these same interval qualities in any major key. Combining $\hat{1}$ and $\hat{3}$, or $\hat{4}$ and $\hat{6}$, or $\hat{5}$ and $\hat{7}$, always results in a M3. A third formed by combining any other scale degrees is always minor quality. And if we simply invert all these intervals, we'll have the entire array of sixths formable within a major key, with the opposite arrangement of qualities (given that major and minor invert to each other):

half steps:	8	9	9	8	8	9	9
interval:	m6	M6	M6	m6	m6	M6	M6
scale degrees:	$\hat{1}$ $\hat{3}$	$\hat{2}$ $\hat{4}$	$\hat{3}$ $\hat{5}$	$\hat{4}$ $\hat{6}$	$\hat{5}$ $\hat{7}$	$\hat{6}$ $\hat{1}$	$\hat{7}$ $\hat{2}$

If we then survey all possible intervals within the same key, we'll have a complete intervallic profile of the tonal system. In fact, we've summarized all these possibilities already. We listed the fourths and fifths formable within C major in Lesson 17.5, when we were examining all the white-key intervals. Here they are again:

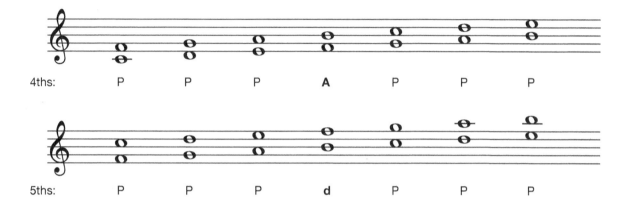

And we studied the seconds (and, by extension, their inversions, sevenths) in Lesson 8, when we first learned about the sizes of steps between consecutive notes in the major scale: WWHWWWH. Here's how it looks if we take consecutive scale degrees and notate them together as seconds, plus their inversions as sevenths:

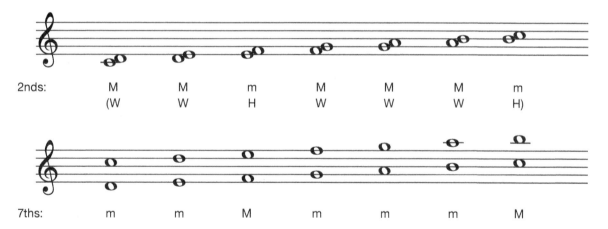

Let's bring all this information together. As we've just seen, there are three ways of forming M3s (or their inversions) between scale tones, and four ways of forming m3s. The display of white-key fourths and fifths shows six perfect and one augmented or diminished. And the scale itself is constructed of a certain ordering of five M2s (whole steps) and two m2s (diatonic half steps). Each interval type is represented a unique number of times:

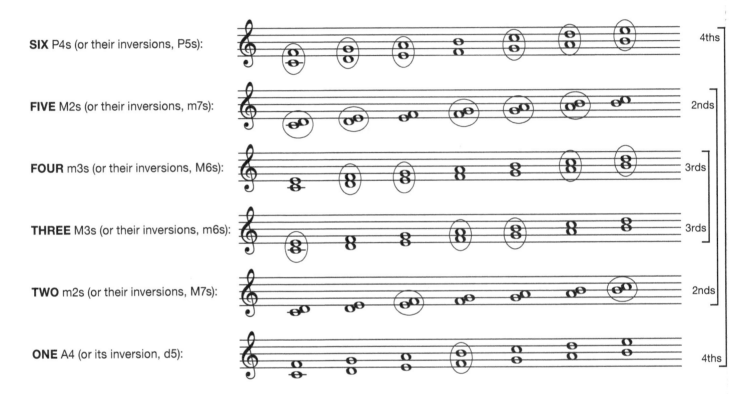

Each interval is special, each has a distinctive profile within the key. The interval that's most prevalent, the P4 (or its inversion, P5), is the foundation for harmonic progressions. The interval that's least prevalent, the A4 (d5)—the only interval on the entire list that's not perfect, major, or minor—has the ability to define a particular tonic: just one occurrence of this interval gives your ear a pretty good idea of what key you're in. The distances with the most even distribution, the thirds, are the building blocks of triads, an important topic of a future lesson.

18.3   COMPOUND INTERVALS

Now let's turn our attention to this melody by Modest Musorgsky:

Meno mosso, pesante   *Pictures at an Exhibition, I*

In each of this melody's first three measures we hear intervals spanning more than an octave. In the first measure it's an octave plus a fourth; in the second, the upper note is one half step higher than before, forming an octave plus a fifth; and in the third measure the melody leaps up two full octaves:

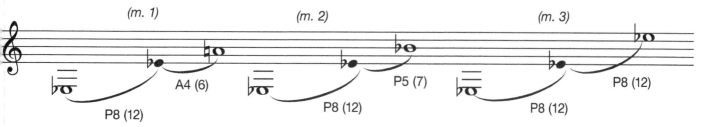

Intervals larger than an octave are known as **compound** intervals, by contrast with the intervals we've studied in previous lessons, called **simple**. The labels for compound intervals simply reflect the wider distance, without changing the quality. The octave-plus-A4 in Musorgsky's first measure is an augmented eleventh (A11). The octave-plus-P5 in the second measure is a P12. The big leap in measure 3 is the upper boundary for compound intervals and is simply known as the **double octave**.

A fourth expands to an eleventh. A fifth expands to a twelfth. The distance of any simple interval increases by seven when it becomes compound:

simple distance	(+ 7 =)	compound distance
2		9
3		10
4		11
5		12
6		13
7		14

It's possible to count the distance in a compound interval just as you do in a simple interval, by stepping through the musical alphabet, alternating lines and spaces from one note to another. But it's not necessary to do this. If you know the label for a simple interval, just add seven to its distance to get its compound equivalent. The quality stays the same. The half-step size increases by the number of half steps in an octave, twelve.

To *identify* a compound interval, first convert it to its simple version. Let's say, for example, that we want to identify this compound interval:

Start by converting it to a simple interval:

Label the simple version, then add seven to the distance to get the label for the compound version. The simple version is an augmented fourth; the compound version is an augmented eleventh.

To *construct* a compound interval, also start by working with its simple equivalent. Let's say we want to construct a minor tenth above B♭. The simple equivalent of a minor tenth is a minor third. So first notate a minor third above B♭, then convert it to compound:

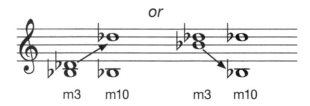

18.4   SUMMARY

We can now expand our earlier chart of interval sizes and enharmonic equivalences (Lesson 17.4) to include compound intervals:

COMPOUND

half steps:	12	13	14	15	16	17	18	19	20	21	22	23	24
double 8ve:												[d15]	P15
14ths:										d14	m14	M14	[A14]
13ths:								[d13]	m13	M13	A13		
12ths:							d12	P12	[A12]				
11ths:					[d11]	P11	A11						
10ths:			[d10]	m10	M10	[A10]							
9ths:	[d9]	m9	M9	A9									
unison:	P8	[A8]											

SIMPLE

half steps:	0	1	2	3	4	5	6	7	8	9	10	11	12
octaves:												[d8]	P8
7ths:										d7	m7	M7	[A7]
6ths:								[d6]	m6	M6	A6		
5ths:							d5	P5	[A5]				
4ths:					[d4]	P4	A4						
3rds:			[d3]	m3	M3	[A3]							
2nds:	[d2]	m2	M2	A2									
unison:	P1	[A1]											

As before, bold boxes highlight intervals formed by the tonic and one other note in a major or minor scale. Labels in brackets show interval spellings that are theoretical possibilities but very uncommon.

Now with the inclusion of compound intervals in vertical alignment with their simple equivalents, we can easily see their relationships: a difference of seven between vertically aligned distances (e.g., thirds and tenths), and a difference of twelve between vertically aligned half-step sizes (e.g., A4/d5 = 6, A11/d12 = 18).

 For suggestions for further listening and online exercises and drills, go to www.oup.com/us/lambert

▶ **STUDY QUESTIONS FOR LESSON 18**

1. Define these terms:
    compound interval
    double octave
    simple interval

2. In an accumulation of all possible pairs of scale degrees from a major scale,
    give the number of occurrences of these intervals:
    P4
    M2
    M3
    m6
    P5
    M7

3. In an accumulation of all possible pairs of scale degrees from a major scale,
    which intervals occur only once?

4. In an accumulation of all possible thirds within a major scale, how many are
    major quality, and how many are minor quality?

5. In an accumulation of all possible sevenths within a major scale, how many are
    major quality, and how many are minor quality?

6. How do you convert a simple interval into a compound interval? After you do
    that, what happens to the quality, distance, and half-step size?

7. How do you convert a compound interval into a simple interval? After you do
    that, what happens to the quality, distance, and half-step size?

EXERCISES FOR LESSON 18

When extracting intervals from a melody, remember to include accidentals from the key signature in your renotations.

A. Renotate each bracketed interval on the blank staff. Use individual accidentals for notes that are sharped or flatted by the key signature. Underneath your renotated intervals, indicate their half-step sizes and interval labels (quality/distance). The first one is done for you.

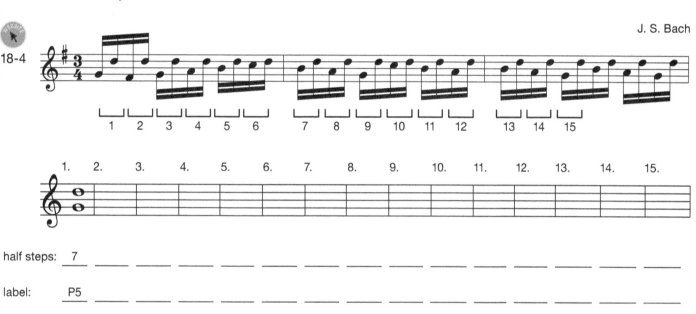

J. S. Bach

18-4

half steps: 7   _____

label: P5   _____

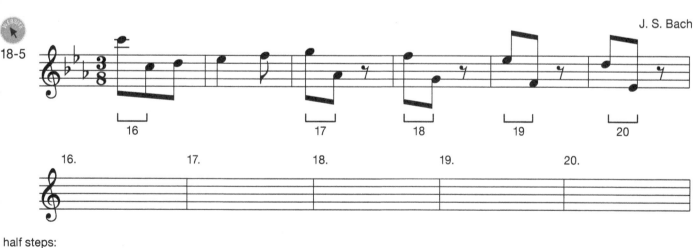

J. S. Bach

18-5

half steps: _____   _____   _____   _____   _____

label: _____   _____   _____   _____   _____

Forming intervals using only notes from a certain scale yields the same distribution of types for any key (Lesson 18.2). No matter what scale you use, you can form **six** P4s (or their inversions, P5s), **five** M2s (m7s), **four** m3s (M6s), **three** M3s (m6s), **two** m2s (M7s), and **one** A4 (d5). Here, for example, are all the thirds formable using only notes from the F major scale:

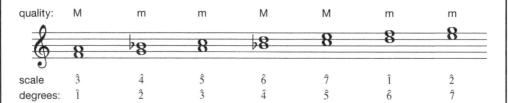

quality:	M	m	m	M	M	m	m
scale	$\hat{3}$	$\hat{4}$	$\hat{5}$	$\hat{6}$	$\hat{7}$	$\hat{1}$	$\hat{2}$
degrees:	$\hat{1}$	$\hat{2}$	$\hat{3}$	$\hat{4}$	$\hat{5}$	$\hat{6}$	$\hat{7}$

Forming thirds using notes of any other major scale will produce the same qualities from the same scale degrees: three major quality, from pairing $\hat{1}$ and $\hat{3}$, or $\hat{4}$ and $\hat{6}$, or $\hat{5}$ and $\hat{7}$; and four minor quality, from pairing $\hat{2}$ and $\hat{4}$, or $\hat{3}$ and $\hat{5}$, or $\hat{6}$ up to $\hat{1}$, or $\hat{7}$ up to $\hat{2}$. If these intervals are all inverted, the qualities and distributions switch (from three major and four minor thirds to three minor and four major sixths).

B. **Notate and annotate the scale tones as indicated. Supply accidentals as needed (don't use key signatures).**

1. Notate all the thirds that can be formed using only notes from the D major scale. Draw a circle around those that are **major** quality.

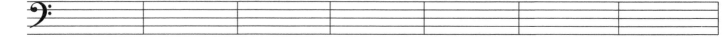

2. Notate all the sixths that can be formed using only notes from the B♭ major scale. Draw a circle around those that are **minor** quality.

3. Notate all the fourths that can be formed using only notes from the A major scale. Draw a circle around the fourth whose quality **isn't perfect**.

4. Notate all the sevenths that can be formed using only notes from the E♭ major scale. Draw a circle around those that are **major** quality.

To label a compound interval, first reduce it to its simple equivalent (Lesson 18.3):

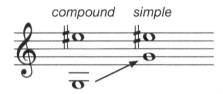

Determine the label for the simple version, then convert that label to compound by adding 7 to the distance (but don't change the quality). Here, the simple interval is **A6**, and its compound equivalent is **A13**.

C. Label the compound intervals (quality/distance).

1. _____ 2. _____ 3. _____ 4. _____ 5. _____ 6. _____ 7. _____ 8. _____

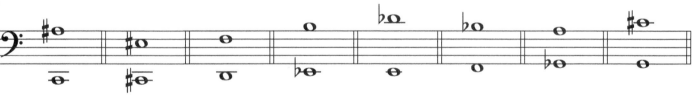

9. _____ 10. _____ 11. _____ 12. _____ 13. _____ 14. _____ 15. _____ 16. _____

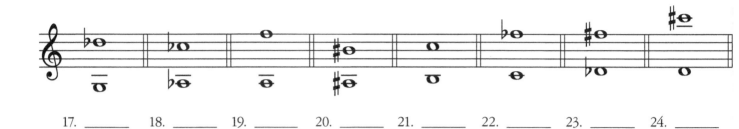

17. _____ 18. _____ 19. _____ 20. _____ 21. _____ 22. _____ 23. _____ 24. _____

To form a compound interval above a given note, first convert the label to its simple equivalent (Lesson 18.3). Notate the simple version and then convert that interval to compound.

For example, to determine the upper note of a d12 above middle C, first write the simple version of this interval, d5 above middle C. Then move the upper note in this interval an octave higher:

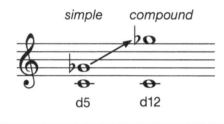

D. Write a note <u>above</u> the given note to form the specified compound interval. Starting with no. 26, write your note in the treble clef (as demonstrated for no. 25).

1. P12   2. m10   3. A11   4. M9   5. A12   6. m10   7. d12   8. m9

9. M10   10. P11   11. m13   12. A10   13. M13   14. A9   15. M14   16. d11

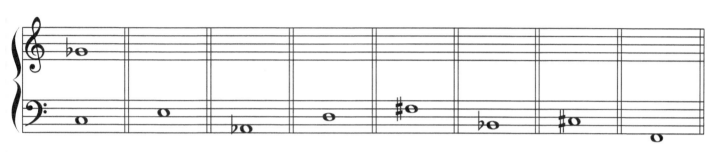

17. m10   18. d10   19. A12   20. M9   21. P11   22. m9   23. M10   24. A11

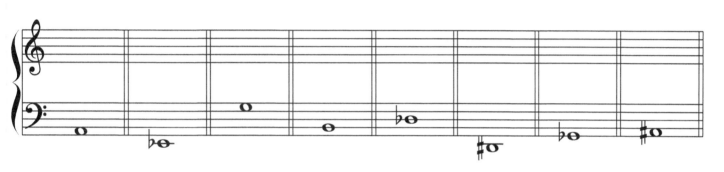

25. d12   26. m10   27. P11   28. M10   29. A12   30. M9   31. M10   32. m14

33. A10   34. P12   35. d14   36. d10   37. d12   38. M13   39. m14   40. P12

ᕫᕯᕤ create!

1. Explore these interval studies from Bartók's *Mikrokosmos*:

   "Melody in Tenths" (book 2, no. 56)

   "Minor Sixths in Parallel Motion" (book 2, no. 62)

   "Thirds" (book 3, no. 71)

   "Diminished Fifth" (book 4, no. 101)

   "And the Sounds Clash and Clang" (book 4, no. 110)

   "Alternating Thirds" (book 5, no. 129)

   "Fourths" (book 5, no. 131)

   "Major Seconds Broken and Together" (book 5, no. 132)

   "Major Seconds, Minor Sevenths" (book 6, no. 144)

2. Explore these interval studies from Fifteen Character Pieces (www.oup.com/us/lambert):

   Minuet

   Ballad

   Scherzo

3. Write a short piano piece (or a duet for some other instrumentation that you can play with a friend) modeled on one or more of these interval studies.

   • Think of ways to create a drama or interplay between intervals of different sizes.

   • Fit your intervallic relationships into an overall formal structure that has a clear beginning, middle, and ending.

   • Also think about the way intervals are presented—melodically or harmonically—and incorporate these ideas within your overall plan.

   • Check over your notation to make sure that your symbols are clear, noteheads are correctly placed, and measures contain the proper number of beats.

LESSON **19**
IRREGULARITIES OF RHYTHM AND METER

19.1   FREE RHYTHM

Regularity has been a basic component of all our previous study of rhythm and meter (Lessons 4, 6, 10, 14). We first asserted that music has a regular **beat** or **pulse**, and we derived **meter signatures** based on regular groupings of those beats.

Now let's consider some instances in which those basic principles don't apply. Imagine speaking the words of the first phrase of "America" as if reciting a poem. Without being restricted to a regular beat, you would most likely emphasize syllables differently than you do when you sing it. For example, when you speak the first phrase ("My country, 'tis of thee / Sweet land of liberty / Of thee I sing"), you probably wouldn't emphasize the word "'tis" as you do when you sing a dotted quarter note on that word on the downbeat of the second measure. You might give more emphasis to other words or syllables, like "thee" in "Of thee I sing," than you do when you sing the melody.

Now imagine creating a new melody for the text of "America," in which the durations of notes are determined entirely by the rhythms of the poetry, not by a grid of regularly spaced beats grouped into equal-size measures. The rhythms of this melody could be widely variable as they follow the stress patterns of the poetry. Any sense of rhythmic or metric regularity could be completely absent, or could disappear and reappear as the poetry dictates. This is called **free rhythm**.

Musical traditions include several examples of rhythm that's controlled by speech patterns. Many arias from operas, oratorios, and cantatas are preceded by **recitatives** in which the performers are free to let the rhythm of the words determine the flow of the music. Recitatives are usually notated with full, complete measures, but performed without a regular pulse, in rhythms determined by the text. Their rhythms are "free" and may differ from one performer to another, just as one actor's delivery of a line of dialogue might differ from another's.

Because American theater music grew out of operatic traditions, many classic American popular songs also begin with an introductory section that works like a recitative. This is called the **verse**; the main melody, known as the **chorus**, comes after.

When we think of classic American popular songs, we usually think of the chorus, not the verse. In fact, many performers omit the verse entirely. Did you know that Irving Berlin's "White Christmas" has a verse? Most of the recordings of this song, including the best-known version by Bing Crosby, don't include it. (Barbra Streisand's does.) Verses of popular songs are generally not as dependent on speech patterns as operatic recitatives are, but their rhythms may still be more freely expressed than the rhythms in the chorus.

The concept of free rhythm applies to any musical performance with beats that are not kept strictly regular. In many types and styles of music, performers take freedoms with beats for expressive purposes—to emphasize a certain word in a song, perhaps, or to dramatize a particular note or notes in an instrumental line. The beat becomes variable, elastic, subject to a performer's discretion. This is called **rubato**.

19.2   IRREGULAR METER

Another exception to our earlier lessons in rhythm and meter arises when the meter signature is not the same in every measure. This is called **irregular meter**. In irregular meter the *beats* are regularly spaced, but the *beat groupings* are variable. Think of it as the counterpart of some types of free rhythm, in which the beat groupings may be regular but the beats themselves irregularly spaced.

Here's an example, from a piano piece by Béla Bartók:

The meter changes help the performer to see patterns in the melody. By placing the A and G on downbeats in measure 3 and 4, for example, the performer is encouraged to place emphasis on these notes. Imagine that same melody notated with equivalent durations but without changing the meter:

In this notation those same notes, the A and G, don't fall on downbeats and aren't automatically and naturally emphasized. In this and in other ways, the regular notation of this melody strips it of its character, dismisses the features that make it interesting and distinctive.

Frequent meter changes didn't become commonplace in western classical music until the twentieth century. In earlier music we find short passages in a different meter, notated without changing the meter signature. Listen, for example, to this excerpt from a piano sonata by Mozart:

The triple meter is very strongly established in the first four measures, especially by the left hand's octaves on downbeats. Starting in measure 5, however, we begin to hear the left-hand octaves every two beats, defining a two-beat grouping through the end of measure 6. After that, starting in measure 7, the meter returns to triple.

The sound of measures 5 and 6, therefore, is not two measures of $\frac{3}{4}$ but three measures of $\frac{2}{4}$:

It's easily perceived as one large measure of triple meter with a half-note beat:

Mozart creates a conflict between the way we experience the meter and the way it looks on the page. This was a favorite technique of many composers of the Baroque, Classical, and Romantic eras. It even has a special name: **hemiola**.

 For suggestions for further listening, go to www.oup.com/us/lambert

▶ STUDY QUESTIONS FOR LESSON 19

1. Define these terms:
   chorus
   free rhythm
   hemiola
   irregular meter
   recitative
   rubato
   verse

2. Why might a composer use meter changes in musical notation?

3. In what era of music history did meter changes become common?

4. What is a common method of creating a sense of temporary meter change without actually changing the meter signature?

▶ RHYTHM READING

▶ **EXERCISES FOR LESSON 19**

When deciding on a beat unit (i.e., the note referenced by the bottom number of the meter signature), remember to account for the distinction between simple and compound meters (Lesson 10). A measure containing six eighth notes, for example, can be notated in either simple meter $\left(\frac{3}{4}\right)$ or compound $\left(\frac{6}{8}\right)$. The grouping and beaming will help you decide which is more appropriate ($\frac{3}{4}$ ♫ ♫ ♫ vs. $\frac{6}{8}$ ♫♫ ♫♫).

A. Count the beats in each measure and insert meter signatures as needed to make the notation correct. Use common meter signatures, with a bottom number of 2, 4, or 8. If the meter in a measure is the same as the previous measure, don't insert that same meter signature again.

Name: _____

In music with an irregular meter, meter changes can be based on repeating pitch patterns.
This melody, for example . . .

. . . could be renotated using meter changes so that each occurrence of the pitch pattern
E–D–C–A–G begins on a downbeat:

B. Each of these melodies is based on a pattern of repeating pitches in variable durations.
For each melody, find the repeating pitch pattern, then renotate the melody using
meter changes so that all the durations remain as they were but the first note of each
repetition of the pitch pattern falls on the downbeat of a measure.

1.

2.

LESSON 19: IRREGULARITIES OF RHYTHM AND METER

3.

4.

5.

✑ create!

Write melodies that contain repeating patterns within the given meter changes. Plan your melodies so that each pattern beginning falls on the downbeat of a measure (as in the Lesson 19B exercises).

1.

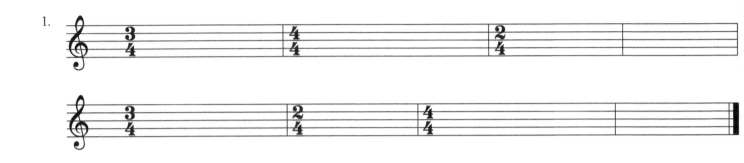

2.

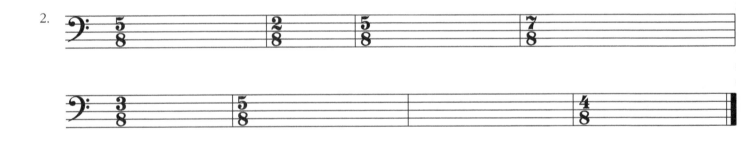

3.

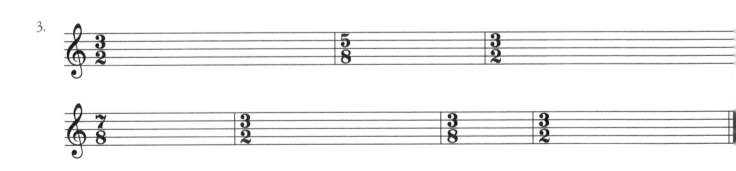

Write melodies in changing meters. Use the lesson examples or music from the *Suggestions for Listening* (www.oup.com/us/lambert) as models.

LESSON **20**

TRIADS

20.1 THREE-NOTE GROUPINGS

Listen to the opening of a well-known piano sonata by Mozart:

One way to explore this music would be to identify interval types, as we did in Lessons 15 through 18. We could, for example, survey the intervals formed by consecutive notes in Mozart's melody, beginning with rising thirds in measure 1 but continuing thereafter with a variety of different interval types (only half and whole steps in measures 2 and 4, a prominent fourth in measure 3, sixths between measures 1 and 2 and 2 and 3, and so forth).

But the pattern in the left hand—known as an **Alberti bass**—encourages us to make larger note groupings. Rhythmically the left hand subdivides into groups of four eighth notes, two groups per measure:

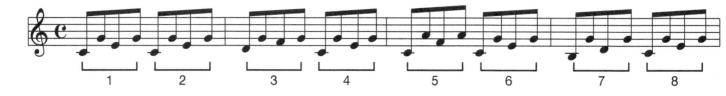

And each group contains three different notes, one repeated. Let's focus, for now, on the most prevalent pitch combination among the groups, the notes C, E, and G occurring in groups 1, 2, 4, 6, and 8. (We'll explore the other groups in future lessons.) These notes occupy adjacent lines on the staff, or if we move them to bass clef, adjacent spaces:

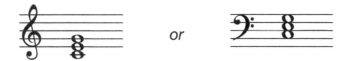

In the musical alphabet, these notes are represented by alternate letters:

One term for C–E–G is **chord**, which simply indicates that they constitute a meaningful combination of three or more notes. More specifically, C–E–G is known as a **triad**—a combination of three notes that may be notated on adjacent lines or spaces, represented by alternate letters in the musical alphabet. The beginning of Mozart's sonata, like many other types and styles of music, is very strongly oriented around the formation of triads.

20.2   TRIAD CHARACTERISTICS

Before we define different types of triads, let's first consider what all triads have in common. When notated on adjacent lines or adjacent spaces, each tone in a triad has a name: the lower note is called the **root**, the middle note is designated the **third**, and the upper note is known as the **fifth**. These names reflect the intervallic distances when the notes are paired off into intervals: The distance from the root to the third is a third, and the distance from the root to the fifth is a fifth. The distance from the third to the fifth is also a third:

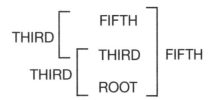

In the triad being expressed frequently in the first four measures of Mozart's sonata, then, C is the root, E is the third, and G is the fifth.

This three-letter combination, C–E–G, is one of seven ways to use letters in the musical alphabet to form a triad. That makes sense: if there are seven different letters in the musical alphabet, then there must be seven possible roots, seven different combinations of three alternate letters:

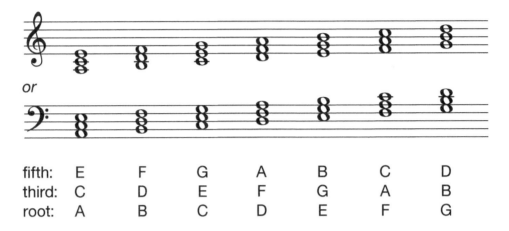

fifth:	E	F	G	A	B	C	D
third:	C	D	E	F	G	A	B
root:	A	B	C	D	E	F	G

So, any triad with a root of C has E as its third and G as its fifth. Any triad with F as its root has A as its third and C as its fifth. And so forth. As we work more and more with triads, you will come to know these seven three-letter combinations by heart.

20.3 MAJOR AND MINOR TRIADS

Now let's be more specific about triad types and characteristics. We'll do that by focusing on the qualities of the intervals within them. The C–E–G triad from Mozart's sonata, for example, has a major third from root to third, a minor third from third to fifth, and a perfect fifth from root to fifth:

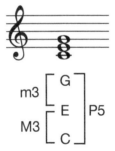

Triads on other roots, however, may have different interval qualities. Look, for example, at the triad presented by the left hand in another well-known Mozart piano sonata:

20-2

The A–C–E triad in the left hand in measures 1 and 3 has a minor third from root to third, major third from third to fifth, and perfect fifth between the root and the fifth:

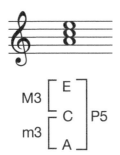

The C–E–G triad from the first example and the A–C–E triad from the second demonstrate the two most common types, or **qualities**, of triads. Both have perfect fifths between root and fifth, but they have different configurations of major and minor thirds within, either major below minor (C–E–G) or minor below major (A–C–E). When the major third is the lower interval, as in C–E–G, we call that **major** quality. When the minor third is the lower interval, as in A–C–E, we call that **minor** quality:

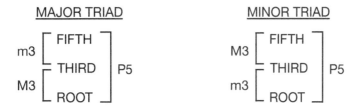

Or, calculating the intervals as half-step spans, a major triad is 4 below 3, and a minor triad is 3 below 4:

Any note may be the root of a triad. Take any note and form one of these combinations of intervals above it, and you will have formed a triad of a certain quality. Identify the triad you form by naming its root and quality: C–E–G is "C major," sometimes abbreviated as "CM," or just "C"; A–C–E is "A minor," abbreviated as "Am."

Forming major and minor triads takes us back to our previous work with major and minor scales. The major triad is essentially an extraction of the first, third, and fifth degrees of the major scale, while the minor triad brings together the first, third, and fifth degrees of the minor scale:

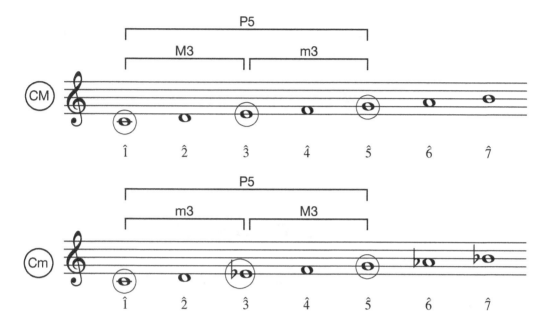

Moving back and forth between major and minor triads on the same root is reminiscent of moving back and forth between parallel major and minor scales. In the first five degrees of parallel scales there is just one different note, the all-important third degree. This same note is likewise the single difference between major and minor triads on the same root. You can change the quality of any major triad to minor simply by lowering the third by one half step, without changing the root or fifth. Conversely, you can change the quality of any minor triad to major by raising the third by one half step while leaving the other two notes as they are:

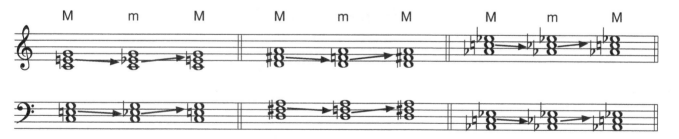

Another way to move between major and minor is to keep the third as it is but move both the root and fifth by half step, either both up (to go from major to minor) or both down (minor to major):

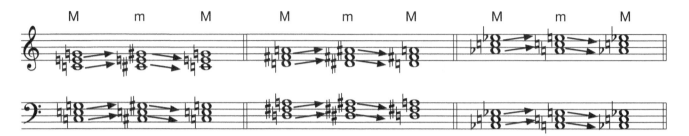

In these shifts you are changing the root, however, and so are not mimicking moves between parallel major and minor scales.

20.4 AUGMENTED AND DIMINISHED TRIADS

Major and minor are by far the most common qualities of triads in music of many styles and cultural traditions. The two other qualities, **diminished** and **augmented**, occur less frequently but still deserve our attention. Because these triad types are structured of thirds and fifths just like major and minor, the process of identifying and constructing them works very similarly.

Claude Debussy moves back and forth between a major triad and a diminished triad in the left-hand part of one of his piano preludes:

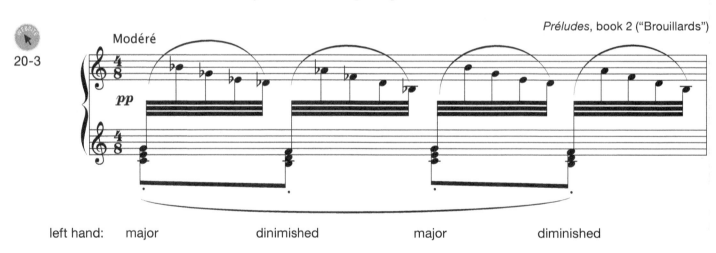

Préludes, book 2 ("Brouillards")

In the diminished triad, both thirds are minor, and the fifth is diminished:

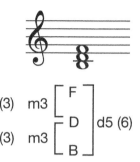

This is the "B diminished" triad, sometimes abbreviated as "B°."

Franz Liszt used augmented triads frequently in his works, including near the end of this virtuosic piano piece, in both hands, with the roots doubled for emphasis:

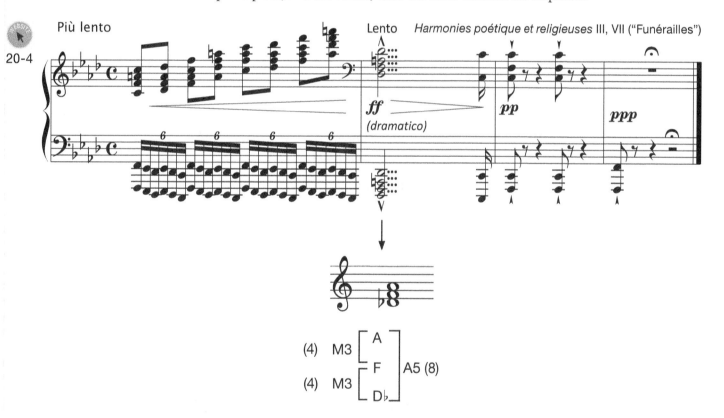

An augmented triad has two major thirds surrounded by an augmented fifth. This one is "D♭ augmented," sometimes abbreviated as "D♭+."

The most important difference between diminished and augmented qualities and the more common major and minor is the quality of the fifth. With a fifth that isn't perfect, diminished and augmented triads have more limited musical functions. They can't, for example, serve as points of harmonic stability, in the sense that major and minor can. Quite the contrary: diminished and augmented triads typically function as moments of instability in harmonic progressions, creating the expectation of more stable harmonies to come.

Here, then, is our complete inventory of triad types:

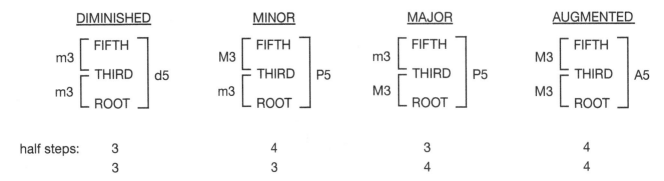

	DIMINISHED			MINOR			MAJOR			AUGMENTED	
m3	FIFTH	d5	M3	FIFTH	P5	m3	FIFTH	P5	M3	FIFTH	A5
	THIRD			THIRD			THIRD			THIRD	
m3	ROOT		m3	ROOT		M3	ROOT		M3	ROOT	

half steps:	3	4	3	4
	3	3	4	4

One way to remember them is to focus on the quality of the intervals:

- In the major or minor triad, the fifth is perfect, but the thirds are different qualities. The thirds are either major below minor (major triad) or minor below major (minor triad).

- In the augmented or diminished triad, the fifth is not perfect (as indicated by the triad name), but the thirds are the same qualities. The thirds are either both major (augmented triad) or both minor (diminished triad).

It's often easiest to form diminished or augmented triads by making half-step alterations of major or minor. To form a diminished triad, for example, you can lower the fifth of a minor triad by one half step. In terms of half steps, you're converting $\frac{4}{3}$ to $\frac{3}{3}$:

You can also create a diminished triad by raising the root of major by one half step ($\frac{3}{4}$ to $\frac{3}{3}$):

An augmented triad can be conceived as a major triad with a raised fifth ($\frac{3}{4}$ to $\frac{4}{4}$):

Or you can form an augmented triad by lowering the root of minor ($\frac{4}{3}$ to $\frac{4}{4}$):

In any of these conversions, be sure not to move notes off their original lines or spaces, even if this means writing an unusual note. If you're raising a note that's already sharp, for example, it becomes double sharp (as in the conversion of F♯ major to F♯ augmented shown above). If you're lowering a note that's already flat, it becomes double flat (as in the conversion of B♭ minor to B𝄫 augmented shown above).

In one rare instance, keeping notes on their original lines and spaces also means notating both a sharped and a flatted note in the same triad, as shown in the B♭ augmented triad above (*). Otherwise we never have a reason to mix sharps and flats in the same triad, of any quality.

20.5   THE CIRCLE OF TRIADS

In working with triads, you may find it helpful to think in relation to major and minor keys, organized like the circle of keys (Lessons 9.3, 12.3). To create a **circle of triads**, simply replace each key in the circle of keys with a triad rooted on the tonic note of that key. Place a C major triad at twelve o'clock, a G major triad at one o'clock, D major at two o'clock, and so forth. In other words, instead of writing a key name or key signature for each key, write a triad created from the first, third, and fifth degrees in the scale of that key.

As you move clockwise around the circle, the fifth of each triad becomes the root of the next one:

etc.

As you move counterclockwise, each root becomes the next fifth:

etc.

The circle of minor triads works the same way. Start with A minor at twelve o'clock and progress clockwise to E minor and B minor, or counter-clockwise to D minor and G minor, and so forth. The pattern of common tones will be the same as it is for major.

Major and minor triads at the same spot on the circle, corresponding to relative major and minor keys, share two common tones. The root and third of major are the third and fifth of minor:

The complete circle is shown below. In the interest of equal time, major triads are notated in treble clef and minor triads in bass clef.

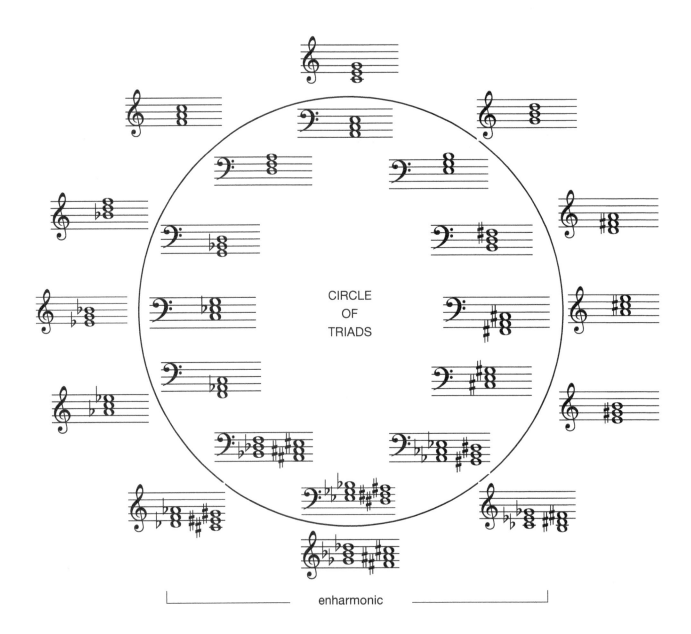

20.6   METHODOLOGY

As a review, let's work through the processes of identifying and constructing triads. If you see a triad and want to know its quality, find the quality of the intervals, using what you know about intervals from previous lessons. Let's say we want to identify these triads:

Break them down into their constituent intervals:

m3 ⌈ B ⌉
   ⌊ G♯ ⌋ P5   M3 ⌈ D ⌉
M3 ⌊ E ⌋   ⌊ B♭ ⌋ P5   m3 ⌈ G ⌉
                m3 ⌊ G ⌋   ⌊ E ⌋ d5   M3 ⌈ E♯ ⌉
                                m3 ⌊ C♯ ⌋   ⌊ C♯ ⌋ A5
                                                M3 ⌊ A ⌋

or:

3 ⌈ B ⌉
  ⌊ G♯ ⌋ 7   4 ⌈ D ⌉
4 ⌊ E ⌋   ⌊ B♭ ⌋ 7   3 ⌈ G ⌉
              3 ⌊ G ⌋   ⌊ E ⌋ 6   4 ⌈ E♯ ⌉
                              3 ⌊ C♯ ⌋   ⌊ C♯ ⌋ 8
                                              4 ⌊ A ⌋

The intervals tell you that the first one is E major (EM), the second is G minor (Gm), the third is C♯ diminished (C♯°), and the fourth is A augmented (A+).

You might also have known this by noticing that the first one, EM, brings together scale degrees $\hat{1}$, $\hat{3}$, and $\hat{5}$ of the E major scale, and the second one, Gm, is $\hat{1}$, $\hat{3}$, and $\hat{5}$ of G minor. The third one, C♯°, could be viewed as a C♯ minor triad with a lowered fifth, or a C major triad with a raised root. You might think of the fourth one, A+, as an A major triad with a raised fifth, or an A♯ minor triad with a lowered root.

Now let's construct. Suppose we want to form these triads:

1. G major (GM)   2. F minor (Fm)   3. A♭ diminished (A♭°)   4. E augmented (E+)

Start by notating all three noteheads on adjacent lines and spaces, without thinking about which ones might need accidentals:

Then add accidentals as needed to produce the correct interval qualities, without moving these notes from these lines or spaces.

The first one, GM, is correct as it is. The thirds are major below minor (in half steps, 4 below 3), as required—$\hat{1}$, $\hat{3}$, and $\hat{5}$ of the G major scale.

To form an F minor triad for the second one, you might start by noticing that it's currently F major, F–A–C. You could then convert F major to F minor by lowering the third to A♭. Or you could just look at the intervals and know that the A needs to be flatted to make the correct configuration of thirds, minor below major (in half steps, 3 below 4). Or just write $\hat{1}$, $\hat{3}$, and $\hat{5}$ of the F minor scale.

For the third one, A♭°, if you're thinking of a diminished triad as a minor triad with a lowered fifth, then you would start by notating A♭ minor, A♭–C♭–E♭, and then lower the fifth to E♭♭. Or perhaps you would start by counting half steps, from A♭ up three to C♭, and from C♭ up another three to E♭♭. In any case you would resist the temptation to renotate the C♭ as B♮ or the E♭♭ as D♮.

In the case of triads with unusual spellings such as A♭ diminished, it may make more sense to start off by converting the root to its enharmonic equivalent, G♯, and spelling a diminished triad on that root as a first step: G♯–B–D. After you've done that, respell *all three* notes of G♯ diminished as A♭– C♭– E♭♭.

The last one, E+, could be formed by taking E major, E–G♯–B, and raising the fifth to B♯ (*not* C♮). Or count four half steps up from E to get G♯ and four half steps up from G♯ to get B♯.

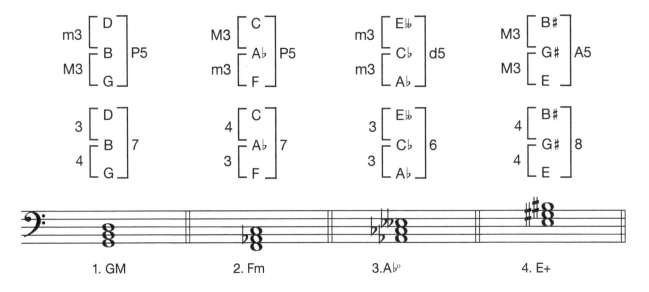

For suggestions for further listening and online exercises and drills, go to www.oup.com/us/lambert

1. Define these terms:
   Alberti bass
   augmented triad
   chord
   circle of triads
   diminished triad
   fifth (of a triad)
   major triad
   minor triad
   quality (of a triad)
   root (of a triad)
   third (of a triad)
   triad

2. How is a "chord" different from a "triad"?

3. What do all triads have in common?

4. Which triad types are formed from two thirds of the same quality?

5. Which triad types have a perfect fifth between the root and fifth?

6. Give two different ways of making these conversions while holding at least one note in common:
   major triad → minor triad
   minor triad → major triad

7. Give the procedure for making these conversions by changing only one note:
   minor → diminished
   diminished → major
   augmented → major
   minor → augmented

8. What is the relationship between the circle of triads and the circle of keys?

9. What is the relationship between triads in neighboring positions (e.g., two o'clock and three o'clock) on the circle of triads?

10. What is the relationship between triads at the same position (e.g., both at ten o'clock) on the circle of triads?

Name: _____

EXERCISES FOR LESSON 20

In Lessons 20.3 and 20.4 we learned several ways of converting the quality of a triad by changing the accidental on one of its notes:

to convert this quality . . .	to this quality . . .	do this:
major	minor	lower the third
minor	major	raise the third
major	augmented	raise the fifth
minor	diminished	lower the fifth
major	diminished	raise the root
minor	augmented	lower the root

The result will be a triad with one different accidental, notated on the same three lines or three spaces.

A. Identify the root and quality (M, m, d, or A) of the given triad. Then rewrite it in the space provided, creating a different triad of the indicated quality by changing the accidental on one note while leaving the other two notes as they are. (The change in accidental may affect any chord tone—root, third, or fifth.) The first one is done for you (lowering the third of CM to make Cm).

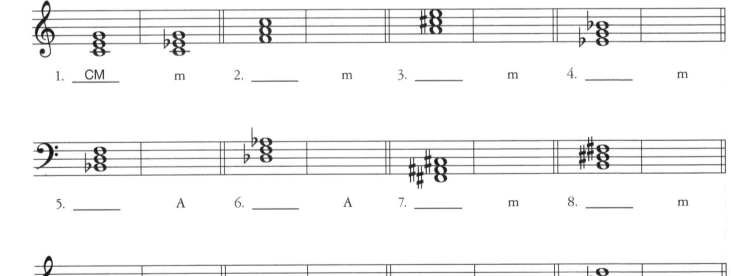

1. __CM__   m   2. _____   m   3. _____   m   4. _____   m

5. _____   A   6. _____   A   7. _____   m   8. _____   m

9. _____   d   10. _____   M   11. _____   M   12. _____   d

284   LESSON 20: TRIADS

13. _____ d   14. _____ M   15. _____ M   16. _____ d

17. _____ A   18. _____ d   19. _____ d   20. _____ m

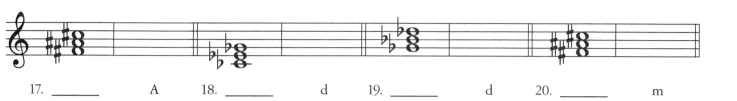

21. _____ M   22. _____ d   23. _____ d   24. _____ d

25. _____ m   26. _____ M   27. _____ m   28. _____ m

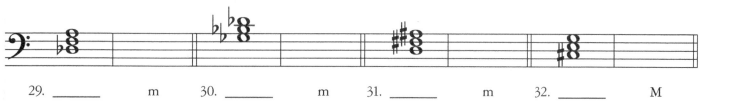

29. _____ m   30. _____ m   31. _____ m   32. _____ M

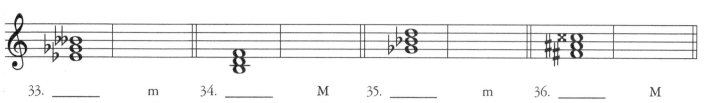

33. _____ m   34. _____ M   35. _____ m   36. _____ M

When notating triads, always place the notes on adjacent lines or adjacent spaces (Lesson 20.5). It's a good idea to write the noteheads on the staff first, before you've determined which, if any, require accidentals.

B. Notate the specified triads.

1. DM   2. C+   3. GM   4. Em   5. A+   6. B♭m   7. C♯M   8. D♭M

9. AM   10. F+   11. G♯°   12. D♯°   13. E♭M   14. Gm   15. B♭m   16. D♯m

17. A°   18. D♭+   19. F♯°   20. B♭M   21. Em   22. B♭°   23. G♯m   24. C♯°

25. E♭+   26. A♯°   27. EM   28. B+   29. F♯+   30 A♭+   31. G♭+   32. Fm

Any single tone can be a member of twelve different triads. It can be the root of four triads (one of each quality), the third of four, and the fifth of four (and $3 \times 4 = 12$). For example, here are the twelve triads in which the note G is the root, third, or fifth:

M   m   d   A   M   m   d   A   M   m   d   A

C. Add accidentals as needed to the darkened noteheads to demonstrate how the tones notated in open noteheads can be members of twelve different triads. Don't add accidentals to any open noteheads.

1.

2.

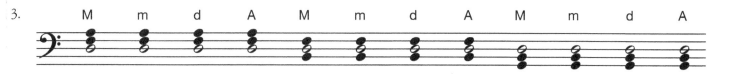

3.

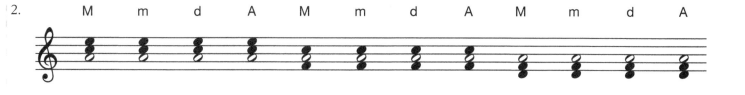

4.

✏ create!

Think about the role of triads in piano accompaniment patterns. In the Alberti bass, which we saw in Mozart's C major sonata at the beginning of this lesson, triad tones are presented one at a time, root-fifth-third-fifth:

In Boat Song (Fifteen Character Pieces) the order is root-third-fifth:

Or you can present the root by itself and the third and fifth together, as in several of the Fifteen Character Pieces (www.oup.com/us/lambert):

Lullaby   Dance   Waltz

In his A minor piano sonata, Mozart simply repeats all three triad tones together:

Experiment with different methods of presenting triads in left-hand accompaniment patterns, using these examples as inspirations. Try different keys, meters, and rhythms. Try using only notes of a single triad, then experiment with patterns that involve more than one triad (as in Dance).

After you've found a pattern you like, improvise a melody in your right hand that goes with it. Try rhythms that are similar to the accompaniment, then try rhythms that aren't. Try pitches that replicate notes in the accompaniment and pitches that don't. If, for example, you create a melody consisting mostly of *adjacent* notes in the scale (steps), you will have set up classic contrast with the notes in the accompaniment taken from *alternate* scale tones (triads).

If you come up with something you like, write it down!

LESSON 21
TRIADS IN PRACTICE

EXPRESSING TRIADS

Let's return to the opening measures of Mozart's well-known C major piano sonata:

In Lesson 20 we noticed recurring C major triads in groups 1, 2, 4, 6, and 8 of the accompaniment. These groups support melody notes that are also members of this triad. In fact, the melody begins by unfolding the root, third, and fifth of C major, C–E–G, in measure 1.

Now let's look at another group and the melody note it supports. In group 5 the left hand starts again on C but then moves the rest of its pattern up a step to A–F–A, while A also sounds in the melody. Although the three different notes in group 5, C, F and A, don't appear on adjacent lines or adjacent spaces as Mozart presents them, it's possible to rearrange them so that they do:

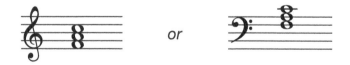

This rearrangement, displaying the notes of a triad on adjacent lines or adjacent spaces, is called **triad form**. When we see these notes in triad form, we recognize the F major triad. The chord in group 5 may not immediately look like F major, because the root F isn't presented first, as the lowest note of the group, but as long as we can rearrange them into triad form, we can consider it an expression of the F major triad.

In one sense, the presentation of the C major triad in groups 1, 2, 4, 6, and 8 is significantly different from the appearance of the F major triad in group 5. Our ears more easily recognize C major as a triad. With its root emphasized on downbeats, it sounds like it has firmer footing than the F major triad in group 5; it sounds more solid, more stable.

In another sense, however, the C major groups and group 5 essentially do the same thing—express triads. They can all be understood by writing notes on the staff in triad form. Whether they look like triads in their original musical presentations is irrelevant to their designations as triads.

In this sense, then, the notion of "triad" is a bit of an abstraction. It carries no particular expectations of a certain arrangement of tones in a musical setting. It only requires that we are able to take those tones out of their context and notate them on adjacent lines or spaces on a staff.

Look at this issue from the perspective of the composer. You have this particular sound, the triad, that you want to use in your composition, and you have abundant options for combining and rearranging its notes to fill different expressive needs. The notes can be unfolded one at a time in a melody, or sounded together to make harmonic support for a melody; they can be colored by repetition and instrumental shading, and so forth. You can do a lot with just three notes.

Now take the perspective of the observer or musical analyst. Because music of many styles and cultural traditions is based on triads, you can learn a lot about a piece of music by exploring just this aspect. There's much more to it than that, of course, but triads are a good place to start, a good indication of what makes the music sound as it does.

21.2   SOME EXAMPLES

Let's explore some triads in different musical contexts. Here's a common way to support the melody of "America," by making each note in the melody part of an expression of a triad:

To see exactly which triad supports each note, take the notes supporting each melody note and rearrange them in triad form:

FM Dm Gm   CM   FM CM   FM Dm BbM   FM   CM Dm   Gm FM CM   FM

In typical fashion, the qualities of these triads are a mixture of major and minor, and they're all formed by combining notes of the F major scale. We'll return to this issue in Lesson 22.

Here's a resplendent display of triads in a keyboard prelude by Johann Sebastian Bach. The right hand presents triad tones one after another, a process known as **arpeggiation**. We hear two triads per measure:

right hand triads: GM   CM   F#°   GM

(pedal point)

The left hand just repeats G, usually doubling a chord tone from the triads, but in one case conflicting with the triad above (first half of measure 2). A repeating note, which may or may not participate with the chords happening around it, is known as a **pedal point**.

Both hands work together to form chords at the beginning of Robert Schumann's *Humoreske*:

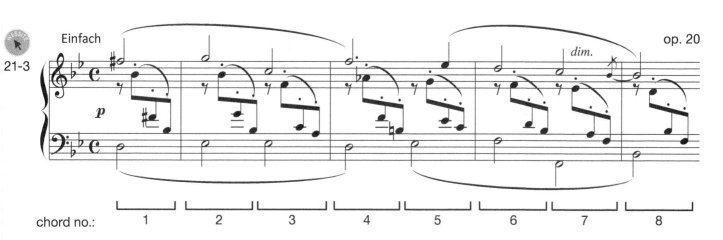

Chords 1, 2, 5, 6, and 8 are expressions of triads. (We'll look at the others in a later lesson.) The first one is augmented quality, using the note F# from outside the key of B♭ major. After that we hear an E♭ major triad at chord 2, a C minor triad at chord 5, and a B♭ major triad repeated in different arrangements as chords 6 and 8:

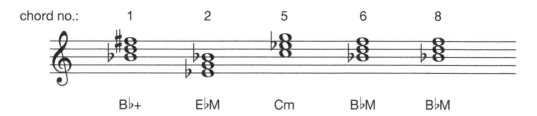

Schumann presents the chords in delicate arpeggiations sandwiched between a simple melody and bass line. In one case, chord 5, the previous melody note (F in chord 4) hangs around for one extra beat before moving to its chord tone (E♭).

In these and countless other examples in music of many types and styles, triads may sound very different from each other, depending on how they are spaced, where and how they're played on the instrument(s), which triad tone is highest or lowest, which notes are duplicated, and abundant other factors. Even triads of the same quality can be made to contrast. By the same token, triads of different qualities can be presented to bring out their similarities. In spite of all this variability, when we've located and identified triads in a piece of music, we've collected some vital information about its sound and structure.

21.3   METHODOLOGY

Because the world of triads is finite and manageable, the process of locating them is fairly straightforward. Learn to recognize the sound of triads and listen for them in meaningful musical groupings. Remember that the notes may appear in any arrangement in a musical setting; your job is simply to collect the notes together and notate them in triad form. After you've done that, you'll know which notes are the root, third, and fifth and will have made a strong start toward understanding the harmony.

As we learned in Lesson 20.2, there are only seven possible combinations of three letters to form a triad:

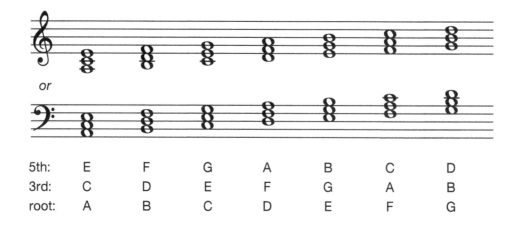

5th:	E	F	G	A	B	C	D
3rd:	C	D	E	F	G	A	B
root:	A	B	C	D	E	F	G

Here's another way to remember the three-letter combinations. Arrange alternate letters of the musical alphabet in a circle:

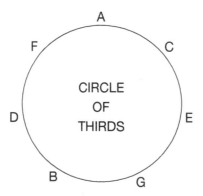

Because the intervallic distance between adjacent letters is 3, it's a **circle of thirds**. Any three adjacent letters in the circle of thirds can be a three-letter combination for a triad spelling. Just choose any letter in the circle as the root of a triad and move clockwise around the circle from that root to the next two and you'll have three letters used in a triad.

So, to locate the root of a triad quickly, you don't even need to concern yourself with the accidentals and interval qualities. You can simply look for a way to form one of the seven three-letter combinations.

For example, suppose we want to identify the triads in these measures:

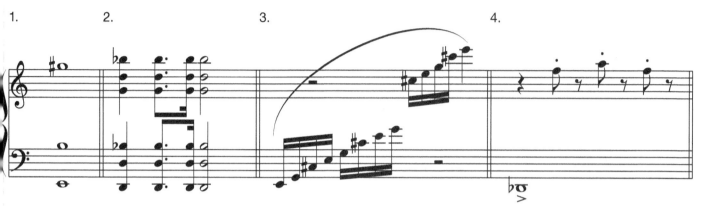

The first one is a widely spaced chord, but it has only three different notes, so we need only find a way to arrange them as a triad. The only way to do it is to use the E–G–B letter combination.

The second one is widely spaced and repetitive, with three notes in each staff, together presenting a rhythm like you might find in a march or fanfare. Even so, only three different letters are represented, in the G–B–D letter combination.

Number 3 is an arpeggio extending upward through four octaves, presenting but a single triad, in the C–E–G letter combination.

And the last one is a much sparer presentation, with a gap of more than three octaves between the hands and just one note repetition (the F in the right hand). As the right hand seems to respond to the left hand, it makes sense to group them together and to consider them an expression of a triad using the D–F–A letter combination.

Now that we know the roots, we can write the triads in triad form on a staff and determine their qualities:

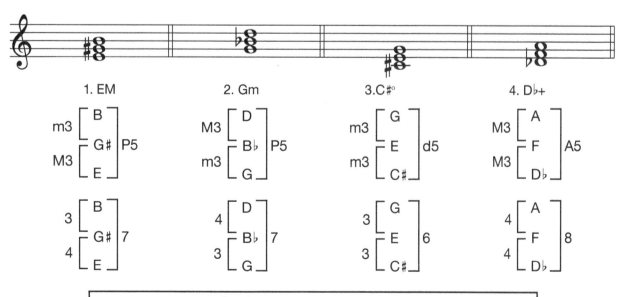

 For suggestions for further listening and online exercises and drills, go to www.oup.com/us/lambert

▶ STUDY QUESTIONS FOR LESSON 21

1. Define these terms:
    arpeggiation
    circle of thirds
    pedal point
    triad form

2. What chord tone is lowest when a triad is notated in triad form?

3. What are the seven three-letter combinations used to spell triads?

4. How can the circle of thirds help with triad spellings?

5. True or false:
    If the letter F is used for the root of a triad, then the third is spelled using the letter A, the fifth with the letter C.
    The root of a triad is always the first note played in the melody.
    The root of a triad is always the lowest note in the original music.
    In piano music, triads may be formed in one hand alone, or by both hands in combination.
    If you find a musical grouping of three notes but you can't somehow arrange them in triad form, then the three notes do not form a triad.

EXERCISES FOR LESSON 21

Here again are the seven three-letter combinations for triads (Lessons 20.2, 21.3):

fifth:	E	F	G	A	B	C	D
third:	C	D	E	F	G	A	B
root:	A	B	C	D	E	F	G

To determine the root of a triad, rearrange its notes into one of these seven combinations. To find its quality, look at the quality of the intervals between the notes (Lessons 20.3, 20.4).

Instructions for exercises A, B, C, and D:

Notate each indicated triad in triad form (on adjacent lines or adjacent spaces) on the staff provided. Use accidentals to indicate which notes (if any) are sharped or flatted in the key (and don't forget added accidentals that carry through the measure). Specify the root and quality (M/m/d/A) of each triad. The first one is done for you.

21-4

A. Mozart, Piano Sonata, K. 545, I

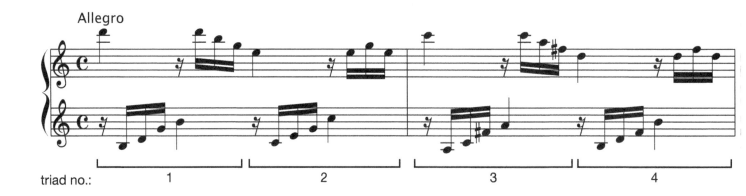

triad no.:   1   2   3   4

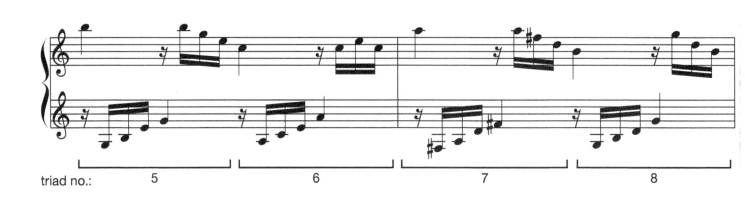

triad no.:   5   6   7   8

triad no.:   1.   2.   3.   4.   5.   6.   7.   8.

root/
quality: GM _____   _____   _____   _____   _____   _____   _____   _____

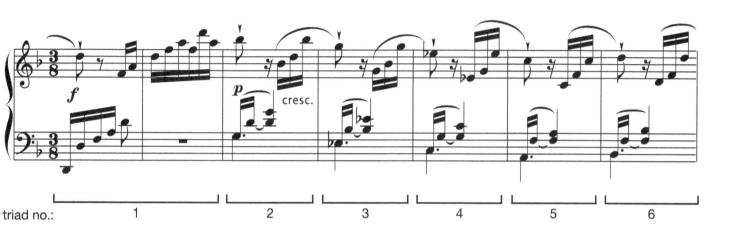

B. Beethoven, Piano Sonata, op. 31, no. 2 ("Tempest"), III

21-5

triad no.:   1   2   3   4   5   6

triad no.:   7   8   9   10   11   12

triad no.:   1.   2.   3.   4.   5.   6.

root/
quality: _____ _____ _____ _____ _____ _____

triad no.:   7.   8.   9.   10.   11.   12.

root/
quality: _____ _____ _____ _____ _____ _____

C. Franz Liszt, "Pace non trovo" (*Petrarch Sonnets*)

21-6

note: Disregard the vocal line, which includes some notes that are not members of the triads being arpeggiated in the piano.

(answers on next page)

triad no.:   1.   2.   3.   4.   5.   6.   7.   8.

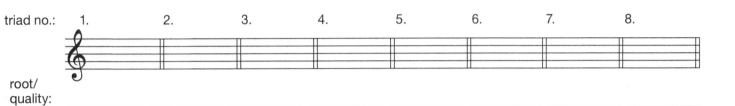

root/
quality: ____ ____ ____ ____ ____ ____ ____ ____

21-7

D. "America the Beautiful," first phrase

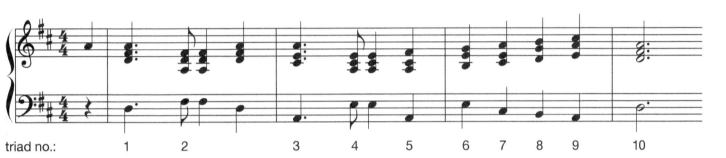

triad no.:   1   2   3   4   5   6   7   8   9   10

triad no.:   1.   2.   3.   4.   5.

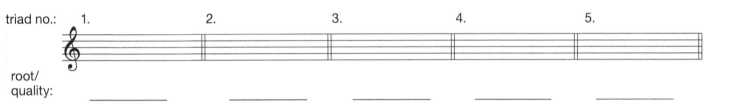

root/
quality: _____   _____   _____   _____   _____

triad no.:   6.   7.   8.   9.   10.

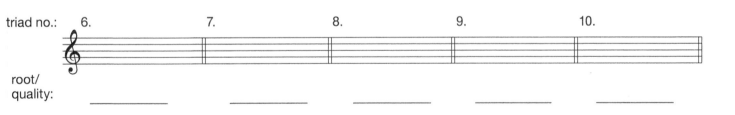

root/
quality: _____   _____   _____   _____   _____

✒ create!

Play this series of shifting triad qualities:

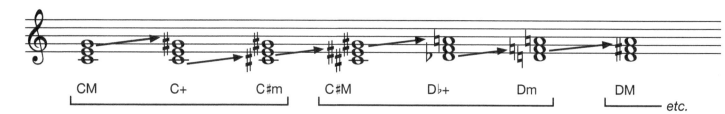

One chord tone moves up a half step from each chord to the next. First major becomes augmented (by raising the fifth). Then augmented becomes minor (by raising the root). Finally, minor becomes major (by raising the third). Then the pattern starts over.

Invent your own patterns of shifting triad qualities. Try involving all four qualities. Try moving tones down at some points in the series. Try shifting two tones instead of one. Try shifting by amounts other than half steps.

Then try different ways of presenting your triad series. Seek inspiration from the musical examples throughout this lesson and written exercises, by Mozart, Bach, Schumann, Beethoven, and Liszt. Here, for example, is a way of presenting the first four triads of the series above in the Alberti bass pattern:

Or we could present these same triads in sweeping arpeggiations, in the manner of Beethoven in his "Tempest" sonata (see Exercise 21B):

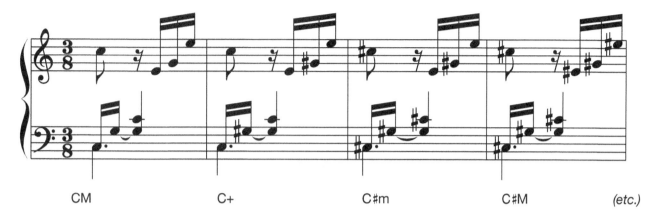

Or try something completely different from the models:

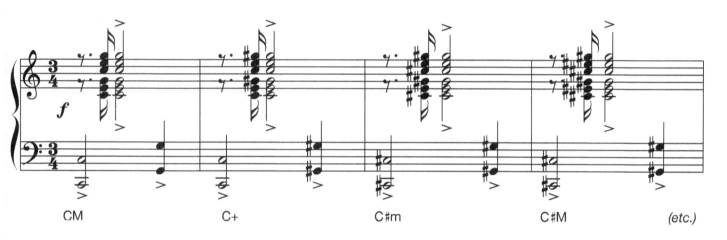

. . . and so forth. Try similar rhythms with different triad series and different rhythms with similar ones. Find ways to highlight the note shifts from one triad to the next. Explore!

LESSON **22**
TRIADS IN MAJOR KEYS

22.1 SCALE DEGREE COMBINATIONS

When we studied major and minor scales in Lessons 8 and 11, we recognized that a scale represents the primary pitch material for music in that key, with the first degree, the tonic, most important of all. More recently we've studied triads and recognized the important roles they play in musical sound and structure.

Now let's merge the two ideas and consider the ways in which scale tones can combine to form triads. If the scale displays primary pitch material, and if triads are an essential feature of the music, then the triads formed by scale tones represent fundamental musical resources.

Let's say we're writing music in the key of F major, or studying music such as the version of "America" we looked at in Lesson 21.2, which is in the key of F major. We'll want to know what triads we can form using only the notes of this scale:

So we build a triad on each scale degree, making sure to use only notes of this scale to form the triads. Most of the notes will be natural, because they're natural in the scale, but all Bs must be flatted, because the B is flatted in the scale:

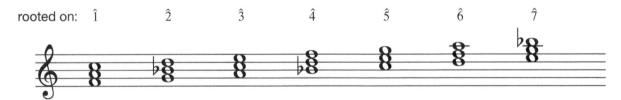

Look at this inventory from the standpoint of the musical alphabet: we've used it three times, as the triad roots (FGABCDE), thirds (ABCDEFG), and fifths (CDEF-GAB). This means, among other things, that every scale tone appears three times, as

304

a root, third, and fifth. Find, for example, the three occurrences of scale degree $\hat{4}$—an easy thing to do, because $\hat{4}$ is the only note with an accidental. This note, B♭, is not only the root of the triad built on $\hat{4}$, but also the third of the triad built on $\hat{2}$, and the fifth of the triad built on $\hat{7}$.

These are the basic harmonic resources for music in the key of F major. Notice that they're triads of varying qualities. The triads built on $\hat{1}$, $\hat{4}$, and $\hat{5}$ are major, while the triads rooted on $\hat{2}$, $\hat{3}$, and $\hat{6}$ are minor, and the triad on $\hat{7}$ is diminished:

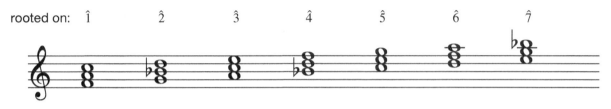

rooted on:	$\hat{1}$	$\hat{2}$	$\hat{3}$	$\hat{4}$	$\hat{5}$	$\hat{6}$	$\hat{7}$
quality:	MAJOR	minor	minor	MAJOR	MAJOR	minor	diminished
3rds:	m	M	M	m	m	M	m
	M	m	m	M	M	m	m
	3	4	4	3	3	4	3
	4	3	3	4	4	3	3

All major keys have this same pattern of qualities: major triads built on $\hat{1}$, $\hat{4}$, and $\hat{5}$; minor triads built on $\hat{2}$, $\hat{3}$, and $\hat{6}$; and a diminished triad built on $\hat{7}$. Here, for example, is the triad inventory for the key of D major:

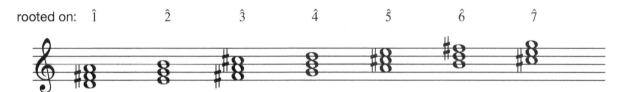

rooted on:	$\hat{1}$	$\hat{2}$	$\hat{3}$	$\hat{4}$	$\hat{5}$	$\hat{6}$	$\hat{7}$
quality:	MAJOR	minor	minor	MAJOR	MAJOR	minor	diminished
3rds:	m	M	M	m	m	M	m
	M	m	m	M	M	m	m
	3	4	4	3	3	4	3
	4	3	3	4	4	3	3

Again, remember that we're using only notes of D major to form these triads. Because F and C are both sharped in the D major scale, they must also be sharped every time they appear in the triad inventory. All the other notes in D major are natural, in the scale and in the triads.

22.2   ROMAN NUMERAL NOTATION

To symbolize each triad of a key we'll use a Roman numeral, which will indicate both the location of the root within the scale and the quality of the triad formed on that scale tone. In the key of F major, use an upper-case "I" to symbolize the major triad rooted on $\hat{1}$, F-A-C; use "ii" to symbolize the minor triad rooted on $\hat{2}$, G-B♭-D; and so forth. To symbolize the diminished triad rooted on $\hat{7}$ (E-G-B♭), use a lower-case "vii" plus a superscripted circle. Prior to the first Roman numeral, always indicate the key.

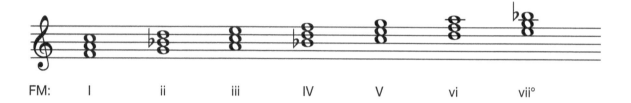

The Roman numerals look exactly the same in any major key. The I, IV, and V chords are always major, written in upper case, no matter what major key you're in. The ii, iii, and vi are always minor, lower case, and the vii° is always diminished, lower case with a superscripted circle. If you're forming a triad using only scale tones from a certain key, just find where its root happens in that key and you'll automatically know its quality.

Think of each triad in a key as a combination of particular scale degrees. The I chord is the marriage of $\hat{1}$, $\hat{3}$, and $\hat{5}$:

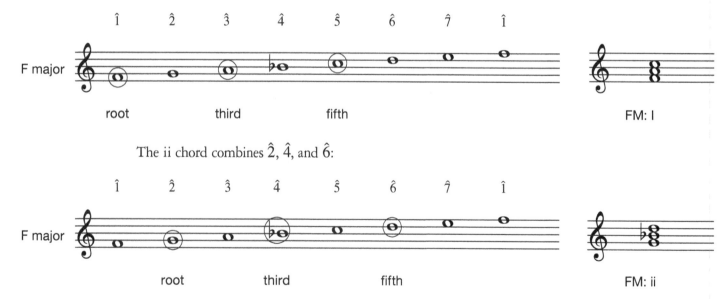

The ii chord combines $\hat{2}$, $\hat{4}$, and $\hat{6}$:

The V brings together $\hat{5}$, $\hat{7}$, and $\hat{2}$:

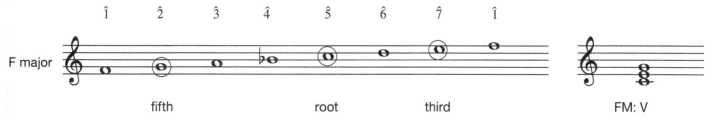

And so forth. Each chord in a key is a unique combination of scale degrees, just as each chord spelling employs a unique combination of three letters from the musical alphabet.

22.3   CHORD FUNCTIONS

To recognize that triads can have particular functions within harmonic progressions, let's adapt the scale degree names (Lesson 8.6). The I chord is rooted on the tonic, so it's the **tonic triad**. The next-most-important triad, the V, is the **dominant triad**, and the chord just below that, the IV, is the **subdominant triad**. That completes the inventory of available *major* triads within a major key. As we noticed in Lesson 8.6, the dominant and subdominant can be arranged by equal distances on either side of tonic:

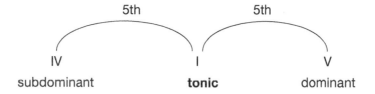

The available minor triads in a major key include the iii, or **mediant triad**, and the vi, or **submediant triad**, also related to tonic by equivalent intervallic distances:

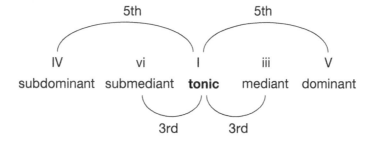

The remaining available triads for major keys are one more minor triad, the ii, or **supertonic triad**, and the only triad that's not major or minor, the vii°, or **leading tone triad**. Here are the chord names as they're ordered in the scale:

I	tonic
ii	supertonic
iii	mediant
IV	subdominant
V	dominant
vi	submediant
vii°	leading tone

The dynamic, dramatic relationship among these triads gives tonal music its vitality and character. Recall, for example, the version of the first phrase of "America" that we looked at in Lesson 21.2, which has triads supporting each note in the melody:

FM	Dm	Gm		CM	FM	CM	FM	Dm	B♭M	FM		CM	Dm	Gm	FM	CM	FM
FM:	I	vi	ii	V	I	V	I	vi	IV	I		V	vi	ii	I	V	I

The tonic triad (I) is, of course, the most common supporting chord. It's also the first triad used, the point of departure, and it's the point of arrival at the end. The next-most-common triad is the dominant (V). Notice the interplay between tonic and dominant throughout these six measures: anytime you hear a dominant, you know that you'll also hear a tonic close by. The other triads we hear, the submediant (vi), supertonic (ii), and subdominant (IV), further enrich this setting of the melody with flavor and variety. Each triad has a role to play, not just to support the melody but also to give momentum and shape to the unfolding musical expression.

 For suggestions for further listening and online exercises and drills, go to www.oup.com/us/lambert

▶ STUDY QUESTIONS FOR LESSON 22

1. Define these terms:
    dominant triad
    leading tone triad
    mediant triad
    subdominant triad
    submediant triad
    supertonic triad
    tonic triad

2. What information does a Roman numeral convey about a triad?

3. What are the Roman numerals of the major triads in a major key?

4. What are the Roman numerals of the other triads (the ones that aren't major) in a major key?

EXERCISES FOR LESSON 22

When you're notating triads built from scale tones of a given key (Lesson 22.1), remember to apply accidentals to notes that are sharped or flatted in the scale of that key. In D major, for example, F and C are both sharped. So when you're writing triads using notes of D major, make sure you've placed a sharp sign in front of all Fs and Cs.

A. Notate the triads in the indicated keys. Write individual sharps or flats as needed (don't use key signatures). The first one is done for you.

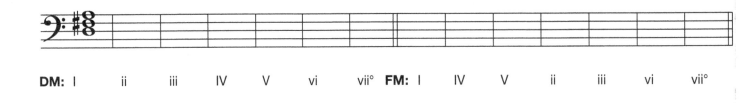

DM: I   ii   iii   IV   V   vi   vii°   FM: I   IV   V   ii   iii   vi   vii°

BM: vi   IV   ii   vii°   V   iii   I   A♭M: I   V   ii   vi   iii   vii°   IV

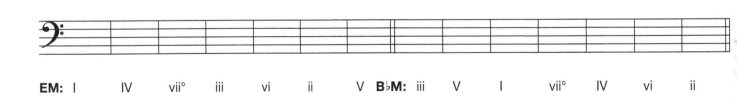

EM: I   IV   vii°   iii   vi   ii   V   B♭M: iii   V   I   vii°   IV   vi   ii

Name: _____

The case of a Roman numeral indicates the quality of the triad it represents (Lesson 22.2). When you label a triad with a Roman numeral, make a clear distinction between upper case (for the triads of major quality, I, IV, and V) and lower case (for the triads of minor quality, ii, iii, and vi, and for the diminished vii°).

B. Write the Roman numerals of the triads in the specified keys. The first one is done for you.

CM: _iii_ ___ ___ ___ ___ ___   DM: ___ ___ ___ ___ ___ ___ ___

GM: ___ ___ ___ ___ ___ ___   F#M: ___ ___ ___ ___ ___ ___ ___

C. Notate the specified triads. Write individual sharps or flats as needed (don't use key signatures).

1. AM: I   2. E♭M: vi   3. CM: V   4. D♭M: vii°   5. G♭M: ii   6. AM: iii   7. E♭M: IV   8. EM: V

9. G♭M: vii°   10. BM: IV   11. AM: vi   12. E♭M: I   13. D♭M: V   14. F#M: ii   15. E♭M: iii   16. AM: vii°

Name: _____

Chord function names reflect a triad's role in harmonic progressions and interrelationships within the key (Lesson 22.3):

I	ii	iii	IV	V	vi	vii°
tonic	supertonic	mediant	subdominant	dominant	submediant	leading tone

D. Find the root of each triad and rewrite it in triad form (on adjacent lines or adjacent spaces) on the lower staff. Then provide the Roman numeral label and function name in the specified key. The first one is done for you.

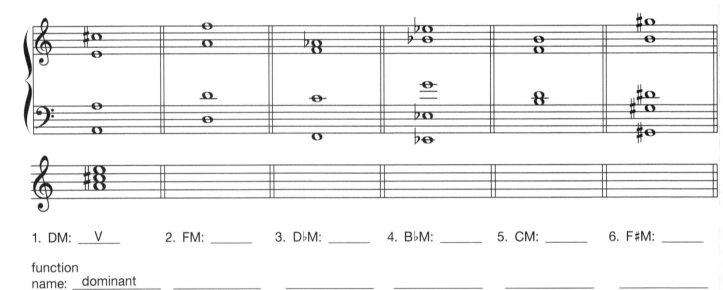

1. DM: __V__   2. FM: _____   3. D♭M: _____   4. B♭M: _____   5. CM: _____   6. F♯M: _____

function
name: __dominant__   _____   _____   _____   _____   _____

7. D♭M: _____   8. FM: _____   9. A♭M: _____   10. E♭M: _____   11. DM: _____   12. CM: _____

function
name: _____   _____   _____   _____   _____   _____

E. Notate each triad in triad form on the staff, using individual accidentals as needed (don't use a key signature). In the space beneath, indicate the Roman numeral of each triad in the key of E♭ major and the function name. The first one is done for you.

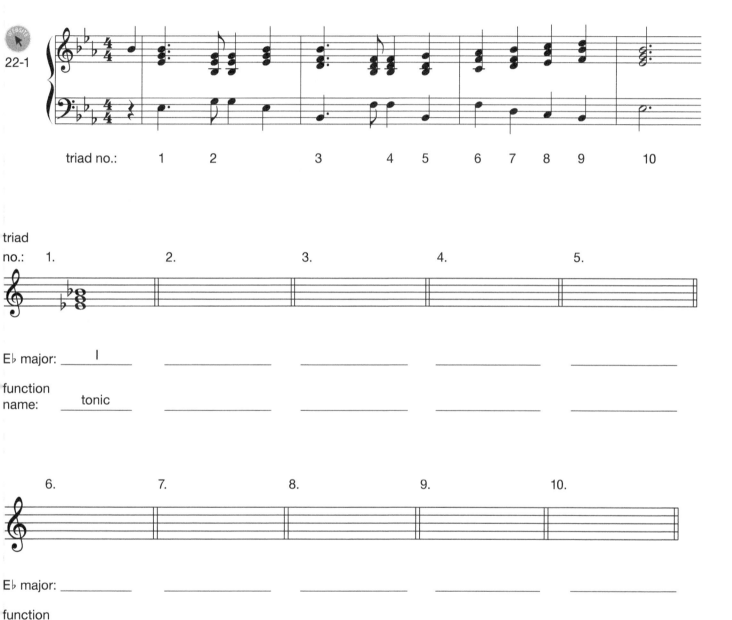

triad no.: 1 2 3 4 5 6 7 8 9 10

triad
no.: 1. 2. 3. 4. 5.

E♭ major: ____I____ _____ _____ _____ _____

function
name: ____tonic____ _____ _____ _____ _____

6. 7. 8. 9. 10.

E♭ major: _____ _____ _____ _____ _____

function
name: _____ _____ _____ _____ _____

 create!

Study this melody and accompaniment, adapted from a sonata for violin and piano by Mozart (K. 296, second movement):

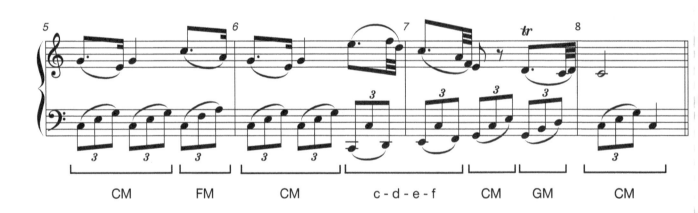

First, the accompaniment. The triplets in the left hand present almost exclusively triads, mostly the tonic C major but also the subdominant F major in measures 1 and 5 and the dominant G major in measures 4 and 7. The only place where the left hand doesn't present triads is the last beat of measure 6, where it jumps down to the low C and works its way up the scale through the first beat of measure 7.

Now focus on the right hand's melody and think about how it relates to accompaniment. Notice how Mozart starts with a little five-note musical idea, or *motive*, and builds his melody around it. Also notice that almost all the notes of the melody belong to the triads being expressed down below. The most dramatic moment in the excerpt is the third beat of measure 6, where the melody leaps up just as the accompaniment jumps down, and new rhythms in the right hand propel the music forward to the ending.

After you've become thoroughly familiar with Mozart's melody and accompaniment, think about other ways of presenting the same or similar ideas. Improvise different accompaniment patterns for these same triads in support of the melody. After you find one you like, write it down.

Also try writing a new melody to go with this same accompaniment. Build your melody around a motive, as Mozart did, but use rhythms that are very different from those in Mozart's melody. Give your melody the same structure as Mozart's—two four-measure phrases with identical beginnings. Find your own ways of heightening the musical drama at the end of measure 6.

LESSON 23
TRIADS IN MINOR KEYS

23.1 TRIAD FORMATIONS USING MINOR SCALES

Here again are the triads we can form using notes of the F major scale, which we studied in Lesson 22:

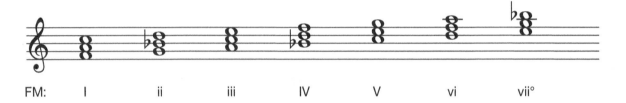

FM: I   ii   iii   IV   V   vi   vii°

In this key and in any major key, the triads rooted on $\hat{1}$, $\hat{4}$, and $\hat{5}$ are major quality, the triads built on $\hat{2}$, $\hat{3}$, and $\hat{6}$ are minor quality, and the triad on $\hat{7}$ is diminished.

Now let's think about the triads we can form from notes of the minor scale. We're already familiar with important differences between major and minor, such as the qualities of the triads rooted on $\hat{1}$. Think about the parallel minor, F minor, for example. The triad rooted on $\hat{1}$ in F minor is the minor triad F–A♭–C, by contrast with the triad rooted on $\hat{1}$ F–A♮–C in F major. To recognize the difference in a Roman numeral label, change to the lowercase ("I" in major, "i" in minor).

Rather than focusing on *parallel* major and minor, however, let's consider *relative* keys. If relative major and minor scales are simply different orderings of the same notes, then the triad inventories for relative major and minor are different orderings of the same triads. We can take the triads of F major, for example, and just re-label them with different Roman numerals to show how they would appear in the relative key, D minor:

FM: I   ii   iii   IV   V   vi   vii°

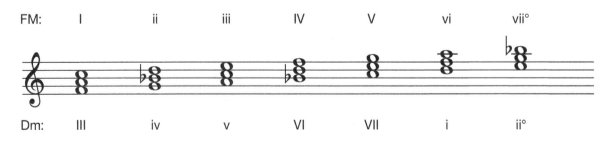

Dm: III   iv   v   VI   VII   i   ii°

316

Because scale degree $\hat{1}$ in the F major scale is the same note as $\hat{3}$ in the D minor scale, the triad rooted on $\hat{1}$ of F major, F–A–C, is identical to the triad rooted on $\hat{3}$ of D minor; FM: I = Dm: III. The triad rooted on $\hat{2}$ of F major, G–B♭–D, is identical to the triad rooted on $\hat{4}$ of D minor; FM: ii = Dm: iv. And so forth. Here are those same triads reordered to start with the D minor i chord:

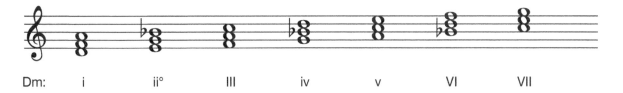

Dm: i   ii°   III   iv   v   VI   VII

Notice the triad qualities. The triads rooted on $\hat{1}$, $\hat{4}$, and $\hat{5}$ are minor, the triads rooted on $\hat{3}$, $\hat{6}$, and $\hat{7}$ are major, and the triad rooted on $\hat{2}$ is diminished. This is true not just in D minor but in any minor key. Here, for example, is the triad inventory for B minor:

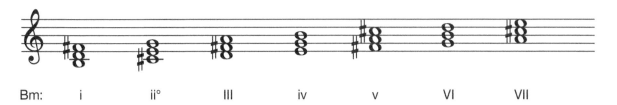

Bm: i   ii°   III   iv   v   VI   VII

Now let's go back to comparing a minor key and its *parallel* major. D major and minor, for example:

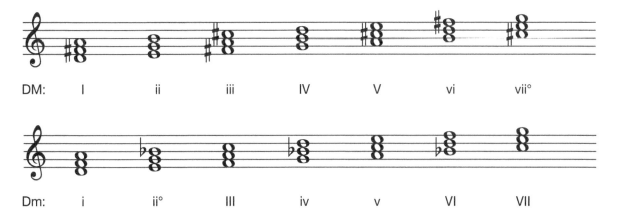

DM: I   ii   iii   IV   V   vi   vii°

Dm: i   ii°   III   iv   v   VI   VII

Compare the triad qualities on each scale degree: each one is different. The triad rooted on $\hat{1}$ is major quality in a major key and minor quality in a minor key; the triad rooted on $\hat{2}$ is minor quality in a major key and diminished quality in a minor key; the triad rooted on $\hat{3}$ is minor quality in a major key and major quality in a minor key; and so forth. This is a big reason that music in minor keys sounds different from music in major keys, even though both use the same collection of triads—three major, three minor, and one diminished.

23.2 ADDITIONAL CONSIDERATIONS FOR MINOR

On the other hand, you may be wondering, what about the *forms* of minor? We learned in Lesson 13 that the natural minor scale is often converted to the harmonic form by raising $\hat{7}$, and to the melodic form by raising $\hat{6}$ and $\hat{7}$:

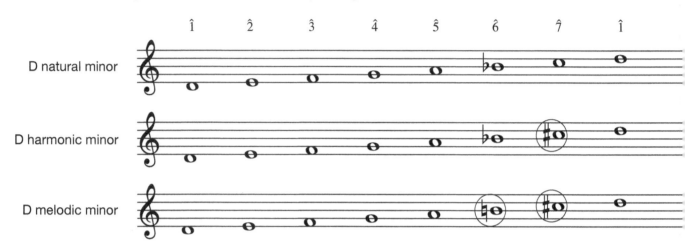

If we're forming triads from scale degrees, and then we alter one or two of those scale degrees, doesn't that affect the qualities of some of the triads?

Yes, it does, although the new qualities aren't all equally important in common musical practice. The raised $\hat{6}$ in melodic minor, for example, is usually a feature of a melody that doesn't have a big impact on chord formations—that's why it's called *melodic* minor. For this reason, we're going to focus only on a couple of cases where the quality differences resulting from harmonic minor are widely found.

The first instance concerns the triad rooted on $\hat{5}$. Suppose, for example, that we're building a triad rooted on this scale degree in D minor, which combines scale degrees $\hat{5}$, $\hat{7}$, and $\hat{2}$. If we're taking those tones from the natural form of the scale, the triad is spelled A–C–E, but if we're taking those tones from the harmonic form, the notes are A–C♯–E:

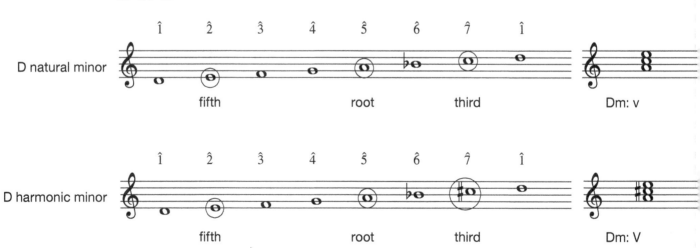

Combining $\hat{5}$, $\hat{7}$, and $\hat{2}$ from the natural form, we've built a minor triad, indicated with a lowercase "v," but combining those same scale degrees from the harmonic form, we've built a major triad, indicated with an uppercase "V."

Composers throughout musical history, writing music in diverse styles, have often made this change when writing music in minor keys, preferring major quality over minor for triads rooted on $\hat{5}$. Here's an example from a piano piece by Robert Schumann:

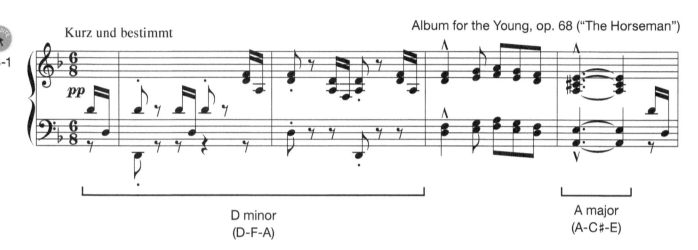

Kurz und bestimmt

Album for the Young, op. 68 ("The Horseman")

23-1

pp

D minor
(D-F-A)

A major
(A-C♯-E)

Evoking the spirit and energy of the "hunt," and the musical tradition of the hunting horns, the music begins with galloping rhythms that gradually introduce the notes of the D minor triad, the primary chord of the key. But when the harmony changes to a triad rooted on A in measure 4, Schumann raises the third to create a major triad. This is the triad rooted on $\hat{5}$, which includes as its third the raised seventh scale degree of the harmonic minor scale.

The other important quality change involving the forms of minor is the triad rooted on $\hat{7}$, which is constructed of scale degrees $\hat{7}$, $\hat{2}$, and $\hat{4}$. If we're taking those scale tones from the natural form of the D minor scale, the triad is spelled C–E–G, but if we're taking those scale tones from the harmonic form, the notes are C♯–E–G:

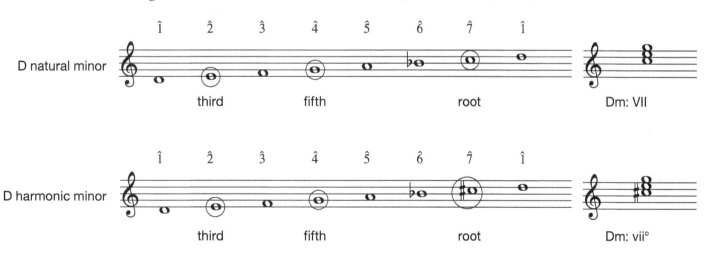

D natural minor

$\hat{1}$ $\hat{2}$ $\hat{3}$ $\hat{4}$ $\hat{5}$ $\hat{6}$ $\hat{7}$ $\hat{1}$

third   fifth   root   Dm: VII

D harmonic minor

$\hat{1}$ $\hat{2}$ $\hat{3}$ $\hat{4}$ $\hat{5}$ $\hat{6}$ $\hat{7}$ $\hat{1}$

third   fifth   root   Dm: vii°

Combining scale tones from the natural form, we've built a major triad, indicated with an uppercase "VII," but combining scale tones from the harmonic form, we've built a diminished triad, indicated by "vii°." Both VII and vii° are commonly used by composers in diverse styles, although usually for different purposes within harmonic progressions.

There is one other triad that includes $\hat{7}$, the triad rooted on $\hat{3}$, but we don't need to concern ourselves with the potential impact of the altered $\hat{7}$ on this triad. Composers usually build triads on $\hat{3}$ in minor keys from the natural form of the scale. The III chord usually stays as it is, as a major triad.

So, to sum up the triad possibilities for music in a minor key, we'll need to account for the variability of scale degree $\hat{7}$ by recognizing two possible qualities for the triad rooted on $\hat{5}$ (v or V), and two for the triad rooted on $\hat{7}$ (VII or vii°). In D minor, for example:

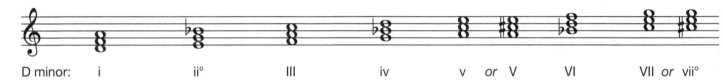

D minor: i   ii°   III   iv   v or V   VI   VII or vii°

The added accidental that converts v to V and VII to vii° must be notated on the staff whenever needed, as in measure 4 of Schumann's piano piece above. It's not something you can add to the key signature. Anytime you write a V or vii° chord in a minor key, you'll need to remember to add the accidental (usually a sharp sign or natural sign, possibly a double sharp) within the staff.

Or if you're studying music in a minor key, you'll have to be likewise attentive to the quality of the triads rooted on $\hat{5}$ and $\hat{7}$. When you encounter a triad rooted on one of these scale degrees, you don't know how to write the label for it until you've listened to it carefully and identified its quality. Visually, look for the altered $\hat{7}$, the accidental that changes v to V and VII to vii°.

The variable qualities of triads rooted on $\hat{5}$ and $\hat{7}$ also affect their names. The name "dominant" is usually applied to the major form of the triad rooted on $\hat{5}$ (V); the minor version (v) is known as the **minor dominant**. The name for the triad rooted on $\hat{7}$ varies along with the scale tone itself (Lesson 11.1): "subtonic" for the triad in the natural form of the scale (VII), and "leading tone" for the triad in the harmonic form (vii°). All the other names are the same as major (Lesson 22.3):

i	tonic
ii°	supertonic
III	mediant
iv	subdominant
v	minor dominant
V	dominant
VI	submediant
VII	subtonic
vii°	leading tone

 For suggestions for further listening and online exercises and drills, go to www.oup.com/us/lambert

STUDY QUESTIONS FOR LESSON 23

1. Define these terms:
   harmonic minor
   minor dominant
   subtonic triad

2. What are the relationships of the Roman numeral labels between relative (major and minor) keys?

3. What are the relationships of the Roman numeral labels between parallel (major and minor) keys?

4. What are the Roman numeral labels for the minor triads in a minor key?

5. What are the Roman numerals of the other triads (the ones that aren't minor) in a minor key?

6. Why does a minor key have two versions of the dominant triad?

7. Why does a minor key have both a subtonic and a leading tone triad?

► EXERCISES FOR LESSON 23

When using the *natural* minor scale to form triads, the quality of the triad rooted on $\hat{5}$ is minor (v) and the quality of the triad rooted on $\hat{7}$ is major (VII). When $\hat{7}$ is raised in the *harmonic* form of minor, however, the qualities of these triads become major (V) and diminished (vii°).

Here are the possibilities in the key of G minor, for example:

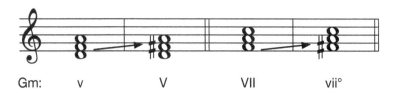

To make the change from v to V, raise the third. To make the change from VII to vii°, raise the root. The note you change is the seventh degree of the scale (F♮ in G natural minor, F♯ in G harmonic minor).

A. Notate v, V, VII, and vii° in the specified keys. Write individual sharps or flats as needed (don't use key signatures).

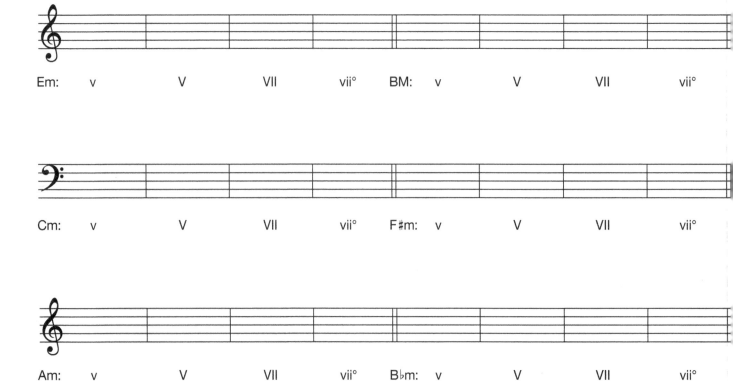

Name: _____

When you're notating triads built from scale tones of a given minor key (Lesson 23.1), remember to apply accidentals to notes that are sharped or flatted in the scale of that key. In E minor, for example, F is sharped. So when you're writing triads using notes of E minor, make sure you've placed a sharp sign in front of all Fs.

In addition, write two versions of the triads on $\hat{5}$ and $\hat{7}$ (Lesson 23.2). The case of the Roman numeral will tell you if the triad rooted on $\hat{5}$ is minor (v) or major (V), and whether the triad rooted on $\hat{7}$ is major (VII) or diminished (vii°).

B. Notate all the specified triads in the keys indicated. Write individual sharps or flats as needed (don't use key signatures). The first one is done for you.

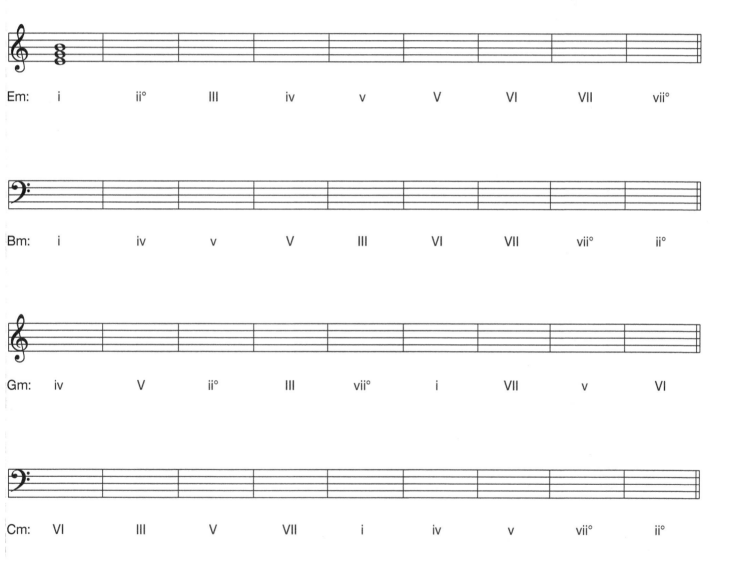

Em:　i　　ii°　　III　　iv　　v　　V　　VI　　VII　　vii°

Bm:　i　　iv　　v　　V　　III　　VI　　VII　　vii°　　ii°

Gm:　iv　　V　　ii°　　III　　vii°　　i　　VII　　v　　VI

Cm:　VI　　III　　V　　VII　　i　　iv　　v　　vii°　　ii°

Name: _____

When you encounter a triad built on $\hat{5}$ or $\hat{7}$ of a minor scale, look for the added accidental that changes its quality. This accidental is the raised seventh degree of the harmonic minor scale, which affects the third of the triad built on $\hat{5}$, and the root of the triad built on $\hat{7}$.

C. Write the Roman numeral labels for the triads in the specified keys. Remember that triads rooted on $\hat{5}$ can be either v or V, and triads rooted on $\hat{7}$ can be either VII or vii°. The first one is done for you.

Am: ___i___ _____ _____ _____ _____ _____ _____ _____

F#m: _____ _____ _____ _____ _____ _____ _____ _____

B♭m: _____ _____ _____ _____ _____ _____ _____ _____

Fm: _____ _____ _____ _____ _____ _____ _____ _____

LESSON 23: TRIADS IN MINOR KEYS

D. Notate the specified triads. Write individual sharps or flats as needed (don't use key signatures).

1. C#m: i   2. E♭m: VI   3. Am: III   4. E♭m: vii°   5. F#m: ii°   6. C#m: III   7. E♭m: iv   8. Cm: iv

9. Gm: v   10. Gm: V   11. Dm: VII   12. Dm: vii°   13. G#m: III   14. G#m: ii°   15. E♭m: VI   16. C#m: iv

17. Fm: vii°   18. B♭m: iv   19. C#m: VI   20. E♭m: i   21. D#m: V   22. C#m: ii°   23. A♭m: III   24. C#M: VII

25. Bm: ii°   26. E♭m: v   27. Fm: VII   28. Am: vii°   29. A#m: V   30. Gm: iv   31. Em: III   32. A♭m: VI

Any major or minor triad is a member of six different major or minor keys.

E. Provide Roman numeral labels for the given triads in three different major keys and three different minor keys.

1.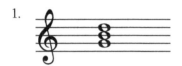

2.

major keys: ___GM: I___   _____   _____

minor keys: ___Em: III___   _____   _____

major keys: _____   _____   _____

minor keys: _____   _____   _____

❧ create!

As we did at the end of Lesson 22, let's use an excerpt adapted from a Mozart violin sonata (K. 377, second movement) as a source of inspiration:

23-2

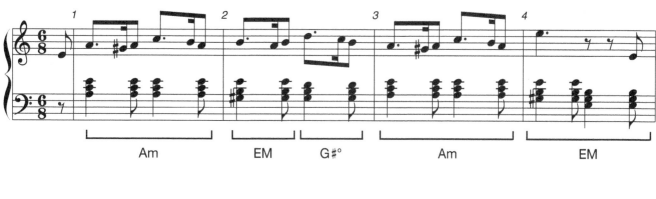

Once again the melody is clearly divided into two four-bar phrases with identical beginnings, built from a motive that appears in every measure. Look carefully at the repeating rhythms in the right hand: Every sixteenth note is surrounded by notes that are also found in the triads below, while the sixteenth notes themselves are absent from those triads.

Now look at the pattern of triads, presented in a repeating rhythm in the left hand. In the midst of all this repetition, the chord sequence in the second phrase (starting in measure 5) is actually fairly different from that of the first phrase, and this brings about some interesting cross-references. Notice, for example, that the melody is the same in measures 2 and 6 but the triads below aren't.

Also notice the distinctive features of triad formations for music in minor keys. Tonic chords are of course prominent, but each time the dominant appears (measures 2, 4, and 7), it's a major triad—its third is the raised $\hat{7}$ of harmonic minor. The chord progression also includes two diminished triads: the leading tone vii° built on the raised $\hat{7}$ in measure 2, and supertonic ii° in measure 6.

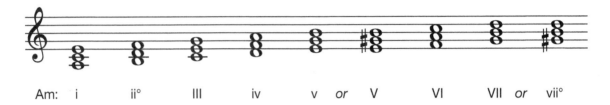

Am: i   ii°   III   iv   v *or* V   VI   VII *or* vii°

Write a different accompaniment for Mozart's melody, and then a different melody for Mozart's accompaniment.

LESSON 24
TRIAD INVERSION

24.1   THE PRINCIPLE OF CHORD INVERSION

When we looked at the first four measures of Mozart's piano sonata in Lesson 21, we noticed the C major triad in left-hand groups 1, 2, 4, 6, and 8, and the F major triad in group 5:

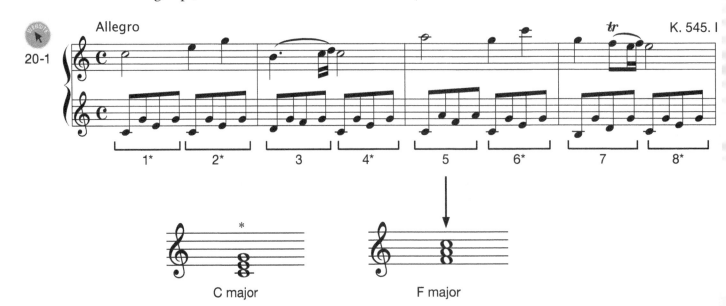

C major   F major

To make these identifications we overlooked the actual arrangements of triad tones. We made no distinction between the appearance of the tones of C major on adjacent lines in the treble clef, and the tones of F major on a line and two spaces, with its fifth, C, placed below its root and third:

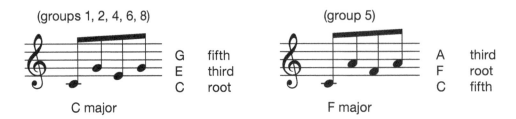

(groups 1, 2, 4, 6, 8)		(group 5)	
	G fifth		A third
	E third		F root
	C root		C fifth
C major		F major	

Now let's go back and pay closer attention to the ways the triad tones are presented. The rearrangement of the tones of the F major triad in group 5 doesn't change the chord's root and quality—the root is still F, and the quality is still major—but it does change the impact of this triad on the listener. Placing the fifth of the triad, the note C, at the bottom gives this triad a weaker, less stable sound. This affects the relations between this triad and the surrounding chords in the harmonic progression.

Placing a note other than the root at the bottom of a triad presentation is known as **inversion**. To invert a chord, shuffle its notes so that a chord tone other than the root sounds at the bottom. That's what Mozart did with the F major triad in the first half of measure 3 of his piano sonata.

24.2 FORMING AND RECOGNIZING TRIAD INVERSIONS

As we observed in Lesson 21, the designation of root and quality is something of an abstraction, stripping away details of musical presentation simply to find an idealized arrangement of notes that we call triad form. With inversion we shift our focus back to the music itself, to the way a composer uses those three notes.

Anytime we want to include a triad in a piece we're composing, or identify a triad in existing music that we're studying, we should be attentive to the possibility of inversion and sensitive to the impact of inversion on a triad's sound and function. The best way to do this is to focus on the lowest note of a given musical context—not the lowest note in triad form, which is always the root, but the lowest note in a particular musical arrangement of the tones of a triad, which could be the root, third, or fifth. What happens with the other two tones above this lowest note isn't as crucial; we need only concern ourselves with which triad tone is underneath.

A particular configuration of triad tones is its **position**. The act of inversion changes a triad's position. Because a triad has three members, it has three possible positions. When the root is lowest, it's in **root position**. When the third is lowest, its position is **1st inversion**. And when the fifth is lowest, its position is **2nd inversion**.

One easy way to derive the positions is to start with a triad in triad form and then move the root up an octave to make 1st inversion. Then convert 1st inversion to 2nd inversion by moving the third up an octave. Here's how that looks for the C major triad:

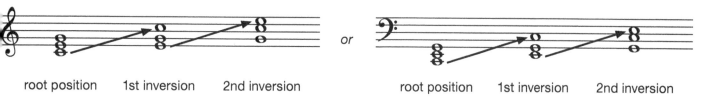

root position   1st inversion   2nd inversion   *or*   root position   1st inversion   2nd inversion

Remember, however, that the position is determined solely by the lowest note. So we could take any of these arrangements and rearrange the upper two notes without changing the triad's position. As long as we haven't changed which note is lowest, the position remains the same:

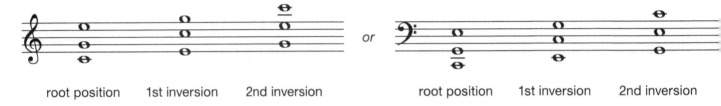

root position   1st inversion   2nd inversion   root position   1st inversion   2nd inversion

We could situate or duplicate the upper notes in any number of ways, but as long as we're not changing the lowest note, we're not altering the chord's position:

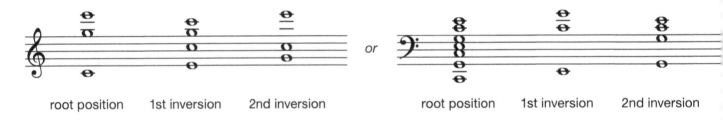

root position   1st inversion   2nd inversion   root position   1st inversion   2nd inversion

The same principles apply if we play this triad in a common piano texture, with all three notes in the right hand and either the root, third, or fifth also in the left. We can rearrange the notes any number of ways in the right hand, but as long as the left hand plays the lowest note, the left hand determines the position:

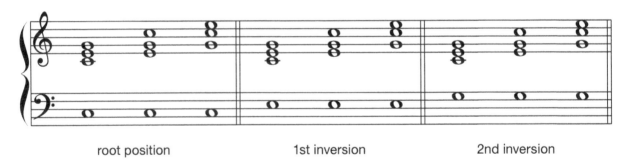

root position   1st inversion   2nd inversion

The principle of inversion can apply in abundant musical settings:

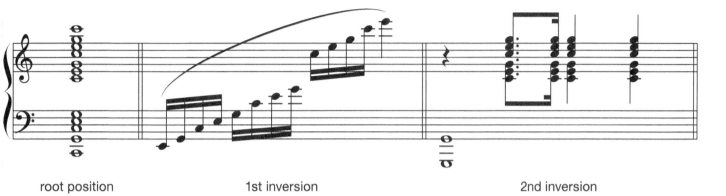

root position   1st inversion   2nd inversion

Remember that "lowest note" isn't necessarily the same as "root." The root is the note at the bottom when you notate it in triad form, on adjacent lines or adjacent spaces. The root may or may not be the lowest note in a given musical presentation. The root may be somewhere else in the texture, while the third or fifth is at the bottom.

24.3 SYMBOLIZING TRIAD INVERSIONS

To designate a triad's position in a given musical setting, we'll use numerical symbols adapted from the tradition of the **figured bass**, a system of chord notation used in music of the Baroque period (1600–1750). To see how figures work for triads, look at the intervallic distances between the lower note and the other two when the three positions are notated in close spacing. Here, for example, are the relevant distances in all three positions of the C major triad:

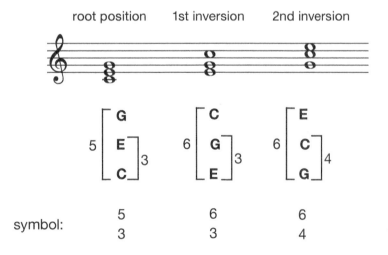

Place one of these symbols to the right of any chord label or Roman numeral to indicate its position: $^5_3$ for root position (root lowest), $^6_3$ for 1st inversion (third lowest), and $^6_4$ for 2nd inversion (fifth lowest). Here's what that looks like for the three positions of the C major triad in close spacing:

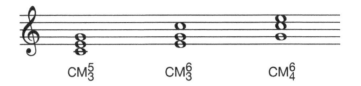

Use these same symbols anytime you want to indicate an inversion, regardless of the note spacing, simply by identifying which chord tone is lowest—root, third, or fifth:

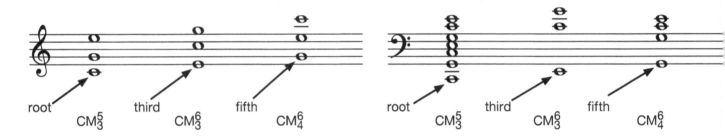

And here's how it looks if we add position labels to the Roman numerals for the version of "America" that we studied in Lessons 21.2 and 22.3:

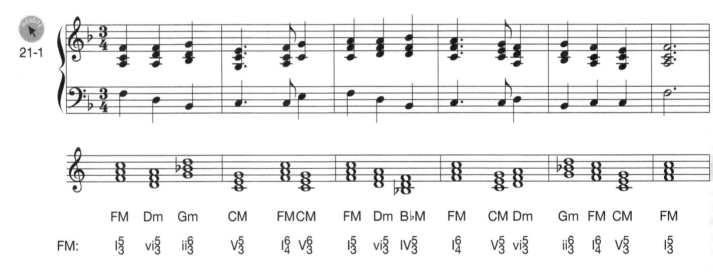

As is often the case, most of the triads are presented in root position. The tonic triads in measures 1, 3, and 6, for example, are labeled I$^5_3$ because their root (F) is the lowest sounding pitch. The three appearances of vi (in measures 1, 3, and 4) are also in root position. But the supertonic triad appears twice in 1st inversion, with the third (B♭) underneath, and so we see two instances of the label ii$^6_3$ (measures 1 and 5), and the dominant triad occurs in both root position (V$^5_3$ in measures 2, 4, and 5) and in 1st inversion (V$^6_3$ in measure 2). The only instances of 2nd inversion in the passage are the I$^6_4$ chords in measures 2, 4, and 5.

24.4   METHODOLOGY

Whether notating or identifying a triad, always start by working with it in triad form, on adjacent lines or adjacent spaces. In other words, disregard the position at first. That's what we've essentially done, for example, with the triad in group 5 of Mozart's piano sonata. We first recognized it as a way of expressing the F major triad in Lesson 21.1, without concern for its specific arrangement of tones. Using the Roman numeral notation from Lesson 22 and inversion symbols from this lesson, we can now give it its complete label:

CM: IV $^6_4$

Or suppose we want to identify this chord in a piece of music in G major:

GM: ?

First, find a way to rearrange its notes, disregarding repetitions, and notate it in triad form, on adjacent lines or adjacent spaces:

(D major)

Now that you know its root is D, you can determine its Roman numeral and position in the key of G. Because D is $\hat{5}$ in G, it's a V chord. And because its original lowest note, F♯, is the third of the D triad, the original arrangement of tones is 1st inversion, or $^6_3$ position:

GM: V $^6_3$

Similarly, suppose you have the task of notating the triad indicated by "B♭M: IV⁶₄." Start by spelling a IV chord in B♭ in triad form. In other words, at first disregard the position:

B♭M: IV

After you're sure that this chord is spelled correctly, notate it in ⁶₄ position, or 2nd inversion, with the fifth, B♭, as the lowest note. Here are four of many ways of doing that:

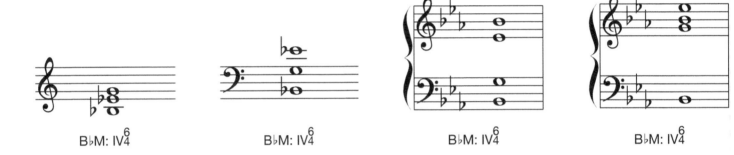

B♭M: IV⁶₄   B♭M: IV⁶₄   B♭M: IV⁶₄   B♭M: IV⁶₄

24.5   CHORAL TEXTURE

Choral texture places the notes of a chord in four different voices, the **soprano** and **alto** in the treble clef and the **tenor** and **bass** in the bass clef. Placement on the staff and stem direction (stems up for soprano and tenor, stems down for alto and bass) helps differentiate one voice part from another:

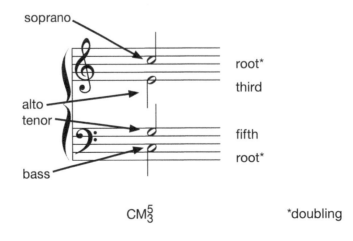

soprano   root*
third
alto
tenor   fifth
root*
bass

CM⁵₃   *doubling

To distribute the three notes of a triad among four voices, one of the triad tones will have to appear twice; this is called a **doubling**. Triads in choral texture often have a doubled root.

A **chorale** is a piece of music for chorus written entirely in choral texture. In the most basic type of chorale, all the voices move together in exactly the same rhythm, as in this phrase from a chorale by Johann Schop ("O Ewigkeit, du Donnerwort," 1642):

24-1

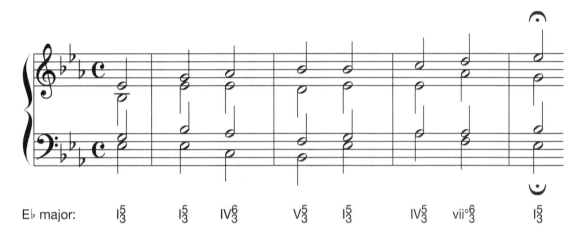

E♭ major: I⁵₃   I⁵₃   IV⁶₃   V⁵₃   I⁵₃   IV⁵₃   vii°⁶₃   I⁵₃

In more sophisticated chorales, such as those of Johann Sebastian Bach, the rhythms of the voices can be more variable and can interact in interesting ways.

 For suggestions for further listening and online exercises and drills, go to www.oup.com/us/lambert

▶ STUDY QUESTIONS FOR LESSON 24

1. **Define these terms:**
   1st inversion
   2nd inversion
   alto
   bass
   choral texture
   chorale
   doubling
   figured bass
   inversion (of a chord)
   position (of a chord)
   root position
   soprano
   tenor
   triad form

2. How is chord inversion similar to interval inversion, and how is it different?

3. Specify the lowest chord tone in:
   root-position triad
   1st inversion triad
   2nd inversion triad

4. Whenever you notate a triad in triad form, you've notated it in root position. Why is the reverse not true: why are all root position triads not necessarily in triad form?

5. What are the figured bass symbols for root position, 1st inversion, and 2nd inversion?

6. Name the indicated voice part(s) in choral texture:
   lowest voice
   highest voice
   voices in the middle
   voices notated in treble clef
   voices notated in bass clef
   voices notated with stems down
   voices notated with stems up

7. When triads are presented in choral texture, which chord tone is often doubled?

▶ EXERCISES FOR LESSON 24

A triad may be presented in three different positions (Lesson 24.3):

This position . . .	*symbolized like this . . .*	*has this chord tone at the bottom . . .*
root position	$\frac{5}{3}$	root
1st inversion	$\frac{6}{3}$	third
2nd inversion	$\frac{6}{4}$	fifth

A. <u>Step 1</u>: Arrange the given notes to form a triad and notate it in triad form (on adjacent lines or adjacent spaces) on the lower staff. <u>Step 2</u>: Specify the quality of the triad (M/m/ d/A) in the blank below. <u>Step 3</u>: Indicate the position of the triad's original presentation ($\frac{5}{3}$ or $\frac{6}{3}$ or $\frac{6}{4}$) in the blank above. The first one is done for you.

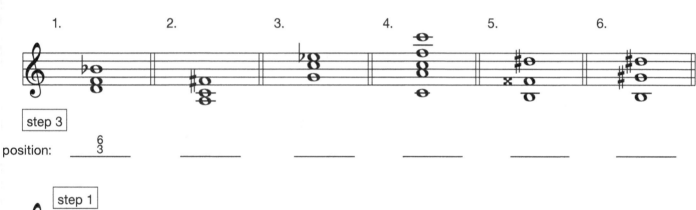

step 3

position: $\frac{6}{3}$ _____ _____ _____ _____ _____

step 1

step 2

quality: ___M___ _____ _____ _____ _____ _____

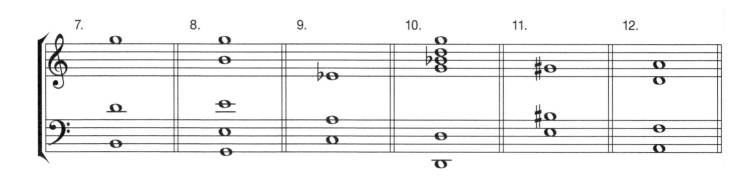

position: ___ ___ ___ ___ ___ ___

quality: ___ ___ ___ ___ ___ ___

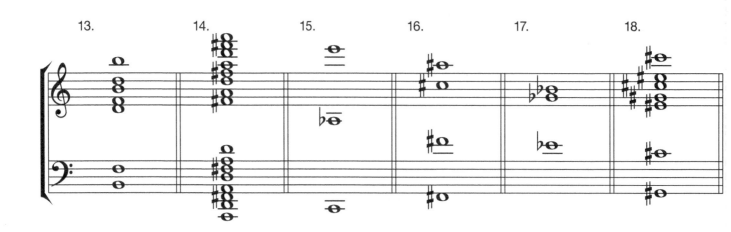

position: ___ ___ ___ ___ ___ ___

quality: ___ ___ ___ ___ ___ ___

Name: _____

A triad has three important properties: root, quality, and position. The first two can be symbolized by a Roman numeral, using scale-degree numbering to indicate the root, and case to indicate quality (Lesson 22.2). The symbol for the third element, position, is placed directly after the Roman numeral (e.g., I$^5_3$, IV$^6_4$; Lesson 24.3).

B. On the blank staff below the chorale, rewrite each chord in triad form. Use sharp signs (not a key signature) to show which notes are sharped in the scale. In the spaces below, label each chord with a Roman numeral in the key of the chorale (D major). Next to the Roman numeral, indicate the position of the triad in its original presentation ($^5_3$ or $^6_3$ or $^6_4$). The first one is done for you.

24-2

1.   2.   3.   4.   5.   6.   7.   8.   9.   10.   11.   12.   13.   14.   15.   16.

1. _____ I$^5_3$ _____   5. _____   9. _____   13. _____

2. _____   6. _____   10. _____   14. _____

3. _____   7. _____   11. _____   15. _____

4. _____   8. _____   12. _____   16. _____

C. On the blank staff below the score, rewrite each numbered chord in triad form. Use flat signs (not a key signature) to show which notes are flatted in the scale. In the spaces below, label each chord with a Roman numeral in the key of F major. Next to the Roman numeral, indicate the position of the triad in its original presentation ($\frac{5}{3}$ or $\frac{6}{3}$ or $\frac{6}{4}$).

24-3

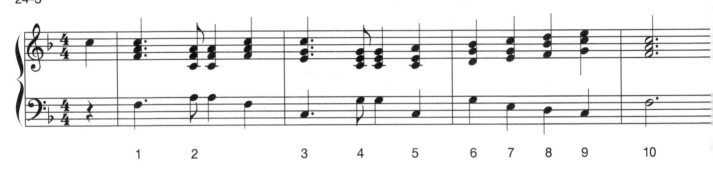

1. _____   2. _____   3. _____   4. _____   5. _____

6. _____   7. _____   8. _____   9. _____   10. _____

The position of a chord is determined by its lowest chord tone, regardless of the spacing or arrangement of the other chord tones above.

D. Write the specified triad in triad form on the treble clef staff. Then write a single note in the bass clef staff to produce a four-note chord of the indicated position. The first one is done for you.

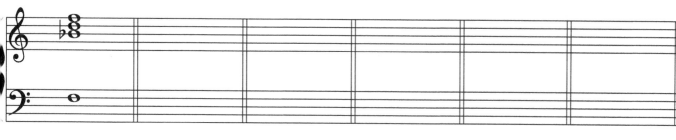

1. B♭M $\frac{6}{4}$ 2. Fm $\frac{5}{3}$ 3. D° $\frac{6}{3}$ 4. B° $\frac{6}{4}$ 5. F+ $\frac{5}{3}$ 6. Bm $\frac{6}{4}$

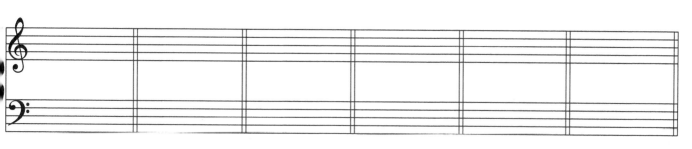

7. AM $\frac{6}{3}$ 8. G♭+ $\frac{6}{3}$ 9. C#° $\frac{6}{4}$ 10. A♭M $\frac{5}{3}$ 11. F#m $\frac{6}{4}$ 12. E° $\frac{6}{3}$

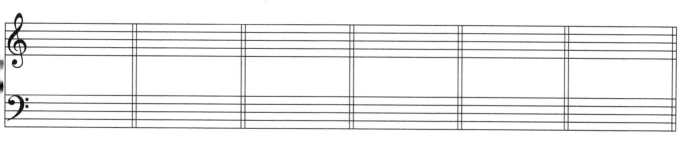

13. D♭M $\frac{5}{3}$ 14. Cm $\frac{6}{4}$ 15. G#° $\frac{6}{3}$ 16. A+ $\frac{6}{4}$ 17. G° $\frac{5}{3}$ 18. E♭° $\frac{6}{4}$

Name: _____

In chords 19–36, use individual accidentals, not a key signature, for notes that are sharped or flatted in the specified key.

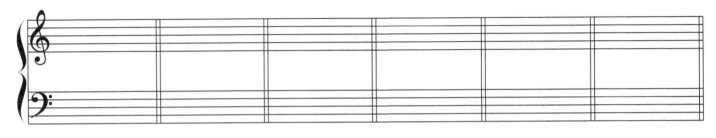

19. CM: I $\frac{5}{3}$ 20. CM: I $\frac{6}{3}$ 21. FM: V $\frac{6}{4}$ 22. AM: IV $\frac{5}{3}$ 23. F♯m: VI $\frac{6}{4}$ 24. Bm: III $\frac{6}{3}$

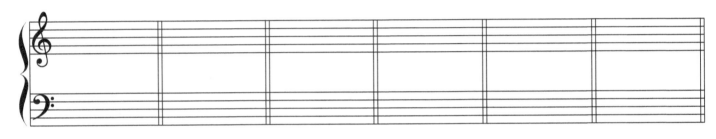

25. EM: vii° $\frac{6}{3}$ 26. A♭M: ii $\frac{5}{3}$ 27. B♭M: iii $\frac{6}{4}$ 28. DM: vi $\frac{6}{3}$ 29. F♯M: I $\frac{6}{4}$ 30. E♭m: III $\frac{6}{3}$

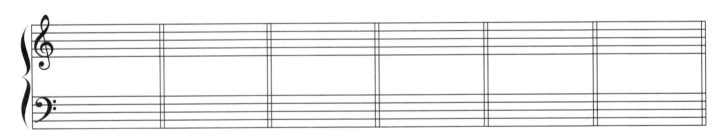

31. Am: v $\frac{5}{3}$ 32. Am: V $\frac{6}{3}$ 33. Gm: ii° $\frac{6}{4}$ 34. D♭M: IV $\frac{5}{3}$ 35. Em: VII $\frac{5}{3}$ 36. Em: vii° $\frac{6}{4}$

✍ create!

In *keyboard texture*, your right hand plays all three notes of a triad in close spacing while your left hand plays one of them (and thus duplicates one of the notes being played by the right hand). Play different triads in keyboard texture, always playing the root with your left hand. Rearrange the notes differently in your right hand, but always keep the root in your left hand. For example, here are some different ways of playing the C major triad in keyboard texture with the root in the left hand:

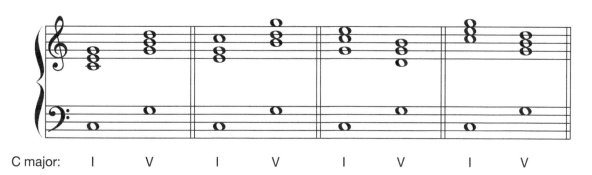

To play one chord after another in keyboard texture, minimize the movements of your hands. If you have a common tone between two consecutive chords, play it again with the same finger. For example, if you are playing I to V in C major, always playing roots in your left hand, *don't* do something like this:

C major: I   V   I   V   I   V   I   V

Instead, connect the right-hand chords with minimal finger movements:

C major: I   V   I   V   I   V   I   V

Big leaps are inevitable between chord roots in your left hand, as long as you're playing both chords in root position.

Whenever possible, move your hands in opposite directions. These two versions of I–V in C major, for example, are both fairly smooth . . .

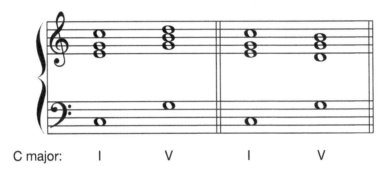

C major: I   V   I   V

. . . but the second one is preferable because the hands move in opposite directions. It also places the common tone (G) in the middle of both right-hand chords.

Play I–V–I in various major keys. Structure each chord in keyboard texture, with the root in your left hand. Make chord connections as smooth as possible and move your hands in opposite directions as much as possible.

Do the same with I–IV–V–I. For example, here's what that progression might look like in C major:

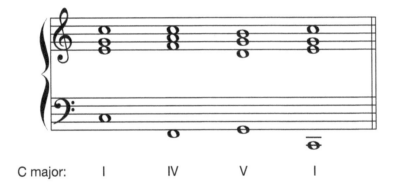

C major: I   IV   V   I

Invent your own chord progressions and play them in keyboard texture. Use progressions found in musical examples elsewhere in this book as points of departure. Try different major or minor keys. Try switching a progression to its parallel mode. Try progressions that sound similar to music you know, and progressions that sound fresh and original.

LESSON **25**
DOMINANT SEVENTH CHORDS

25.1   ENRICHING TRIADS

In earlier lessons we found a lot to discover in the first six measures of "America." Now let's jump ahead to the ending. Here's how triads could be used to support the final patriotic exultation:

By rearranging the notes of the music into triad form, we can see each melody note is supported by some configuration of the notes of a triad, either the I, IV, or V.

Now listen to the difference if we make one small change in the penultimate chord. Instead of C-E-G in the right hand for the second syllable in "freedom," B♭-E-C:

25-2

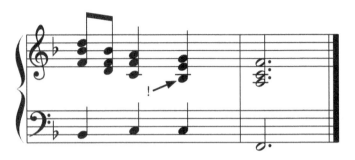

Adding the B♭ introduces dissonance into the chord. The B♭ is the upper note of a dissonant minor seventh with the C down below, and the lower note of a dissonant augmented fourth with the E above:

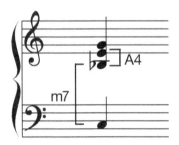

This makes a subtle difference in the character of the sound, gives it a little extra richness. It also introduces a strong expectation that the dissonance will soon disappear—will be *resolved*—when this dominant chord progresses to the tonic chord that follows.

Let's examine this new chord. We begin by taking all the notes in the chord, from both hands, and rearranging them on a single staff, just as we've been doing with triads (Lesson 21). The new note, the B♭, adds another note on top of the C major triad when notated in triad form, extending it to the next line or space above:

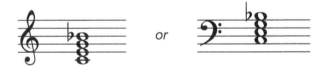

Because the additional note lies a seventh above the root, the entire sonority is known as a **seventh chord**. The new chord tone is known as the "seventh"; the other three tones are still called the root, third, and fifth.

Don't confuse this instance of the word "seventh" with other uses of this word or number, such as "seventh degree of the scale." The phrase "seventh of the chord" or "chord seventh" *doesn't* refer to a specific key, just to a specific note at the top of a chord. "Seventh scale degree" *does* refer to a specific key, and may or may not have relevance to a specific chord.

In a seventh chord, the seventh adds another third on top of a triad. And like a triad, the four notes of any seventh chord can be notated on adjacent lines or adjacent spaces, represented by alternate letters in the musical alphabet. We've already learned the seven three-letter combinations for triads (Lesson 20.2); now we have seven *four-letter* combinations for seventh chords:

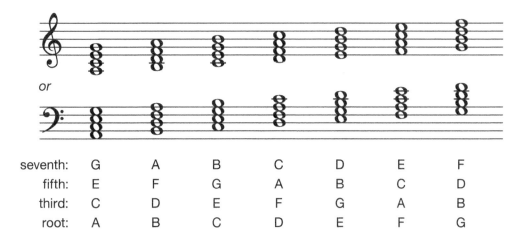

seventh:	G	A	B	C	D	E	F
fifth:	E	F	G	A	B	C	D
third:	C	D	E	F	G	A	B
root:	A	B	C	D	E	F	G

We can use the **circle of thirds** to keep track of seventh-chord letter combinations, as we did with triad spellings (Lesson 21.3). Choose any letter in the circle as a root of a seventh chord and move clockwise from that root to the next three and you'll have four letters used to spell a seventh chord.

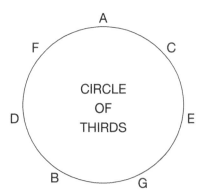

The revised ending of "America" is typical of seventh chords in harmonic practice: we added a seventh to a V chord, creating "V⁷." This is by far the most common usage for seventh chords in many styles of music. Seventh chords are certainly possible rooted on other scale degrees, but they aren't as common as the seventh chord rooted on $\hat{5}$. Because its root is the dominant in the key, it's often called the **dominant seventh**. The addition of the seventh to the dominant triad gives it stronger momentum to progress to the next chord, which is usually a triad rooted on $\hat{1}$. That's the way it works in our revised ending of "America."

25.2   PRINCIPLES OF CONSTRUCTION

Let's explore the structure of the dominant seventh chord. It's built on a major triad, and the quality of the seventh interval between bottom and top is minor:

$$
\text{MAJOR TRIAD} \left[\begin{matrix} \mathbf{B}\flat \\ \begin{matrix} \mathbf{G} \\ \mathbf{E} \\ \mathbf{C} \end{matrix} \end{matrix} \right] \text{m7 (10)}
$$

We use these two bits of information—the quality of the triad, and the quality of the seventh—to designate chord quality. Because this chord combines a *major* triad with a *minor* seventh, its quality is **major-minor**, abbreviated "Mm^7."

As a stacking of thirds, the Mm^7 is, from bottom to top, M3-m3-m3, or half-step spans 4-3-3:

$$
\begin{aligned}
\text{m3 (3)} &\left[\begin{matrix} \mathbf{B}\flat \\ \mathbf{G} \end{matrix} \right. \\
\text{m3 (3)} &\left[\begin{matrix} \mathbf{G} \\ \mathbf{E} \end{matrix} \right] \text{d5 (6)} \\
\text{M3 (4)} &\left[\begin{matrix} \mathbf{E} \\ \mathbf{C} \end{matrix} \right.
\end{aligned}
$$

You can also think of the Mm^7 chord as an overlapping of a major triad (C–E–G) with a diminished triad (E–G–B$\flat$). Later in this lesson we'll learn about other qualities of seventh chords, built on different qualities of triads and sevenths.

Perhaps the most important interval in this type of seventh chord is the diminished fifth, also known as the tritone, between the third and seventh. (At the beginning of this lesson we noticed this interval in inversion, as the B$\flat$–E augmented fourth, in the revised ending of "America.") As we learned in Lesson 18, the tritone holds a special presence within the family of intervals formable within a major scale. Of the seven scale-degree combinations that form fifths, for example, only the fifth from $\hat{7}$ up to $\hat{4}$ is diminished quality; all the others are perfect.

Now think about all the scale degrees used to form a dominant seventh chord. Here they are in F major:

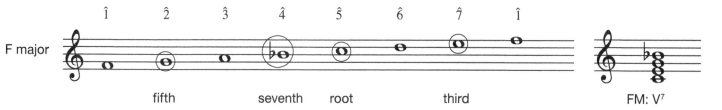

The dominant triad, formed by $\hat{5}$–$\hat{7}$–$\hat{2}$, is already a crucial chord in harmonic progressions, the primary counterpart to the tonic. With the addition of the seventh ($\hat{4}$) and the formation of the tritone between $\hat{7}$ and $\hat{4}$, it gains even greater strength and distinction. Its momentum to progress to tonic is even more powerful.

25.3 INVERSION OF SEVENTH CHORDS

Listen again to the opening of Mozart's C major piano sonata:

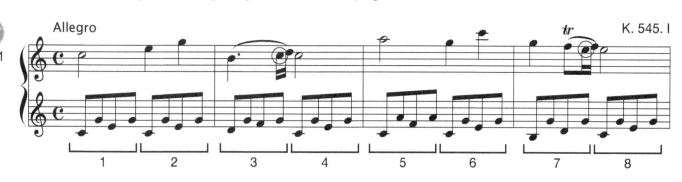

As we've seen, triads support the melody in groups 1, 2, 4, 5, 6, and 8 of the accompaniment (Lessons 20.1, 21.1). Let's turn our attention to the groups we've skipped over, 3 and 7, including all the notes in both hands except for those that are circled in the right-hand melody, which are decorative nonchord tones. In both groups, it's possible to rearrange the chord tones as dominant seventh chords, analogous to our previous rearrangements of triads (Lesson 21):

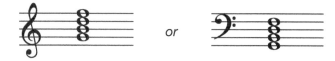

This is the G Mm[7] chord, V[7] in the key of C:

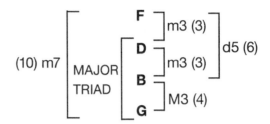

As presented in groups 3 and 7, however, the G Mm[7] chord is inverted; its root isn't the lowest sounding note. In group 3 the chord is inverted to place its fifth, D, at the bottom, and in group 7 it's inverted to place its third, B, as the lowest sounding note. These are two of the four possible positions of this chord:

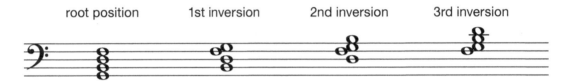

Just as with triads, root position means the root is lowest, 1st inversion means the third is lowest, and 2nd inversion means the fifth is lowest. When the seventh is lowest we'll call that **3rd inversion**.

The symbols for these positions are again based on intervallic distances (not half-step sizes!) between the lowest note and each of the others in close spacing, adapting figured bass notation:

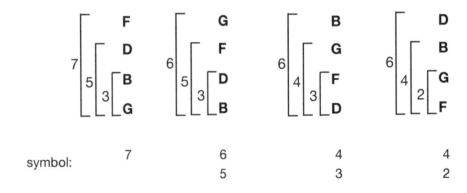

For seventh chords, however, we abbreviate. The distances from the lowest note to the others within a root position seventh chord, for example, are 7, 5, and 3, but for the symbol we use only the 7. The symbols for the other positions are similarly derived. As usual, place the symbol next to the root/quality or Roman numeral:

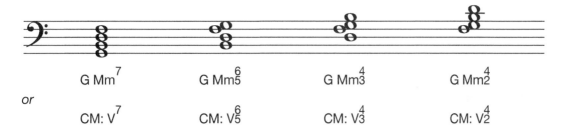

So the chords in groups 3 and 7 are properly labeled V$\overset{4}{3}$ and V$\overset{6}{5}$:

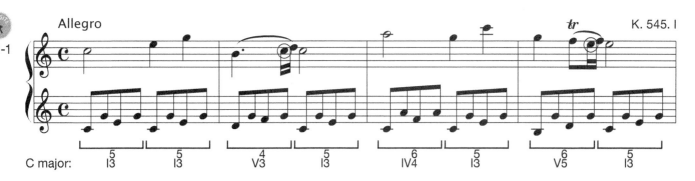

The uses of inversion in groups 3 and 7 (and for the IV chord in group 5) allow minimal finger movements from one group to the next in the left hand, in contrast with the wide-ranging melody above.

25.4   FIVE TYPES OF SEVENTH CHORDS

Let's revisit another example from a previous lesson (21.2), Schumann's *Humoreske*:

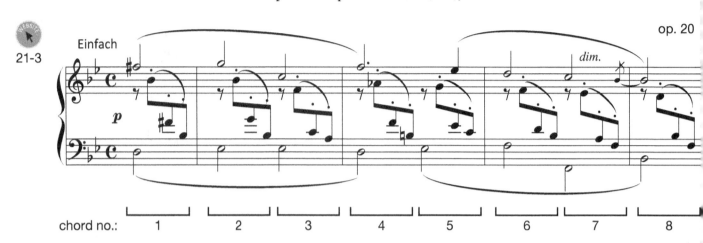

Two of the chords we skipped over when we looked at this excerpt in Lesson 21.2, numbered 3 and 7, are different positions of the dominant seventh chord in the key of B♭:

Chord 3 is 3rd inversion and chord 7 is root position of this Mm^7 chord.

The other chord we haven't yet looked at, chord 4, is a seventh chord of a different quality, which we can identify, as usual, by rearranging the notes to appear on adjacent lines or adjacent spaces:

In this type both the triad and the seventh are diminished:

(9) d7 — dim. triad: B, D, F, A♭ with m3 (3) intervals

Because it's based on a diminished triad, it's called a **diminished seventh chord**. Because the seventh is also diminished, its complete name is **fully diminished**, by contrast with another type that's based on a diminished triad plus m7, known as **half-diminished**:

```
                      A ┐
                        ┤ M3 (4)
                      F ┘
(10) m7 ┌ dim. ┌        ┐
        │ triad │      D ┤ m3 (3)
        │       │        ┘
        │       │      B ┐
        └       └        ┘ m3 (3)
```

In all there are five common qualities of seventh chords, including the dominant seventh and two diminished types. Here's a notation of all of them rooted on E:

quality	m	M	m	M	m
of thirds:	m	m	M	m	m
	M	M	m	m	m
half-step	3	4	3	4	3
spans:	3	3	4	3	3
	4	4	3	3	3
sevenths:	m	M	m	m	d
triads:	M	M	m	d	d
quality:	Mm	MM	mm	half-diminished	fully diminished

The first two are based on major triads, only the third one is based on the minor triad, and the last two are both based on diminished triads. Other combinations of a triad and a seventh are possible (for example, minor triad plus major seventh), but uncommon.

In the American popular tradition, it's also common to stack other notes above triads, in addition to (or instead of) sevenths. The added note can be indicated as a superscript, just as it is for seventh chords. It's also common to add notes with half-step alterations, such as "$D^{7\flat 9}$." As long as you have a solid understanding of intervals and triads, it's usually pretty easy to figure out what the symbols indicate.

 For suggestions for further listening and online exercises and drills, go to www.oup.com/us/lambert

▶ STUDY QUESTIONS FOR LESSON 25

1. Define these terms:
    3rd inversion
    circle of thirds
    dominant seventh chord
    fully diminished seventh chord
    half-diminished seventh chord
    major-minor seventh chord
    seventh chord

2. What are the names of the chord tones in a seventh chord?

3. What do all types of seventh chords have in common?

4. What scale degrees are used to spell a dominant seventh chord?

5. What are the seven four-letter combinations used to spell seventh chords?

6. How can the circle of thirds help with seventh-chord spellings?

7. Specify the lowest chord tone in:
    root-position seventh chord
    1st-inversion seventh chord
    2nd-inversion seventh chord
    3rd-inversion seventh chord

8. What are the figured bass symbols for the four positions of a seventh chord?

EXERCISES FOR LESSON 25

To write all four positions of a seventh chord, start with root position $\binom{7}{}$ and move the root to the top to make 1st inversion $\binom{6}{5}$. Then move the new low note up to create 2nd inversion $\binom{4}{3}$. Perform the same procedure one more time to make 3rd inversion $\binom{4}{2}$.

In minor keys, an upper case "V^7" indicates a dominant seventh chord based on a major-quality triad, using the raised $\hat{7}$ of harmonic minor:

A. Notate the specified dominant seventh chords in root position, 1st inversion, 2nd inversion, and 3rd inversion, all in close spacing. Use accidentals as needed (don't use key signatures).

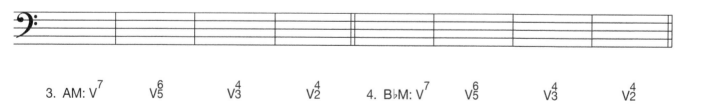

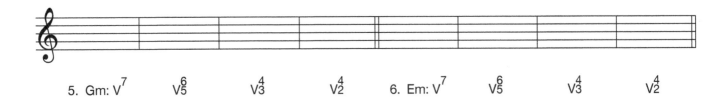

5. Gm: V^7 V$^6_5$ V$^4_3$ V$^4_2$ 6. Em: V^7 V$^6_5$ V$^4_3$ V$^4_2$

When identifying or spelling seventh chords, use the same procedure we used for triads (Lesson 21). At first disregard the position and renotate the chord on adjacent lines or adjacent spaces. After you're sure you've found the root, then focus on the position.

B. Step 1: Arrange the given notes to form a dominant seventh chord and notate it in root position, on adjacent lines or adjacent spaces, on the lower staff. Step 2: In the blank below, specify the key in which each chord would be labeled V^7. Step 3: In the blank above, indicate the chord's position (^{7} or $^6_5$ or $^4_3$ or $^4_2$). The first one is done for you.

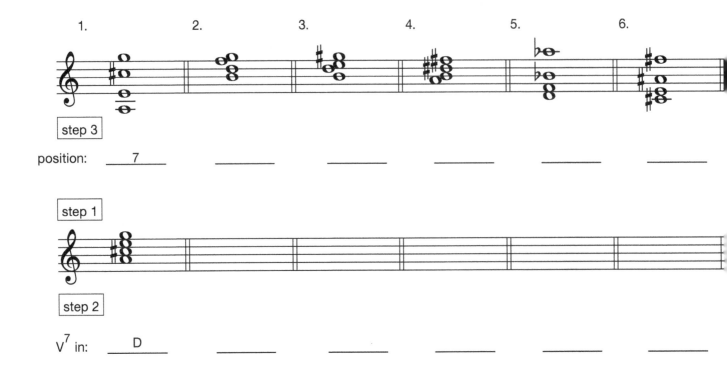

step 3

position: 7   _____   _____   _____   _____   _____

step 1

step 2

V^7 in: D   _____   _____   _____   _____   _____

7.   8.   9.   10.   11.   12.

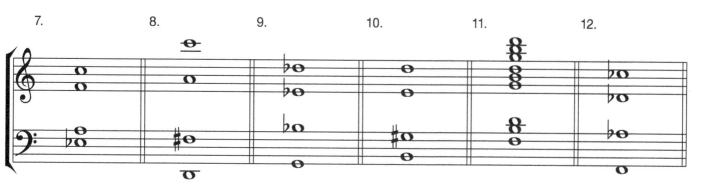

sition: _____   _____   _____   _____   _____   _____

V⁷ in: _____   _____   _____   _____   _____   _____

13.   14.   15.   16.   17.   18.

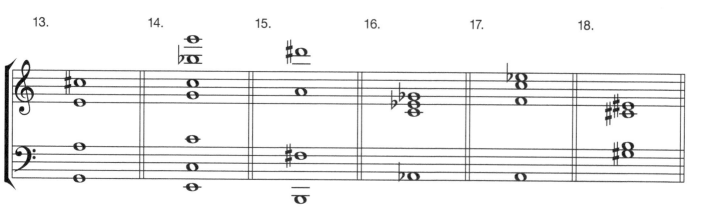

sition: _____   _____   _____   _____   _____   _____

V⁷ in: _____   _____   _____   _____   _____   _____

Symbolize inversions of seventh chords following the same procedure you use for inversions of triads, by placing the numerical position label directly after the Roman numeral (Lesson 25.3).

C. On the blank staff below the chorale, rewrite each chord as a triad or seventh chord in closely spaced root position (on adjacent lines or adjacent spaces). Use flat signs (not key signatures) to show flatted notes in the scale. In the spaces below, label each chord with a Roman numeral in the key of the chorale (F major). Next to the Roman numeral, indicate the position of the chord in its original presentation ($\frac{5}{3}$ or $\frac{6}{3}$ or $\frac{6}{4}$ or ^{7} or $\frac{6}{5}$ or $\frac{4}{3}$ or $\frac{4}{2}$). The first one is done for you.

25-3

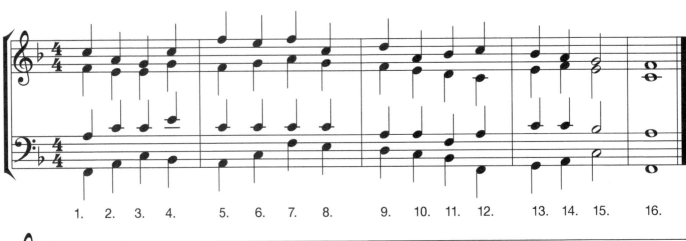

1. 2. 3. 4.   5. 6. 7. 8.   9. 10. 11. 12.   13. 14. 15.   16.

1. _____$\frac{5}{13}$_____   5. _____   9. _____   13. _____

2. _____   6. _____   10. _____   14. _____

3. _____   7. _____   11. _____   15. _____

4. _____   8. _____   12. _____   16. _____

D. On the blank staff below the score, rewrite each chord on adjacent lines or adjacent spaces. Use sharp signs (not a key signature) to show which notes are sharped in the scale. Immediately above your notations, label each original chord with a Roman numeral in the key of G major. Next to the Roman numeral, indicate the position of the chord in its original presentation $\left(\begin{smallmatrix}5\\3\end{smallmatrix}\text{ or }\begin{smallmatrix}6\\3\end{smallmatrix}\text{ or }\begin{smallmatrix}6\\4\end{smallmatrix}\text{ or }^7\text{ or }\begin{smallmatrix}6\\5\end{smallmatrix}\text{ or }\begin{smallmatrix}4\\3\end{smallmatrix}\text{ or }\begin{smallmatrix}4\\2\end{smallmatrix}\right)$**. The first two are done for you.**

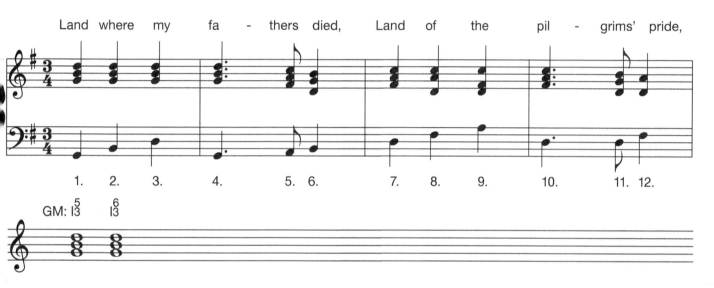

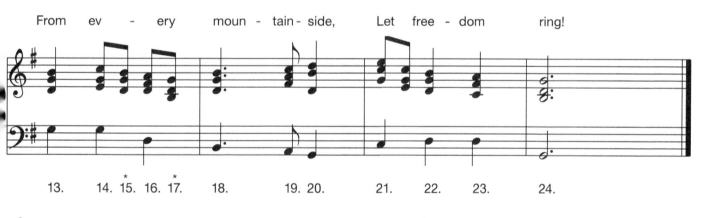

*Chord 15 shares a bass note with chord 14 (G), and chord 17 shares a bass note (D) with chord 16. Be sure to include those shared bass notes when you determine the position of chords 15 and 17.

Name: _____

A seventh chord may be presented in four different positions (Lesson 25.3):

position:	root position	1st inversion	2nd inversion	3rd inversion
symbol:	7	$^6_5$	$^4_3$	$^4_2$
bottom note:	root	third	fifth	seventh

E. <u>Step 1</u>: Notate the given chord in root position, close spacing (on adjacent lines or adjacent spaces) on the top staff. <u>Step 2</u>: Notate that same chord on the grand staff, with one note in the bass clef and three in the treble. Use the position label $\left(^7 \text{ or } ^6_5 \text{ or } ^4_3 \text{ or } ^4_2\right)$ to determine which note goes in the bass clef. The first one is done for you.

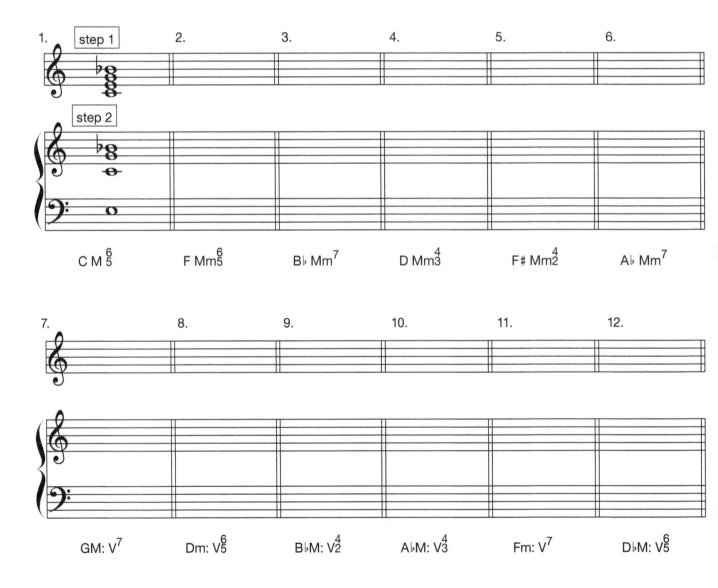

1. step 1   2.   3.   4.   5.   6.

step 2

C M $^6_5$ F Mm$^6_5$ B♭ Mm^7 D Mm$^4_3$ F# Mm$^4_2$ A♭ Mm^7

7.   8.   9.   10.   11.   12.

GM: V^7 Dm: V$^6_5$ B♭M: V$^4_2$ A♭M: V$^4_3$ Fm: V^7 D♭M: V$^6_5$

✍ create!

Some music is notated in *lead sheet* format, which is just a single melody and chord symbols. Here, for example, is what a lead sheet might look like for "Happy Birthday":

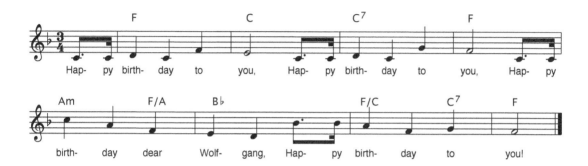

You can probably guess what the chord symbols mean. A single uppercase letter indicates a root-position major triad. Upper case plus "m" indicates root-position minor. The superscripted "7" indicates a root-position seventh chord. The slash notation indicates chord inversion: The letter after the slash is the bass note (so "F/A" indicates F major with A in the bass, also known as 1st inversion).

Try singing "Happy Birthday" while you play the indicated chords on piano or guitar.

In jazz and show tunes the chord symbols can include other notations, as shown in the piano-vocal score for Ballad (Fifteen Character Pieces, www.oup.com/us/lambert). For example, "Gmaj9" indicates a G major seventh chord (Lesson 25.4) plus a major ninth above the root (G–B–D–F♯–A). The symbol "D9" indicates a dominant seventh chord on D plus a major ninth above the root (D–F♯–A–C–E). The notation "sus4" indicates the addition of a fourth above the root displacing the third ("D9sus4" = D–G–A–C–E). Gadd6 indicates the G major triad plus an added sixth above the root (G–B–D–E). And so forth.

Try writing some melodies of your own and notate them in lead sheet format. Start with something simple like "Happy Birthday." As you work out the notes of the melody, work out the chords that go with them. Figure out how you would play your melodies and chords on piano or guitar, or how you would play only the chords to accompany a singer.

After you've tried writing some simple melodies, try following more sophisticated models, like a pop song or show tune you like (or Ballad). One possibility is to focus your creative energies on the chords and rhythms of the accompaniment and then write a melody. But you might also start by writing a melody (and lyric?) that is so catchy and inventive, it doesn't need a flashy accompaniment—in fact, it's best supported by chords and rhythms that are spare and unobtrusive. Ultimately, if you like the way your song sounds, it's because you've fashioned a melody and accompaniment that relate in perfect interplay.

LESSON 26
MUSIC IN MOTION

26.1   COMPOSERS AND PERFORMERS

When you get to know a piece of music really well, it becomes a part of you. It breathes with you, grows with you, helps shape your perceptions and sensibilities. You mold it with your personality and feelings, and it reciprocates. The notes written on the page become less and less important, more and more like starting points for discovery. What you play or sing—the actual "music" floating through the air—can't actually be represented on five lines and four spaces. It's too personal, too ineffable.

The chain of communication from composer-notator to performer to listener has always offered artistically productive challenges. A tempo, or the shaping of a melody, or the interpretation of a poetic text, can be widely variable from one performer to another, and may even vary from one performance to the next by the same musician. Composers customarily prepare their scores with great care and precision, but unless they're doing all the performing themselves, they're just one part of the artistic process.

The contributions of the performer are more overtly felt in some cultural traditions than in others. Music in many cultures is learned by imitation and oral transmission and never notated at all. The art of improvisation, in its infinite variety in music all over the world, may be completely performer-driven or may be structured by some sort of creative source, perhaps a composer, perhaps just a leader or a collective. Ultimately, unless we're trying to assign legal shares, or royalty claims, or bragging rights, it doesn't really matter; we don't really need to assess and explain the roles in a creative enterprise. It's all just art, just exploring the imagination.

Users of the system of musical notation we've learned in this book have various ways of addressing and accommodating these issues. Much of the music known as "jazz" exists only in the ears of listeners at the moment of its performance (and perhaps its electronic re-creation, if it's recorded), without ever being fully notated. But some notation is usually required, even if just a melody and chord symbols to use as a starting point. Scores for big-band jazz usually require more extensive notational cues. Whatever the circumstances, the notation of jazz typically expects performers to take liberties, especially with regard to rhythm.

Take a look, for example, at the customary notation of the first melodic phrase of a jazz classic, "In the Mood":

A jazz performer knows not to interpret these rhythms literally but to stretch and compress in idiomatic ways. The notes on the beats are actually played slightly longer than eighth notes, and notes off the beats are slightly shorter. The overall effect is a close approximation of what we called a "compound," or three-part, subdivision of the beat in Lesson 10. A more accurate notation of how these measures are actually performed would look more like $\frac{12}{8}$ than $\frac{4}{4}$:

This performance style is known as **swing**. Many printed scores include no specific instructions to swing the notes but just assume that performers will know not to play them straight. When specific instructions are provided, you might see the directive "swing eighths" written above the first measure, or a notation something like this:

Of course, any music *can* be swung. You can change the character of even the most solemn dirge by swinging the rhythms and perhaps speeding it up a bit. Adapters have been doing this since the beginning of jazz, looking for whole new ways to hear classics. Some of the most successful swing adaptations of traditional concert repertoire were jazz vocal versions of music by Johann Sebastian Bach made by a vocal group, the Swingle Singers, in the 1960s. Gospel musicians often take hymns conceived in straight rhythms and perform them in swung rhythms, with inspirational results.

26.2   SYNCOPATION

Another type of early jazz generally kept the eighths straight, not swung, but shifted important notes away from main beats. Pianists specializing in popular music around the turn of the twentieth century began to refer to this technique as "ragged time." To keep a very steady pulse in the left hand while playing notes at different times in the right hand was known as "ragging." Eventually a new art form emerged: **ragtime**.

Here's an example, from the main theme of Scott Joplin's "The Entertainer":

In typical fashion, the left hand establishes a very steady eighth-note pulse. The right hand, however, sometimes plays notes at the same time as the left hand but sometimes doesn't. Look at the three notes marked by asterisks in the right hand: These notes begin between left-hand pulses and then sustain through the next left-hand pulse. Rhythmically, they create a pattern of stresses in the melody that doesn't always line up with the regular eighth-note stress pattern in the accompaniment. A conflict between the stress pattern defined by the meter (here, reinforced by the left hand) and the stress pattern created by the various notated rhythms (right hand) is known as **syncopation**.

Syncopation is the defining feature of ragtime music, but it's also found in music of many other styles and eras. Here's an example from Igor Stravinsky's orchestral music for his ballet, *Firebird*:

Here the stress pattern of the meter is three beats per measure, but notice how often the notes of the melody don't coincide with beats. In fact, only two notes in the excerpt—the last note of measure 2, and the last note of measure 4—*do* occur on beats. The stress pattern of the melody is almost entirely at odds with the quarter-note beats. The melody is almost entirely syncopated.

And here's one more example of syncopation, from a piano sonata by Mozart:

26-3

In this case the stress pattern of the meter, three quarter-note beats per measure, is strongly affirmed by the two lower lines moving stepwise down the scale in parallel tenths. But the stress pattern of the upper line, the stems-up notes in the treble clef, is constantly off the beat, consistently syncopated. It gives the impression that it's lagging behind the lower parts, constantly trying but failing to catch up. Notice what happens if we shift the upper melody back by one eighth note, so that it does line up:

26-4

It's a series of first inversion triads. Here they are in triad form:

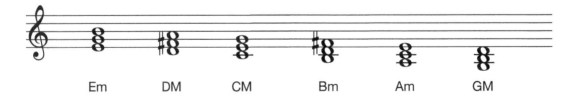

Mozart's syncopated upper line continually delays the formation of the triads. What we hear instead on each quarter-note beat is a dissonance created when the interval of a seventh is formed between the top and bottom notes. Each time the melody moves down a step, from a seventh to a triad member, an accented dissonance gives way to a consonance on the offbeats, and then it starts all over again.

 For suggestions for further listening, go to www.oup.com/us/lambert

STUDY QUESTIONS FOR LESSON 26

1. Define these terms:
   ragtime
   swing
   syncopation

2. How are swing eighths different from regular eighths?

3. Are "swing eighths" more similar to simple meter or compound meter?

4. What rhythmic technique is a distinguishing feature of ragtime?

5. In music that is syncopated, what two aspects work in opposition to each other?

RHYTHM READING

(straight 8ths—or try swinging!)

13. 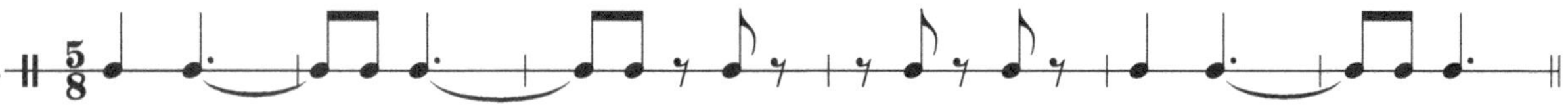

14. 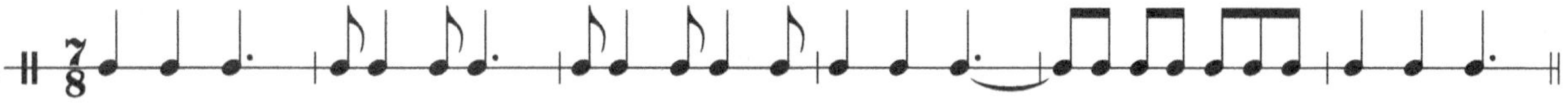

15. 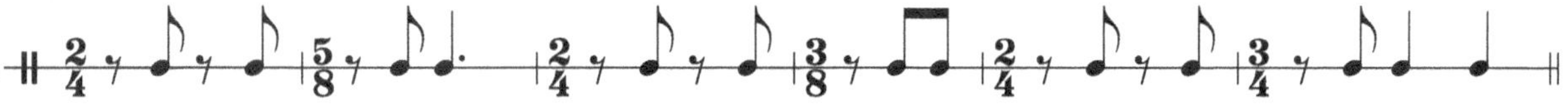

16. 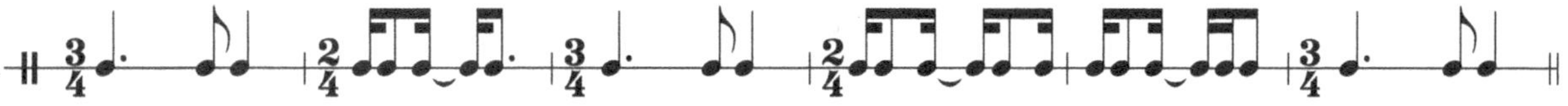

17. 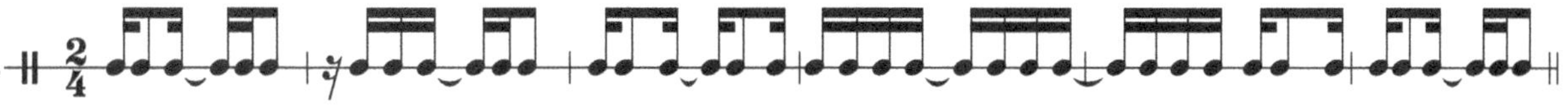

18. 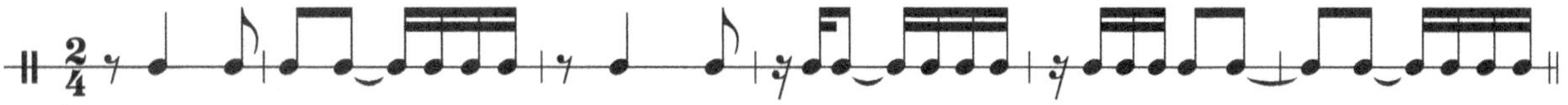

19. 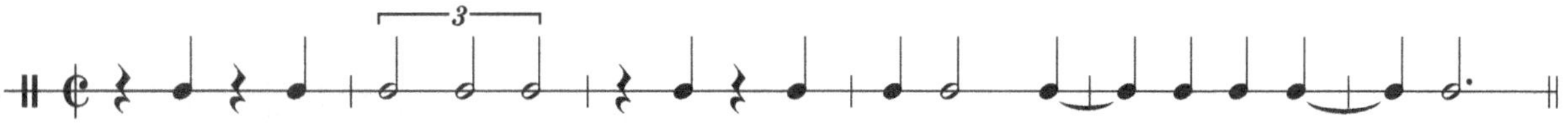

20. 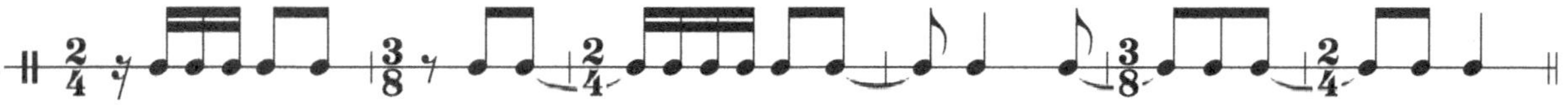

21. 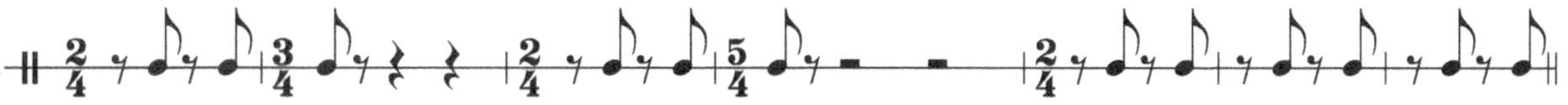

22. 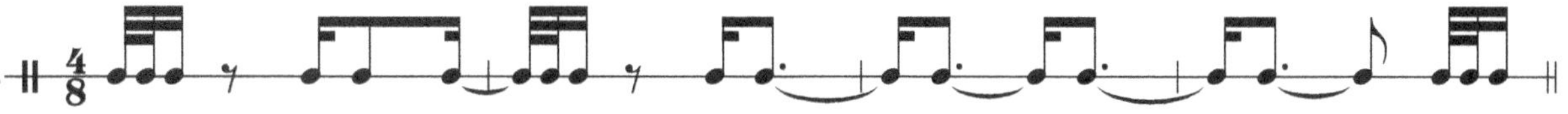

23. 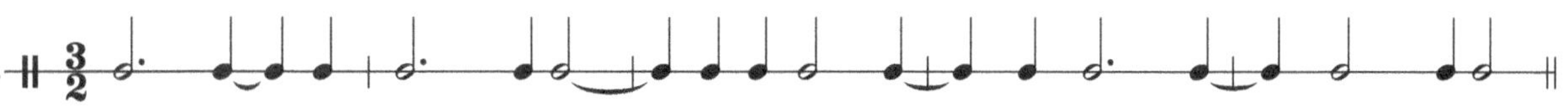

24. 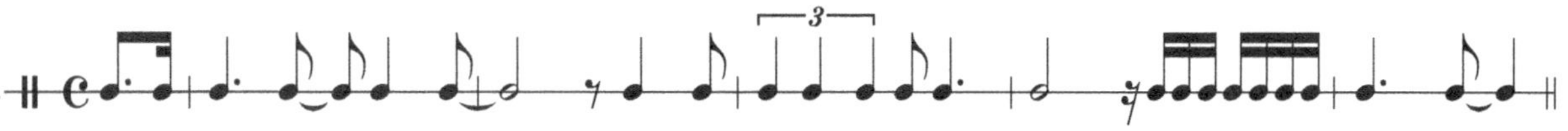

► EXERCISES FOR LESSON 26

To create a syncopated version of a melody, shift selected notes from beats to offbeats. Suppose, for example, you start with this melody:

A syncopated version might go something like this:

The new version simply takes the first two notes of each measure in the original melody and shifts them one half beat later, so that they fall between the beats. It also shifts the last note of the melody one half beat earlier, making it arrive before the first beat of the final measure. These are just some of the possibilities.

Rewrite the given melody using syncopated rhythms. There is no single best or correct answer! As long as the new version has the correct number of beats per measure, and shifts selected notes from beats to offbeats, it will be correct.

✧ create!

1. Listen to some sets of themes and variations such as:

   - Johann Sebastian Bach (1685–1750), Aria with Thirty Variations ("Goldberg Variations"), BWV 988 (1741).

   - Wolfgang Amadeus Mozart (1756–1791), Twelve Variations on "Ah, vous dirai-je, Maman," K. 265 (1781–82).
     - The theme is better known as "Twinkle, Twinkle Little Star" or "The Alphabet Song."

   - Ludwig van Beethoven (1770–1827), Thirty-Three Variations on a Waltz by Diabelli, op. 120 (1823).

   - Johannes Brahms (1833–1897), Variations on a Theme by Haydn, op. 56a (1873).

   - Béla Bartók (1881–1945), "Variations on a Folk Tune," *Mikrokosmos*, book 4, no. 112 (1926, 1932–39).

   - Paul Hindemith (1895–1963), *Symphonic Metamorphosis after Themes by Carl Maria von Weber*, second movement (1943).

   - George Gershwin (1898–1937), *"I Got Rhythm" Variations* (1934).

   - Alec Wilder (1907–1980), Theme and Variations (1945).

   - Benjamin Britten (1913–1976), *The Young Person's Guide to the Orchestra: Variations and Fugue on a Theme of Henry Purcell*, op. 34 (1945).

   - "Heroes and Villains" (Beach Boys [Brian Wilson, Van Dyke Parks], from *Smiley Smile*, 1967).
     - Think of the initial verse ("I've been in this town so long...") as the theme and listen for variations. In the remainder of the song, the only section that *isn't* a variation of that theme is the chorus ("Heroes and Villains . . .").

2. Write your own set of theme and variations, for piano or some other instrumentation. Here are some things to think about:

   - One possibility is to use an existing theme as the basis of your variations (a common choice; see above). Choose a melody that's not too long or complex.

   - You could also write a theme of your own to use as the basis for the variations. Keep it short and simple. Use a theme from one of the pieces listed above as a model, or a melody from Fifteen Character Pieces (www.oup.com/us/lambert) such as Lullaby or Boat Song or Folk Song.

   - Think of different ways of changing your theme to make a variation, drawing inspiration from the models listed above. In addition to melodic embellishment, try changing the mode or meter or style.

   - As you probably noticed when studying the models, variation sets often progress from simplicity toward complexity, from variations in which features of the theme are prominent and recognizable, to variations in which features of the theme are hardly present at all.

   - Produce an overall formal structure that's clear and easy for the listener to follow. Classic variation sets are clearly sectionalized, with breaks or pauses between variations.

   - Check over your notation to make sure that your symbols are clear, noteheads are correctly placed, and measures contain the proper number of beats.

APPENDIX A:
Glossary

1st inversion	A presentation of a *chord* with its *third* as the lowest sounding pitch.
2nd inversion	A presentation of a *chord* with its *fifth* as the lowest sounding pitch.
3rd inversion	A presentation of a *seventh chord* with its *seventh* as the lowest sounding pitch.
8va basso	A score notation indicating to play one *octave* lower than written.
accidental	The generic term for symbols that indicate adjustments to a notated pitch: *sharp* (♯), *double sharp* (𝄪), *flat* (♭), *double flat* (♭♭), *natural* (♮).
Aeolian mode	The sixth rotation of the *major scale*, also known as *natural minor*, with the whole (W) and half-step (H) sequence WHWWHWW (e.g., the A *white-key scale*).
Alberti bass	An accompaniment pattern common in piano music of the classical era in which chord tones are played separately in patterns, most commonly low-high-middle-high.
alto	The lower treble-clef voice in four-part choral music.
alto clef	A *clef sign* specifying note names on a *staff* such that the middle line is *middle C*. See *C clef*.
anacrusis	A note or group of notes preceding the first primary *downbeat* (the "Oh" in "Oh, say can you see . . ."). Also known as *pickup note* or *upbeat*.
arpeggiation	The presentation of one *triad* tone after another.
ASA standard	A method of *pitch* labeling in which middle C is designated "C_4."
augmented interval	A perfect or major *interval* expanded by one *chromatic half step* (i.e., without moving the notes to different lines and/or spaces).
augmented triad	A three-note *chord* built from a major third on top of another major third, with an augmented fifth between the outer notes; in half-step spans, 4+4 (e.g., C–E–G♯).
balanced meter	An organization of *beats* and *stress patterns* such that each *measure* can be divided into parts of equivalent durations (e.g., $\frac{4}{4}$, $\frac{6}{8}$).
bar	See *measure*.
bar line	The vertical line denoting the division of music into *measures*, as defined by the *meter signature*.
bass	The lower bass-clef voice in four-part choral music.
bass clef	A symbol specifying note names on a *staff* such that the fourth line up is the F below *middle C*.
beam	A thick line connecting flagged notes (such as *eighth notes* or *sixteenth notes*) and used in place of flags to enhance readability.
beat	A regularly spaced impulse often underlying musical performance.
breve	A duration equivalent to twice the value of a *whole note*.

clef	A *clef sign* showing the location of *middle C* and most commonly placed either centered on the middle line of the *staff* (*alto clef*) or centered on the fourth line of the *staff* (*tenor clef*).
orale	Music in *choral texture*, with the voices moving in identical or very similar rhythms to proclaim a text.
oral texture	Music in four sung parts, usually notated with two parts in the *treble clef* (*soprano* and *alto*, typically sung by female voices), and two parts in the *bass clef* (*tenor* and *bass*, typically sung by male voices).
ord	A meaningful grouping of at least three notes, as in the *triad*.
orus	1. The repeated strain of a song (as opposed to the *verse*, which may be different each time); 2. In the American tradition, the main melody of a song (which may or may not be preceded by a *verse* in *free rhythm*).
romatic half step	The notation of two adjacent keys on the piano using notes on the same line or space on the *staff* (e.g., C–C♯).
romatic scale	A series of notes separated by *half steps*.
cle of fifths	See *circle of keys*.
cle of keys	The circular arrangement of keys (*major* and/or *minor*) according to the number of *accidentals* in their *key signatures*, as if displacing the numbers on a clock face, and including three places (five o'clock, six o'clock, and seven o'clock) holding pairs of *enharmonic keys*. Often called the *circle of fifths* because the fifth scale degree of any key is the first scale degree of the next key clockwise.
cle of thirds	The circular arrangement of alternate letters in the *musical alphabet*, displaying letter combinations for *triads* among three adjacent letters, or *seventh chords* among four adjacent letters.
cle of triads	The circular arrangement of triads (*major* and/or *minor*) according to the position of their *roots* in the *circle of keys*.
f sign	A symbol specifying the names of lines and spaces on a *staff*.
mon time	$\frac{4}{4}$ *meter* (notated as **C**).
npound interval	A pairing of two notes separated by more than an *octave* but less than a *double octave*.
npound meter	An organization of *beats* into *measures* in which each beat is divided into three parts. In a *meter signature* for compound meter, the top number divided by three indicates the number of beats per measure, and the bottom number indicates which note value is grouped in threes to represent one beat.
t time	$\frac{2}{2}$ *meter* (notated as **¢**).
atonic half step	The notation of two adjacent keys on the piano using notes on a neighboring line and space on the *staff* (e.g., C–D♭).
atonic mode	Any rotation of the scale represented by the white keys within one *octave* on the piano.
ninished interval	A perfect or minor *interval* reduced by one *chromatic half step* (i.e., without moving the notes to different lines and/or spaces).
ninished seventh chord	A four-note *chord* built from a *diminished triad* plus an additional note forming a seventh with the triad *root*. If the quality of the seventh is minor, the chord type is *half-diminished* (e.g., D–F–A♭–C, or 3+3+4 half-step spans); if the quality of the seventh is

	diminished, the chord type is *fully diminished* (e.g., D–F–A♭–C♭, or 3+3+3 half-step spans).
diminished triad	A three-note *chord* built from a minor third on top of another minor third, with a diminished fifth between the outer notes; in half-step spans, 3+3 (e.g., C–E♭–G♭).
distance (of an interval)	The number of scale degrees spanned by the notes in an *interval*, including both notes in the counting.
dominant	The fifth degree of a *major* or *minor scale*.
dominant seventh chord	A four-note *chord* built from a *major triad* plus an additional note forming a minor seventh with the triad *root* (e.g., D–F♯–A–C, 4+3+3 half-step spans).
dominant triad	The *triad* built on the fifth scale degree within a key, with scale-degree $\hat{7}$ as its *third* and scale-degree $\hat{2}$ as its *fifth*.
Dorian mode	The second rotation of the *major scale*, with the whole (W) and half-step (H) sequence WHWWWHW (e.g., the D *white-key scale*).
dotted note	A duration that has been extended by half of its value (e.g., ♩. = ♩ + ♪).
double bar	Two vertical lines usually demarcating an important sectional division or ending within a score.
double flat	The symbol (♭♭) indicating an adjustment to a notated pitch by two *half steps* down.
double octave	In the span of three consecutive notes with identical labels (e.g., C–C–C), the distance from the first to third.
double sharp	The symbol (𝄪) indicating an adjustment to a notated pitch by two *half steps* up.
doubling	Placement of the same part of a *chord* (e.g., *root*, *third*, or *fifth*) in two different voices.
doubly augmented interval	A perfect or major *interval* expanded by two *chromatic half steps* (i.e., without moving the notes to different lines and/or spaces).
doubly diminished interval	A perfect or minor *interval* reduced by two *chromatic half steps* (i.e., without moving the notes to different lines and/or spaces).
doubly dotted note	A duration that has been extended by ¾ of its value (e.g., ♩.. = ♩ + ♪ + ♬).
duple meter	Two beats per measure.
eighth note	A duration equivalent to half the value of a *quarter note*.
eighth rest	A duration of silence equivalent to half the value of a *quarter rest*.
enharmonic equivalence	Different spellings of identical sounds. Can apply to *pitches* or *intervals* or *triads* or *seventh chords* or *keys* (etc.).
family (of scales)	The collection of all possible rotations of a scale (e.g., the group of *white-key scales*).
F clef	See *bass clef*.
fifth (of a triad)	The upper note of a triad when notated in *triad form*.
figured bass	A tradition of numbers and symbols indicating the *positions* (i.e., *inversions*) of *chords*.
flat sign	The symbol (♭) indicating an adjustment to a notated pitch by one *half step* down.
forms of minor	The three versions of the minor scale (*natural*, *harmonic*, and *melodic*).
free rhythm	Music performed without a regular *beat*.
fully diminished seventh chord	A four-note *chord* built from a *diminished triad* plus an additional note forming a diminished seventh with the triad *root* (e.g., D–F–A♭–C♭, 3+3+3 half-step spans).

clef	See *treble clef.*
and staff	The coupling of a *treble clef* and *bass clef* staff, as in most piano music.
lf-diminished seventh chord	A four-note *chord* built from a *diminished triad* plus an additional note forming a minor seventh with the triad *root* (e.g., D–F–A♭–C, 3+3+4 half-step spans).
lf note	A duration equivalent to twice the value of a *quarter note.*
lf rest	A duration of silence equivalent to twice the value of a *quarter rest.*
lf step	The distance between two adjacent keys on a piano. Can be notated as *chromatic* or *diatonic.*
rmonic interval	Two notes making a meaningful grouping and sounding simultaneously.
rmonic minor	A *form* of the minor scale created by raising scale degree $\hat{7}$ of the *natural minor* scale by one *chromatic half step.*
miola	A stress pattern contradicting the notated *meter* to suggest a different meter (e.g., stressing every other beat in consecutive measures of $\frac{3}{4}$).
erval	The pairing of two notes, characterized by its *quality*, *distance*, and size in *half steps.*
version (of an interval)	Flipping the two notes in an *interval* so that the bottom note becomes the top note.
version (of a chord)	The presentation of the members of a chord so that a note other than its *root* is the lowest sounding pitch.
ian mode	The ancient name for what we now call the *major scale*, with the whole (W) and half-step (H) sequence WWHWWWH (e.g., the C *white-key scale*).
egular meter	Music that changes *meter signatures* frequently, possibly in consecutive measures.
y	The primary sound of tonal music, represented by its *tonic note* and *scale.*
y signature	The notation, in standard form, of all the sharps or flats in the key of the music, placed immediately after the *clef sign.*
ding tone	The seventh degree of a *major* or *harmonic* or *melodic minor* scale.
ding tone triad	The *triad* built on the seventh scale degree in a major or harmonic or melodic minor scale, with scale-degree $\hat{2}$ as its *third* and scale-degree $\hat{4}$ as its *fifth.*
ger line	An extension of the *staff* up or down, using short parallel lines spaced like the staff lines.
crian mode	The seventh rotation of the *major scale*, with the whole (W) and half-step (H) sequence HWWHWWW (e.g., the B *white-key scale*).
dian mode	The fourth rotation of the *major scale*, with the whole (W) and half-step (H) sequence WWWHWWH (e.g., the F *white-key scale*).
jor interval	A combination of two notes both taken from the *major scale* starting on the lower note with *distance* 2, 3, 6, or 7.
jor-minor seventh chord	Another name for the *dominant seventh chord*, because it combines a *major triad* with a *minor seventh.*
jor mode	See *major scale, Ionian mode.*
jor scale	A series of *scale degrees* completing an *octave* and using every letter of the *musical alphabet*, with the whole (W) and half-step (H) sequence WWHWWWH (e.g., the *Ionian mode*, or C *white-key scale*).
jor seventh chord	A four-note *chord* built from a *major triad* plus an additional note forming a major seventh with the triad *root* (e.g., D–F♯–A–C♯, 4+3+4 half-step spans).

major triad	A three-note *chord* formed by combining the first, third, and fifth degrees of the *major scale*. In terms of intervals: M3 below m3, or half-step spans 4 below 3.
measure	An organization of music, using *bar lines*, into units defined by the *meter signature*.
mediant	The third degree of a *major* or *minor scale*.
mediant triad	The *triad* built on the third scale degree within a key, with scale-degree $\hat{5}$ as its *third* and scale-degree $\hat{7}$ as its *fifth*.
melodic interval	Two notes making a meaningful grouping and sounding consecutively.
melodic minor	A *form* of the minor scale created by raising degrees $\hat{6}$ and $\hat{7}$ of the *natural minor* scale, each by one *chromatic half step*.
meter	The organization of *beats* into meaningful units by *bar lines*.
meter signature	A stacking of two numerals placed immediately after the *key signature* and giving important information about the notation of rhythm. In *simple meter*, the top number of the meter signature indicates the number of beats per measure, and the bottom number indicates which note value represents one beat. In *compound meter*, the top number divided by three indicates the number of beats per measure, and the bottom number indicates which note value is grouped in threes to represent one beat. The meter signature is placed at the beginning of the score and does not appear again unless the meter changes.
middle C	The name for the white key just to the left of a group of two black keys roughly in the center of the piano keyboard, with a frequency of approximately 262 Hz.
minor dominant	The *triad* rooted on the fifth degree of the *natural minor scale*, with $\hat{7}$ as its *third* and $\hat{2}$ as its *fifth*.
minor interval	A combination of two notes both taken from the *natural minor* scale starting on the lower note with *distance* 3, 6, or 7. The "minor second" is another name for *diatonic half step*.
minor mode	See *minor scale, Aeolian mode*.
minor scale	A series of *scale degrees* completing an *octave* and using every letter of the *musical alphabet*, with the whole (W) and half-step (H) sequence WHWWHWW (e.g., the *Aeolian mode*, or A *white-key scale*).
minor seventh chord	A four-note *chord* built from a *minor triad* plus an additional note forming a minor seventh with the triad *root* (e.g., D–F–A–C, 3+4+3 half-step spans).
minor triad	A three-note *chord* formed by combining the first, third, and fifth degrees of the *minor scale*. In terms of intervals: m3 below M3, or half-step spans 3 below 4.
Mixolydian mode	The fifth rotation of the *major scale*, with the whole (W) and half-step (H) sequence WWHWWHW (e.g., the G *white-key scale*).
musical alphabet	A–B–C–D–E–F–G.
natural minor	The unaltered *form* of minor (i.e., same as *minor scale* or *Aeolian mode*, as demonstrated by the A *white-key scale*).
natural sign	The symbol (♮) indicating the absence of a *flat* or *sharp* for a *pitch*, as when a previously indicated *accidental* (perhaps from a *key signature*) is negated.
octave	The distance spanned by two consecutive notes with identical labels (e.g., C–C).
octave symbol	A score notation indicating to play one *octave* higher than written.

rallel keys (or scales)	*Major* and *minor keys* or *scales* with the same *tonic* note.
dal point	A held or repeated note, often in the low register, that may or may not be consonant with concurrent chord formations.
ntatonic scale	Any five-note scale, but usually indicating the scale consisting of the black keys on the piano.
rfect interval	A combination of two notes both taken from the *major* or *minor* scale starting on the lower note with *distance* 1, 4, 5, or 8.
rygian mode	The third rotation of the *major scale*, with the whole (W) and half-step (H) sequence HWWWHWW (e.g., the E *white-key scale*).
kup note	See *anacrusis*.
ch	The highness or lowness of sound, often specified using notes of certain durations on a *staff* with a *clef*.
ition (of a chord)	The specification of exactly which member of a chord is the lowest sounding pitch.
lse	See *beat*.
adruple meter	Four beats per measure.
ality (of an interval)	A designation reflecting scale membership of the notes in an *interval*. Intervals drawn from *scales* with *tonic* as the lower note have *perfect*, *major*, or *minor* qualities. Otherwise their qualities are *diminished* or *augmented*.
ality (of a triad)	The classification of three-note chords according to the quality of their intervals, as *major* (M3+m3, 4+3 half steps), *minor* (m3+M3, 3+4), *diminished* (m3+m3, 3+3), or *augmented* (M3+M3, 4+4).
arter note	A duration equivalent to half the value of a *half note*.
arter rest	A duration of silence equivalent to half the value of a *half rest*.
intuple meter	Five beats per measure.
intuplet	Division of a beat into five parts.
gtime	A forerunner of jazz featuring oom-pah accompaniments and *syncopated* melodies.
itative	A passage of *free rhythm* focused on text declamation, usually preceding an aria or duet in an opera or other vocal genre.
ative keys	*Major* and *minor scales* with the same *key signatures*.
t	A notation of silence.
ythm	Musical durations and their organization.
t (of a triad)	The lower note of a triad when notated in *triad form*.
t position	A presentation of a *chord* with its *root* as the lowest sounding pitch.
bato	Variations in *tempo* made by a performer for expressive purposes. From the Italian word for "stolen," as when an elongated beat, for example, "steals" some extra time for itself.
le	A series of notes filling an *octave* and holding specific relevance to a certain musical sound or tradition.
le degree	A note in a *scale*, often identified by an Arabic numeral topped by a caret ($\hat{1}$ $\hat{2}$ $\hat{3}$ $\hat{4}$ $\hat{5}$ $\hat{6}$ $\hat{7}$).
tuple meter	Seven beats per measure.

seventh chord	A four-note *chord* built from a *triad* plus an additional note forming a minor seventh with the triad *root*.
sextuplet	Division of a beat into six parts.
sharp sign	The symbol (♯) indicating an adjustment to a notated pitch by one *half step* up.
simple interval	A pairing of two notes separated by less than an *octave*.
simple meter	An organization of *beats* into *measures* in which each beat is divided into two parts. In a *meter signature* for simple meter, the top number indicates the number of beats per measure, and the bottom number indicates which note value represents one beat.
sixteenth note	A duration equivalent to ¼ the value of a *quarter note*.
sixteenth rest	A duration of silence equivalent to ¼ the value of a *quarter rest*.
solfège symbols	The system of assigning words to scale degrees, originating with Guido of Arezzo in the early eleventh century. The syllable names have evolved over the years, but in current American usage are as follows: $\hat{1}$ = do, $\hat{2}$ = re, $\hat{3}$ = mi, $\hat{4}$ = fa, $\hat{5}$ = sol, $\hat{6}$ = la, $\hat{7}$ = ti.
soprano	The upper treble-clef voice in four-part choral music, usually carrying the primary melody.
staff	The arrangement of five parallel lines used in conventional musical notation.
subdominant	The fourth degree of a *major* or *minor scale*.
subdominant triad	The *triad* built on the fourth scale degree within a key, with scale-degree $\hat{6}$ as its *third* and scale-degree $\hat{1}$ as its *fifth*.
submediant	The sixth degree of a *major* or *minor scale*.
submediant triad	The *triad* built on the sixth scale degree within a key, with scale-degree $\hat{1}$ as its *third* and scale-degree $\hat{3}$ as its *fifth*.
subtonic	The seventh degree of the *natural minor scale*.
subtonic triad	The *triad* built on the seventh scale degree within a *natural minor scale*, with scale-degree $\hat{2}$ as its *third* and scale-degree $\hat{4}$ as its *fifth*.
supertonic	The second degree of a *major* or *minor scale*.
supertonic triad	The *triad* built on the second scale degree within a key, with scale-degree $\hat{4}$ as its *third* and scale-degree $\hat{6}$ as its *fifth*.
swing	A style of music characterized by unequal divisions of the beat, giving more time to notes on the beat and less to notes between beats.
syncopation	A conflict between the stress pattern of the notated rhythms and the stress pattern defined by the *meter*.
tempo	The speed of the beat.
tenor	The upper bass-clef voice in four-part choral music.
tenor clef	A *clef sign* specifying note names on a *staff* such that the fourth line up is *middle C*. See *C clef*.
third (of a triad)	The middle note of a triad when notated in *triad form*.
tie	A curved line connecting two durations, indicating that they are to be combined as one single duration.
tonic	The first degree of a *major* or *minor scale*, indicating the most important note in the *key*.

nic triad	The *triad* built on the first scale degree within a key, with scale-degree $\hat{3}$ as its *third* and scale-degree $\hat{5}$ as its *fifth*.
ransposition	Shifting music to another key, without changing the meter or rhythm.
eble clef	A symbol specifying note names on a *staff* such that the second line up is the G above *middle C*.
iad	A three-note *chord*.
iad form	An arrangement of three notes that occupy adjacent lines or spaces in the staff, represented by alternate letters in the musical alphabet. The possibilities are limited to seven three-letter combinations:

E	F	G	A	B	C	D
C	D	E	F	G	A	B
A	B	C	D	E	F	G

iple meter	Three beats per measure.
iplet	The division of a beat into three parts.
itone	Another name for the augmented fourth (which spans three whole tones, thus the name) or diminished fifth.
nbalanced meter	An organization of *beats* and *stress patterns* such that each *measure* can be divided into parts of non-equivalent durations (e.g., $\frac{5}{4}$, $\frac{7}{8}$).
nison	Different musicians or instruments performing the same note.
bbeat	See *anacrusis*.
rse	1. The part of a song preceding the chorus, which may have different text each time it's performed; 2. In the American tradition, the prefatory section leading to the main melody of a song, often in *free rhythm*.
hite-key scales	Scales that fill octaves using only piano white keys, stepping through the entire *musical alphabet*.
hole note	A duration equivalent to four *quarter notes* or two *half notes*.
hole rest	A duration of silence equivalent to four *quarter rests* or two *half rests*.
hole step	The distance spanned by two *half steps*. Always notated using adjacent letters in the musical alphabet, on a neighboring line and space in the *staff*.
hole-tone scale	A series of *whole steps* filling an octave.

APPENDIX B:
A Brief Guide to Common Musical Symbols and Markings

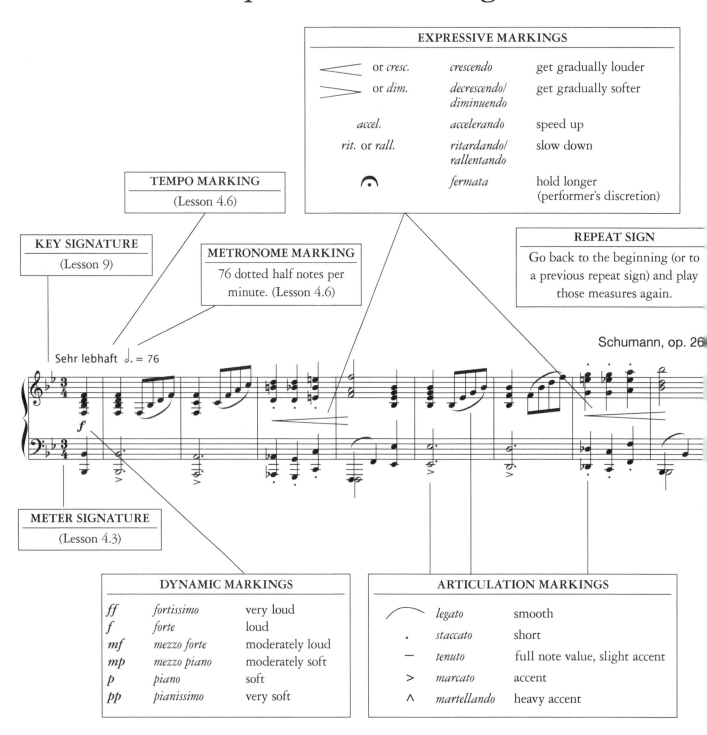

EXPRESSIVE MARKINGS

< or *cresc.*	*crescendo*	get gradually louder
> or *dim.*	*decrescendo/ diminuendo*	get gradually softer
accel.	*accelerando*	speed up
rit. or *rall.*	*ritardando/ rallentando*	slow down
⌢	*fermata*	hold longer (performer's discretion)

TEMPO MARKING

(Lesson 4.6)

KEY SIGNATURE

(Lesson 9)

METRONOME MARKING

76 dotted half notes per minute. (Lesson 4.6)

REPEAT SIGN

Go back to the beginning (or to a previous repeat sign) and play those measures again.

Schumann, op. 26

Sehr lebhaft ♩. = 76

METER SIGNATURE

(Lesson 4.3)

DYNAMIC MARKINGS

ff	*fortissimo*	very loud
f	*forte*	loud
mf	*mezzo forte*	moderately loud
mp	*mezzo piano*	moderately soft
p	*piano*	soft
pp	*pianissimo*	very soft

ARTICULATION MARKINGS

⌢	*legato*	smooth
.	*staccato*	short
—	*tenuto*	full note value, slight accent
>	*marcato*	accent
∧	*martellando*	heavy accent

384

APPENDIX C:
Mini-Dictionary of Score Indications

tempo	*(It.)* Return to the original tempo.
ccelerando (accel.)	*(It.)* Get gradually faster.
d libitum (ad lib.)	*(Lat.)* Freely.
dagio	*(It.)* Tempo marking: very slow (approx. 56 beats/minute). See also *langsam, largo, lent.*
gitato	*(It.)* With energy and excitement.
llegretto	*(It.)* Tempo marking: moderately fast (approx. 100 beats/minute). See also *etwas bewegt, un peu animé.*
llegro	*(It.)* Tempo marking: fast (approx. 120 beats/minute). See also *animé, bewegt, schnell.*
ndante	*(It.)* Tempo marking: moderately slow (approx. 84 beats/minute). See also *mässig langsam, très modéré.*
ndantino	*(It.)* Slightly faster than *andante.*
nimato	*(It.)* With vigor and animation.
nimé	*(Fr.)* Tempo marking: fast (approx. 120 beats/minute). See also *allegro, bewegt, schnell.*
ssai	*(It.)* Very, extremely. See also *sehr, très.*
usdruck	*(Ger.)* Expressively. See also *espressivo.*
ewegt	*(Ger.)* Tempo marking: fast (approx. 120 beats/minute). See also *allegro, animé, schnell.*
antabile	*(It.)* In a singing style. See also *gesangvoll.*
on fuoco	*(It.)* With fire and passion.
rescendo (cresc.)	*(It.)* Get gradually louder. May be indicated by a widening wedge (<).
ecrescendo (decresc.)	*(It.)* Get gradually softer. May be indicated by a narrowing wedge (>). See also *diminuendo.*
iminuendo (dim.)	*(It.)* Get gradually softer. May be indicated by a narrowing wedge (>). See also *decrescendo.*
olce	*(It.)* Softly, sweetly.
olente	*(It.)* Mournfully, sadly. See also *doloroso.*
olore	*(It.)* Painfully, with anguish.
oloroso	*(It.)* Mournfully, sadly. See also *dolente.*
lig	*(Ger.)* Tempo marking: very fast (approx. 148 beats/minute). See also *lebhaft, vif, vite, vivace.*
egante	*(It.)* Elegantly.
mpfindung	*(Ger.)* With feeling.

Energico	*(It.)* With energy.
Espressivo	*(It.)* Expressively. See also *ausdruck*.
Etwas bewegt	*(Ger.)* Tempo marking: moderately fast (approx. 100 beats/minute). See also *allegretto, un peu animé*.
Etwas langsam	*(Ger.)* Tempo marking: slow (approx. 66 beats/minute). See also *lento, un peu lent*.
Expressivo	*(It.)* Passionately.
Forte (*f*)	*(It.)* Loud.
Forte-piano (*fp*)	*(It.)* Start loud (*forte*) and become immediately soft (*piano*).
Fortissimo (*ff*)	*(It.)* Very loud.
Ganz schnell	*(Ger.)* Tempo marking: extremely fast (approx. 160 beats/minute). See also *presto, sehr lebhaft, très vif*.
Gesangvoll	*(Ger.)* In a singing style. See also *cantabile*.
Grandioso	*(It.)* In a stately manner.
Grave	*(It.)* Tempo marking: extremely slow (approx. 40 beats/minute). See also *sehr langsam, très lent*.
Grazioso	*(It.)* Gracefully.
Langsam	*(Ger.)* Tempo marking: very slow (approx. 56 beats/minute). See also *adagio, largo, lent*.
Larghetto	*(It.)* Slightly faster than *largo*.
Largo	*(It.)* Tempo marking: very slow (approx. 56 beats/minute). See also *adagio, langsam, lent*.
Lebhaft	*(Ger.)* Tempo marking: very fast (approx. 148 beats/minute). See also *eilig, vif, vite, vivace*.
Legato	*(It.)* Smoothly.
Légèrement	*(Fr.)* Lightly. See also *leggiero, leicht*.
Leggiero	*(It.)* Lightly. See also *légèrement, leicht*.
Leicht	*(Ger.)* Lightly. See also *légèrement, leggiero*.
Lent	*(Fr.)* Tempo marking: very slow (approx. 56 beats/minute). See also *adagio, largo, langsam*.
Lento	*(It.)* Tempo marking: slow (approx. 66 beats/minute). See also *etwas langsam, un peu lent*.
L'istesso tempo	*(It.)* At the same speed.
Maestoso	*(It.)* Majestically.
Marcato	*(It.)* Accented.
Martellando	*(It.)* Heavily accented.
Mässig bewegt	*(Ger.)* Tempo marking: moderate (approx. 92 beats/minute). See also *moderato, modéré*.
Mässig langsam	*(Ger.)* Tempo marking: moderately slow (approx. 84 beats/minute). See also *andante, très modéré*.
Meno mosso	*(It.)* At a slightly slower tempo.
Mezzo forte (*mf*)	*(It.)* Moderately loud.
Mezzo piano (*mp*)	*(It.)* Moderately soft.

Moderato	*(It.)* Tempo marking: moderate (approx. 92 beats/minute). See also *mässig bewegt, modéré*.
Modéré	*(Fr.)* Tempo marking: moderate (approx. 92 beats/minute). See also *mässig bewegt, moderato*.
Morendo	*(It.)* Fade to nothing. See also *niente*.
niente	*(It.)* Fade to nothing. See also *morendo*.
pesante	*(It.)* Heavily.
pianissimo (*pp*)	*(It.)* Very soft.
piano (*p*)	*(It.)* Soft.
poco a poco	*(It.)* Little by little.
portamento	*(It.)* Gliding from one note to another.
presto	*(It.)* Tempo marking: extremely fast (approx. 160 beats/minute). See also *ganz schnell, sehr lebhaft, très vif*.
rallentando (rall.)	*(It.)* Slow down. See also *ritardando*.
risoluto	*(It.)* With resolve and determination.
ritardando (rit.)	*(It.)* Slow down. See also *rallentando*.
rubato	*(It.)* Taking liberties with the rhythm for expressive purposes.
ruhig	*(Ger.)* Peaceful.
schnell	*(Ger.)* Tempo marking: fast (approx. 120 beats/minute). See also *allegro, animé, bewegt*.
sehr	*(Ger.)* Very, extremely. See also *assai, très*.
sehr langsam	*(Ger.)* Tempo marking: extremely slow (approx. 40 beats/minute). See also *grave, très lent*.
sehr lebhaft	*(Ger.)* Tempo marking: extremely fast (approx. 160 beats/minute). See also *ganz schnell, presto, très vif*.
sempre	*(It.)* Always.
sforzando (*sfz*)	*(It.)* Extremely forceful accent.
simile	*(It.)* In the same way.
sostenuto	*(It.)* Held, sustained.
staccato	*(It.)* Short.
subito	*(It.)* Suddenly.
tenuto	*(It.)* Full note value, slight accent.
tranquillo	*(It.)* Calmly.
très	*(Fr.)* Very, extremely. See also *assai, sehr*.
très lent	*(Fr.)* Tempo marking: extremely slow (approx. 40 beats/minute). See also *grave, sehr langsam*.
très modéré	*(Fr.)* Tempo marking: moderately slow (approx. 84 beats/minute). See also *andante, mässig langsam*.
très vif	*(Fr.)* Tempo marking: extremely fast (approx. 160 beats/minute). See also *ganz schnell, presto, sehr lebhaft*.

Un peu animé	*(Fr.)* Tempo marking: moderately fast (approx. 100 beats/minute). See also *allegretto, etwas bewegt.*
Un peu lent	*(Fr.)* Tempo marking: slow (approx. 66 beats/minute). See also *etwas langsam, lento.*
Vif	*(Fr.)* Tempo marking: very fast (approx. 148 beats/minute). See also *eilig, lebhaft, vite, vivace.*
Vite	*(Fr.)* Tempo marking: very fast (approx. 148 beats/minute). See also *eilig, lebhaft, vif, vivace.*
Vivace	*(It.)* Tempo marking: very fast (approx. 148 beats/minute). See also *eilig, lebhaft, vif, vite.*

INDEX